AF265830

THE AMERICAN PRESIDENCY

The American Presidency

Disclaimer:
This book is intended for informational and educational purposes. It reflects the author's interpretation of historical events and is not intended as political advocacy or
endorsement of any party, candidate, or ideology.

First edition: 2026
ISBN: [978-0-9991650-2-7]

Cover design by the author
Interior design by the author
Maps and Photos are digital illustrations modified by the author

Learning Innovations
Learning Innovations is an independent educational publisher dedicated to evidence-based, nonpartisan works in history, civics, and science. Our publications emphasize clarity,
historical context, and intellectual independence, with the goal
of supporting informed citizenship and lifelong learning.

DEDICATION

For readers who seek to understand how history has shaped the political life of our nation

Epigraph

*"If men were angels, no government would be neces-
sary. If angels were to govern men, neither external nor internal controls on government would be necessary."*

— James Madison, Federalist No. 51

AUTHORS NOTES

Over years of reading American history and presidential biography, I found that while there were excellent works on individual presidents and specific eras, there were relatively few single-volume resources that offered clear, concise portraits of every president within the broader development of the office itself. This book grew from a desire to assemble such a resource—one that could be read sequentially or consulted often as a practical reference.

The goal of this work is understanding rather than persuasion. The American presidency has evolved across more than two centuries through war, expansion, crisis, reform, and renewal. Each president has entered the office shaped by his time and circumstances, and each has left a distinct imprint on the institution. By presenting brief but structured accounts of presidential lives alongside the political and historical contexts in which they governed, this book seeks to illuminate both the individuals and the office they held.

Interpretations of presidential success and failure inevitably vary across generations, and recent administrations are often viewed through the lens of ongoing public debate. Where appropriate, this book presents widely accepted historical assessments while acknowledging that the reputations of more recent presidents will continue to evolve as new scholarship and distance from events allow for fuller evaluation.

This is not a work of political advocacy. It is intended as a readable civic reference for people who wish to better understand the United States as a country and the longitudinal development of its highest office. Hopefully, it will also encourage readers to further explore the presidents and the system in which they operate.

Contents

THE EARLY PROGRESSIVE ERA — 151

MARKET AUTONOMY — 173

THE NEW DEAL AND WORLD WAR — 183

THE POST AND COLD WAR — 197

PUBLIC MISTRUST AND CRISIS MANAGEMENT — 223

THE CONTEMPORARY PRESIDENCY — 253

THE ARC OF THE OFFICE — 291

WHY DEMOCRACY WILL PREVAIL — 293

PREFACE

This book was not written by a professional historian, nor does it pretend to be a comprehensive academic treatment of the American presidency. It was written by a citizen—curious, skeptical, and deeply interested in how the presidency and democracy functions over time.

For more than decade, I have studied the American presidency in depth. This study began not as a scholarly pursuit, but as a response to a moment of modern political anxiety. Following Donald Trump's election in 2016, many voices—across media, academia, and public discourse—warned of catastrophic and even existential consequences for the United States. Institutions would collapse. Norms would vanish. The republic itself, some claimed, would not survive.

Yet history did not end.

That disconnect between prediction and reality prompted a question that sits at the heart of this book: Have Americans experienced moments like this before—and if so, how did the presidency, and the nation, fare? To answer that question honestly required stepping back from contemporary politics and examining the full arc of the office itself.

What I discovered is that nearly every generation believes it is living through an unprecedented crisis—and that nearly every generation is both right and wrong. Presidents have governed through wars, depressions, assassinations, scandals, social upheaval, and bitter polarization. Many were denounced in their own time as dangerous, incompetent, corrupt, or unfit. Some were later vindicated. Others were not. Almost all were more complicated than their reputations suggest.

This book presents concise, biographies of each president, focusing on five core elements: their ascent to the presidency, their family life, their major accomplishments, the major criticisms they faced, and their ultimate legacy. The goal is not to persuade the reader toward admiration or condemnation, but to provide a grounded, accessible framework for understanding how each presidency influenced the country—often in ways very different from how it was perceived at the time.

My perspective is admittedly practical rather than academic. I am less interested in ideological purity or theoretical models than in outcomes and unintended consequences. History, viewed from a distance, tends to reward humility. Leaders rarely control events as fully as their supporters or critics assume. The presidency is powerful, but it is also constrained—by institutions, by public opinion, by economic realities, and by human limitations.

If this book has a thesis, it is a modest one: that the American presidency is more resilient, more flawed, and more human than our modern political discourse allows. Understanding that reality does not diminish the importance of the office—it clarifies it.

This work is offered in the spirit of inquiry rather than authority. It was written with the deliberate aim of maintaining historical balance. In an era of pronounced political polarization, I have tried to examine each presidency within its constitutional and institutional context rather than through a contemporary partisan lens. Readers are encouraged to disagree, to question, and to explore further. If the book succeeds, it will not tell you what to think about the presidents of the past but help you think more clearly about the presidency in the present.

— PAUL SCHMITZ

Acknowledgments

This book grew out of many years of reading, reflection, and an enduring interest in the history of the American presidency. Although it has been largely an individual effort, I am grateful to the authors, historians, and scholars whose work has shaped modern understanding of the presidents and the office they held. Their careful research and thoughtful interpretations made this volume possible and provided the foundation upon which it rests. Any errors or omissions in this volume are entirely my own.

I am especially appreciative of family and friends who offered encouragement throughout the writing and revision of this manuscript. Their patience and support during the long process of organizing, refining, and completing the work were invaluable.

Finally, I extend my thanks to the readers who share an interest in the American presidency. It is my hope that this book serves as a useful and enduring reference for those who wish to better understand the office and its place within the broader American story.

INTRODUCTION

This book is designed to be both comprehensive and flexible. While it can be read straight through from the founding to the present, it is equally suited for selective reading or thematic exploration.

Presidents are grouped into historical eras rather than treated as an uninterrupted chronology. These eras reflect shifts in constitutional practice, economic structure, party systems, and global context. Each era opens with an interpretive overview that frames the dominant challenges and institutional dynamics of the period. Readers unfamiliar with a given era may find it helpful to begin with these essays before turning to individual presidents.

Each presidential chapter follows a consistent structure. This format is intended to encourage comparison across presidencies and to prevent overemphasis on any single achievement or failure. The biographical summaries emphasize proportion and context, which are assessed based on the information, constraints, and norms available at the time they were made, not solely by later outcomes. Where historical judgment remains contested—particularly for recent presidents—that uncertainty is acknowledged explicitly.

Finally, this book does not require agreement to be useful. It requires only patience, curiosity, and a willingness to view the presidency across time rather than through the urgency of the present.

BIRTH OF THE PRESIDENCY

For much of the colonial period, Americans viewed themselves as Englishmen entitled to the same political rights enjoyed in Britain. Local assemblies, town meetings, and colonial courts fostered habits of political participation that made arbitrary rule increasingly unacceptable. When Parliament imposed new taxes in 1763, colonial resistance drew heavily on constitutional arguments, not revolutionary ideology. As John Adams later recalled, "The Revolution was in the minds of the people, and this was effected from 1760 to 1775." Political independence would come later; the first battles were over legitimacy and authority.

Public opinion hardened as compromise repeatedly failed. Thomas Paine's Common Sense[1] gave voice to a growing impatience with monarchy, arguing that hereditary rule was incompatible with liberty. "A government of our own is our natural right," Paine wrote, urging Americans to see separation not as rebellion, but as necessity. Yet even then, many colonists hesitated. The step from resistance to independence was momentous, committing the colonies to a war against the world's most powerful empire. What followed was not a smooth march toward nationhood, but a series of uncertain experiments in war, diplomacy, and governance, each revealing new weaknesses in the young republic's political structure and forcing leaders to reconsider how authority should be organized.

THE DECLARATION OF INDEPENDENCE (1776)

The Declaration of Independence was not merely an announcement of separation, but a legal and philosophical justification for revolution. Drafted primarily by Thomas Jefferson and adopted on July 4, 1776, it drew heavily on Enlightenment Ideals (page 295), especially those of John Locke, asserting that legitimate governments exist to secure natural rights and derive authority from the consent of the governed. When a government becomes destructive of those ends, the people possess the right to alter or abolish it. This framing was intended not only to unify the colonies but to persuade foreign powers that the American cause rested on universal principles.

---

1 Thomas Paine, Common Sense (1776) was a widely read pamphlet that argued in clear, direct language for American independence, rejected monarchy, and helped mobilize popular support for separation from Great Britain.

The Declaration also functioned as an indictment of King George III, listing grievances meant to demonstrate a pattern of tyranny. These included dissolving legislatures, obstructing justice, maintaining standing armies in peacetime, and imposing taxes without consent. While some charges were rhetorically exaggerated, the cumulative case transformed political protest into a claim of national independence. The document forced colonial leaders into an irrevocable commitment to separation and recast the conflict as a war between sovereign entities rather than a domestic rebellion.

The Revolutionary War (1775–1783)

The war (Figure 1) began as a series of local clashes between colonial militias and British troops but quickly became a prolonged struggle in which the Americans faced major disadvantages in training, funding, and equipment. George Washington's principal achievement was strategic endurance: preserving the Continental Army despite repeated setbacks and chronic shortages. He understood that survival itself could defeat an empire operating far from home and under growing political strain.

International support proved decisive. French military and naval assistance after 1778 transformed the conflict into a global war that stretched British resources. The victory at Yorktown (Figure 2) in 1781, where American and French forces trapped General Cornwallis's army, effectively ended major combat operations. Independence, however, had never been guaranteed. Without foreign intervention and sustained political will, the rebellion might well have failed. The war left the new nation heavily indebted, politically fragmented, and uncertain how to convert military success into stable governance.

The Treaty of Paris (1783)

The Treaty of Paris (Figure 3) formally recognized the United States as an independent nation and granted territorial boundaries extending to the Mississippi River.

American negotiators secured terms that exceeded most expectations, laying the groundwork for future westward expansion and economic development. These gains, however, also introduced new challenges, including unresolved relations with Native American nations and the geographic expansion of slavery.

More immediately, the treaty exposed the weaknesses of the government under the Articles of the Confederation. Congress lacked the power to enforce treaty provisions, regulate commerce, or compel states to meet financial obligations. British troops remained in frontier forts, and diplomatic tensions persisted. Political independence had been achieved, but the machinery of national authority remained dangerously inadequate.

THE U.S. CONSTITUTION (1787–1788)

The transition from the Articles of Confederation to the United States Constitution emerged from widespread recognition that the confederal system created during the Revolutionary era was insufficient to sustain a stable national government. Ratified in 1781, the Articles established a loose union of sovereign states with a weak central authority that lacked the power to levy taxes, regulate interstate commerce, or enforce national laws. Economic instability, mounting war debts, interstate tariff disputes, and episodes such as Shays' Rebellion[2] underscored the inability of the Confederation Congress to maintain order or provide coherent fiscal and defense policy. Many political leaders concluded that republican government itself might be imperiled without structural reform.

In response, delegates from twelve states convened at the Constitutional Convention in Philadelphia in May 1787, initially tasked with revising the Articles but soon turning toward drafting an entirely new governing framework. The framers sought to balance the need for stronger national authority with safeguards against tyranny, producing a federal system that divided power between national and state governments and separated authority among executive, legislative, and judicial branches. Key compromises—such as the Great (Connecticut) Compromise establishing a bicameral legislature and the *Three-Fifths Compromise regarding representation—reflected efforts to reconcile large and small state interests, as well as sectional differences between North and South*[3]. The resulting

---

2 Shays' Rebellion refers to a brief uprising in 1786–1787 by struggling farmers in Massachusetts who were facing heavy taxes, mounting debts, and the loss of their land after the American Revolution. Led by Daniel Shays, the protesters shut down local courts to stop foreclosures and debt trials. The rebellion was eventually put down by state forces, but it alarmed national leaders by showing how weak the central government was under the Articles of Confederation.

3 Fehrenbacher, Don E. The Slaveholding Republic: An Account of the United States Government's Relations to Slavery. New York: Oxford University Press, 2001.

Constitution created mechanisms for taxation, regulation of commerce, national defense, and law enforcement absent under the Articles.

Ratification between 1787 and 1788 required approval by conventions in nine of thirteen states and provoked vigorous public debate between Federalists, who supported the new Constitution, and Anti-Federalists, who feared centralized power and insufficient protections for individual liberties. The Federalist Papers, authored by Alexander Hamilton, James Madison, and John Jay, articulated the philosophical and structural rationale for the new framework, emphasizing checks and balances, federalism, and the extended republic as safeguards of liberty. To secure broader support, Federalists agreed to add a Bill of Rights, ratified in 1791, guaranteeing fundamental civil liberties. The Constitution thus replaced the Articles of Confederation with a more resilient and adaptable system of governance, establishing the durable institutional foundations of the modern United States.

At the Constitutional Convention, a central question was whether the United States would function primarily as a confederation of sovereign states or as a single consolidated national republic. Many *delegates believed the new government's legitimacy rested on the continued political importance of the states, which had been the original holders of sovereignty after independence.* Allowing states to control the selection of presidential electors preserved their role as essential political units within the federal system. Each state, regardless of size, received electoral votes equal to its total representation in Congress, ensuring that the presidency would be chosen through a process reflecting both the people and the states as constituent members of the Union.

This arrangement reinforced the concept of federalism—a balance between national authority and state sovereignty. Smaller states feared domination by populous states under a direct national vote, while larger states sought representation proportional to population. The Electoral College blended these concerns by tying electoral strength partly to population (House representation) and partly to equal state representation (Senate seats). *In this way, the presidency derived authority not solely from a national popular majority but from a coalition of states, underscoring that the Union was a partnership of states whose consent and participation were fundamental to the structure and legitimacy of the new constitutional order.*

Bridge to the First Presidency

With independence secured and a constitutional framework in place, the central question was no longer whether self-government was possible, but whether it could function in practice. The presidency, created cautiously and with little historical precedent, was designed to provide leadership while remaining bound by law. When George Washington assumed office in 1789, he did so not merely as a victorious general, but as the first test of whether republican executive power could exist without sliding into monarchy or disorder. The precedents set during his administration would define the office for generations and shape the conduct of every president who followed.

The Electoral System. The Constitution established an indirect system for electing the president through the Electoral College rather than by direct popular vote[4]. Each state received electors equal to its representation in Congress, and state legislatures determined how those electors were chosen. Electors cast two votes for president; the candidate with a majority became president and the runner-up became vice president. If no majority existed, the House of Representatives chose the president. This system reflected a compromise between election by Congress and direct popular vote, preserved a strong role for the states within the federal system, and balanced influence between large and small states through combined House and Senate representation.

The framers created this structure largely out of distrust of direct democracy and practical concerns about communication and voter knowledge in a vast 18th-century republic. They hoped a body of electors would act as an informed buffer against demagoguery and regional favoritism while reinforcing federalism. The system also indirectly incorporated the Three-Fifths Compromise[5], giving slaveholding states greater electoral influence.

---

4 Federalist No. 68 (Hamilton). Keyssar, Alexander. Why Do We Still Have the Electoral College? Cambridge, MA: Harvard University Press, 2020. Ross, Tara. Enlightened Democracy: The Case for the Electoral College. 2nd ed. Los Angeles: Colonial Press, 2019.

5 Historians generally view the Three-Fifths Compromise as emblematic of the founding era's tension between republican ideals and the realities of slavery. It preserved unity in 1787 but also entrenched sectional divisions that would shape national politics until the Civil War and the Reconstruction amendments abolished slavery and eliminated the compromise's constitutional basis.

The Party System

The Constitution established enduring institutions—the presidency, Congress, and the judiciary—but it did not anticipate the emergence of organized political parties. The founders hoped that competing interests could be managed within a framework of separated powers, yet disagreements over fiscal policy, executive authority, and foreign relations quickly produced political coalitions. These coalitions soon evolved into formal parties that organized elections, structured legislative behavior, and increasingly defined the boundaries of acceptable policy debate.

Over time, wars, economic crises, territorial expansion, industrialization, and social movements repeatedly disrupted existing alignments, producing new coalitions and dissolving old ones. Parties collapsed, merged, and re-formed, often retaining institutional continuity while radically altering their social bases and policy priorities. American political development is therefore best understood not as a static two-party system, but as a sequence of party systems shaped by long-term social change and punctuated by periods of electoral realignment (Figure 4).

For presidents, these party systems constitute the political environment in which leadership is exercised. Coalition strength affects legislative support, policy feasibility, and public legitimacy. Some presidents emerge during periods of stability and govern as managers of established arrangements; others preside over transitions that redefine party identities and national priorities. Evaluating presidential performance thus requires attention not only to personal leadership, but also to the partisan structures that condition what any administration can realistically achieve.

THE FOUNDING ERA
1789-1824

The American presidency was created in uncertainty. The Constitution established a single executive but left much of the office undefined. The Founders (page 297) feared monarchy, demagoguery, and concentrated power, yet they also understood that effective governance required energy, decisiveness, and national leadership. The presidency emerged from this, not as a fully formed institution, but as an experiment.

George Washington's presidency set the most enduring precedents of the era, not through bold assertions of power, but through restraint. By deferring to Congress on domestic legislation, respecting judicial independence, and voluntarily relinquishing office after two terms, Washington established norms that proved more influential than any constitutional clause. His administration demonstrated that executive authority could be exercised firmly without becoming personal or permanent, embedding legitimacy through moderation rather than force. As times changed and crisis emerged the presidency adapted and power has generally become more concentrated in the executive as described in later eras.

The early republic also revealed that consensus would not last. Political parties emerged and ideological divisions hardened between Federalists and Democratic-Republicans. John Adams' presidency exposed the fragility of civil liberties during national threat, while Thomas Jefferson's election marked a pivotal moment: the first peaceful transfer of power between rival parties. That transition affirmed that the presidency did not belong to any individual or faction.

During this early period, presidential power remained tempered but significant in consequence. Jefferson's Louisiana Purchase stretched constitutional interpretation. James Madison's wartime leadership during the War of 1812 exposed weaknesses in the executive branch yet also reinforced civilian control of the military and the importance of congressional authorization. James Monroe's presidency, often remembered for stability, masked unresolved tensions over slavery, territorial expansion, and national identity.

Collectively, the presidents of the founding era established the executive as a constitutional branch while demonstrating that the office remained malleable. The presidency was neither dominant nor marginal; it functioned as one component of a deliberately designed system of checks and balances that resists both paralysis and tyranny.

The founding era thus set the baseline against which all later expansions of presidential power would be measured. It demonstrated that strength could coexist with restraint, and that the durability of the presidency depended as much on what presidents declined to do as on what they chose to do. The tensions embedded in the office at its creation—between energy and accountability, leadership and limitation—would recur throughout American history, shaping every subsequent era.

George Washington (1789-1797)

Early Life and Background

George Washington was born on February 22, 1732, in Westmoreland County, Virginia, into a moderately prosperous planter family that belonged to the Virginia gentry but not its political elite. His childhood was shaped by plantation life along the Potomac and Rappahannock rivers and by a practical, locally focused education rather than the classical schooling common among elite colonial families. The death of his father, Augustine Washington, when George was eleven proved formative, ending any prospect of education in England and pushing him toward early responsibility and self-discipline. Influenced strongly by his older half-brother Lawrence, a British military officer who introduced him to imperial culture and Virginia's leading circles, Washington absorbed ideals of honor, service, and reputation at a young age. By his late teens, his training in mathematics and surveying enabled him to work as a professional surveyor, marking an early transition from dependent youth to self-reliant adulthood and setting the foundation for his later military and political career.

Washington gained frontier experience as a surveyor and then as a Virginia militia officer during the French and Indian War[6], where both his ambition and early mistakes taught him important lessons about leadership, discipline, and the limits of colonial authority within the British Empire. After resigning his commission in 1758, Washington devoted himself to managing Mount Vernon, transforming it into a profitable and diversified plantation while serving intermittently in the Virginia House of Burgesses, where he quietly opposed British taxation policies. His return to military life came in 1775, when the Second Continental Congress appointed him commander in chief of the Continental Army, a role in which he demonstrated resilience, patience, and an ability to hold together a fragile revolutionary force despite repeated setbacks. Washington's voluntary resignation of his commission at the end of the Revolutionary War solidified his reputation for republican virtue and civilian supremacy, making him the nation's most trusted figure and the natural choice to preside over the Constitutional Convention and, ultimately, to become the first president of the United States.

Domestic Life

Washington's domestic life was defined by duty and personal restraint rather than warmth or intimacy. In 1759, he married Martha Dandridge Custis, a wealthy widow with two young children, and together they established Mount Vernon as one of Virginia's most prominent plantation households. Although the marriage produced no children of their own, Washington acted as a devoted stepfather and later guardian to Martha's grandchildren. He managed Mount Vernon with close attention to agricultural advances, finances, and social

---

6 George Washington's early military experience came during the French and Indian War (1754–1763), the North American theater of the larger Seven Years' War between Britain and France. Serving as a young Virginia militia officer, he gained practical training in frontier warfare, logistics, and command, while early defeats and later service under British General Edward Braddock provided lasting lessons in discipline and leadership. The conflict established Washington's regional reputation and shaped his understanding of military organization and imperial authority, experience that proved invaluable during the American Revolution.

obligations. He frequently hosted guests and maintained the expectations of a leading Virginia household. At the same time, Washington's domestic life was inseparable from the institution of slavery; he enslaved hundreds of people over his lifetime, relying on their labor to sustain his household and estate. Washington found personal satisfaction in order, routine, and the responsibilities of family and home, viewing domestic stability as an essential foundation for public service.

POLITICAL AFFILIATION AND GOVERNING STYLE

Washington did not affiliate formally with any political party, and he regarded factionalism as a threat to republican stability. In practice, however, his administration quickly became associated with Federalist policies, particularly those advanced by Alexander Hamilton. Washington's governing style was deliberative and cautious. He solicited competing viewpoints, weighed them privately, and decided firmly once judgment was reached.

Washington's most significant contributions were operational: he made the executive branch function. He established cabinet members, clarified the president's role as chief executive, and affirmed civilian control of the military without spectacle. These practices were not dictated by constitutional text. They were choices—made deliberately.

In foreign affairs, Washington articulated and enforced a policy of neutrality. His Neutrality Proclamation asserted executive authority in diplomacy at a moment when entanglement in European war could have been fatal to the young republic. The policy disappointed allies abroad and angered domestic partisans, but it preserved national independence when institutional capacity remained fragile.

ACCOMPLISHMENTS AND VISION

Washington's accomplishments evolved between his first and second terms, reflecting the transition from institutional creation to institutional preservation. During his first term, Washington focused on making the new constitutional system operational. His administration established the executive departments, implemented federal taxation, stabilized public credit through assumption of state debts, and operationalized the judiciary, transforming constitutional text into functioning governance. These actions were not merely administrative; they created the conditions under which federal authority could be exercised consistently across states. Washington's support for Hamilton's financial program—though controversial—provided the fiscal foundation necessary for national survival and international credibility, anchoring the presidency within a workable framework of law, finance, and enforcement.

In his second term, Washington's priorities shifted toward preserving national stability amid foreign war and domestic polarization. His Neutrality Proclamation asserted executive authority in foreign affairs at a moment when legislative guidance was limited and international entanglement posed existential risk. The suppression of the Whiskey Rebellion[7] demonstrated that federal law would be enforced without reverting to military rule or personal dominance, reinforcing civilian supremacy and constitutional process. Washington's decision to step down after two terms, while not legislated, proved among his most consequential acts: it embedded the principle of voluntary restraint as a governing norm. Collectively, Washington's two terms established the presidency as a durable institution—capable of energy without autocracy and authority without permanence.

CRITICISMS AND CONTROVERSIES

Washington's presidency was not without controversy. His support for Hamilton's economic agenda provoked opposition from agrarian and states' rights advocates, who feared excessive centralization. Critics argued that policies such as the national bank exceeded constitutional authority and favored commercial interests over farmers.

Washington's ownership of enslaved people remains a central moral contradiction. While he expressed private misgivings about slavery and took steps toward emancipation in his will, his presidency did not challenge the institution. This silence reflected both personal caution and the political realities of maintaining fragile national unity.

---

7 The Whiskey Rebellion was an uprising by western Pennsylvania farmers protesting a federal excise tax on distilled spirits. President George Washington's decisive use of federal militia power to suppress the resistance affirmed the new Constitution's authority and the federal government's ability to enforce its laws.

Legacy

Washington's legacy rests foremost on his indispensable role in establishing the legitimacy and durability of the American republic. As commander of the Continental Army, he provided the steady leadership necessary to secure independence against a global superpower, maintaining cohesion among often-fractious colonial forces and civilian authorities. Yet his greatest contribution arguably came after victory, when he voluntarily relinquished military power and later stepped down after two presidential terms, setting a durable precedent for civilian supremacy and the peaceful transfer of authority. As the nation's first president, Washington defined the contours of the executive office—shaping cabinet governance, establishing neutrality in foreign affairs, enforcing federal law during the Whiskey Rebellion, and supporting the creation of a stable national financial system under Alexander Hamilton. In doing so, he transformed an abstract constitutional framework into a functioning government capable of commanding both domestic loyalty and international respect.

Washington's enduring historical significance lies in his model of restrained, institution-centered leadership at a moment when republican government remained fragile and unproven. He consistently prioritized national unity over regional or factional interests, warning in his Farewell Address against partisan division, sectionalism, and entangling alliances—concerns that have echoed across subsequent centuries of American political development. Ultimately, his legacy is that of a founder who embodied republican virtue, institutional restraint, and a commitment to constitutional order, establishing precedents that shaped the presidency and helped secure the long-term stability of the United States.

The Issue of Slavery. George Washington freed his enslaved people through a legal decision made late in life. Over time, Washington grew increasingly uneasy with slavery, influenced by Enlightenment ideals, the contradictions between slavery and the principles of the American Revolution, practical difficulties managing enslaved labor at Mount Vernon, and the moral views of those around him, including Alexander Hamilton and the Marquis de Lafayette. By the 1790s, he privately expressed the belief that slavery should end through a lawful, gradual process, though he avoided public advocacy to preserve national unity.

Washington acted on these views in his 1799 will. He ordered that the 123 enslaved people he personally owned be freed upon Martha Washington's death, and he provided for the care, education, and financial support of the young, elderly, and infirm among them—an unprecedented provision for a major Virginia planter. He delayed emancipation until Martha's death to avoid breaking up families, since many enslaved people at Mount Vernon were legally owned by the Custis estate and intermarried with those that Washington owned; immediate emancipation would have forced painful separations. In practice, Martha freed Washington's enslaved people in 1801, about a year after his death, out of concern for her own safety. Washington thus became the only major Founding Father to free all the enslaved people he personally owned, doing so through careful legal planning that balanced moral conviction, family considerations, and the legal constraints of slavery in Virginia.

John Adams (1797-1801)

Early Life and Background

John Adams was born in 1735 in Braintree, Massachusetts, into a modest but respected Puritan family, where his childhood was shaped by rural labor, strict moral expectations, and a strong sense of civic duty. His father, a farmer and local official, insisted that Adams pursue education rather than agriculture, setting him on a path that contrasted with his own early inclinations toward outdoor work and independence. Though not an outstanding student at first, Adams gradually developed intellectual discipline through classical study and religious instruction, ultimately enrolling at Harvard at age sixteen. These early experiences formed the foundation of Adams's lifelong belief in law, education, and public service as the pillars of a stable republic.

John Adams's professional career began in law after graduating from Harvard and studying law in Worcester. His defense of British soldiers after the Boston Massacre in 1770, while unpopular, established his commitment to the rule of law over public passion. Adams soon moved into revolutionary politics, serving as a delegate to the Continental Congress, where he played a central role in advocating independence and shaping early American governance. During the Revolutionary War, he became one of the nation's most important diplomats, helping secure French support and later negotiating the Treaty of Paris, which formally ended the war. After independence, Adams continued in public service as U.S. minister to several European nations, vice president under George Washington, and ultimately as the second president of the United States, bringing to each role a lawyer's respect for institutions, balance, and constitutional order.

DOMESTIC LIFE

John Adams's domestic life was defined by a deeply consequential partnership with his wife, Abigail Smith Adams, whom he married in 1764. Their marriage was intellectually engaged and emotionally close, sustained largely through extensive correspondence during Adams's long absences in public service. Abigail managed the household and family finances in Braintree while raising their children, including John Quincy Adams, and served as Adams's most trusted confidante and advisor. The demands of revolutionary and diplomatic life placed strain on the family, but their shared commitment to education, moral responsibility, and republican virtue reinforced both their marriage and their public roles. Adams's home life thus functioned not as a retreat from politics, but as a formative extension of his political thought and character.

POLITICAL AFFILIATION AND GOVERNING STYLE

A Federalist by conviction, Adams believed strongly in the rule of law, constitutional order, and the importance of executive authority. Unlike Washington, however, he lacked both the unifying stature and the political flexibility needed to manage emerging partisan divisions. Adams governed with a strong sense of personal responsibility and moral duty, often resisting political compromise even when pragmatism might have served him better.

Adams insisted on independence from party leadership, particularly from Alexander Hamilton, whose influence within the Federalist Party he distrusted. This independence left Adams politically isolated. His governing style was principled, prioritizing correctness over coalition-building.

ACCOMPLISHMENTS AND VISION

Adams's presidency was defined by his commitment to preserving American independence and stability during a period of intense international and domestic pressure. Facing escalating tensions with revolutionary France, Adams strengthened the U.S. Navy and managed the Quasi-War[8], an undeclared naval conflict in the Atlantic. Despite strong Federalist support for a full-scale war, Adams pursued diplomacy, ultimately securing the Convention of 1800, which ended hostilities and preserved American neutrality[9]. This decision reflected his central vision: safeguarding the young republic from entangling alliances and costly wars that could threaten its fragile institutions. Adams also oversaw the continued development of federal authority, including the strengthening of the executive branch and the establishment of a more capable national defense.

Adams's broader vision centered on the rule of law, balanced government, and the cultivation of civic virtue. A principal architect of American independence and a leading political thinker of the founding generation, he believed that durable republican government required strong institutions capable of checking both popular excess and concentrated power. He supported the development of an independent judiciary, signing the Judiciary Act of 1801, which expanded the federal court system and helped shape the long-term structure of American juris-

---

8 The Quasi-War was an undeclared naval conflict between the United States and France from 1798 to 1800, arising after France began seizing American merchant ships amid tensions following the Jay Treaty with Britain. Diplomatic efforts collapsed during the XYZ Affair (1797–1798), when French intermediaries—later labeled "X, Y, and Z"—demanded bribes and loans before formal negotiations could proceed. Public outrage in the United States fueled a surge of anti-French sentiment, accelerated naval expansion, and pushed the young republic toward armed conflict at sea, ultimately resolved by the Convention of 1800.

9 Founding-era American neutrality was a strategic doctrine of non-alignment in European power struggles, designed to safeguard the young republic's sovereignty, commerce, and internal cohesion until it was strong enough to assert itself more fully on the world stage.

prudence. Though his presidency was politically contentious, Adams's leadership emphasized constitutional stability, national sovereignty, and the careful stewardship of the republic during its formative years.

Criticisms and Controversies

Adams' presidency is most criticized for the passage of the Alien and Sedition Acts[10], which restricted immigration and criminalized criticism of the federal government. Enacted amid fears of foreign subversion and domestic unrest, the laws represented a serious violation of civil liberties and contradicted foundational principles of free expression. Adams did not initiate the legislation, but he signed it into law and failed to prevent its enforcement.

The acts provoked widespread opposition and accelerated partisan polarization. Jefferson and Madison's responses, including the Virginia and Kentucky Resolutions, challenged federal authority and introduced doctrines of nullification. Adams' inability—or unwillingness—to restrain Federalist excesses remains the central stain on his presidency.

Legacy

John Adams's legacy rests foremost on his unwavering commitment to the rule of law and the institutional stability of the early American republic. As a principal advocate for independence and a leading diplomat in securing French support and negotiating the Treaty of Paris (1783), Adams helped establish the United States as a legitimate sovereign nation. His presidency was marked by the formidable challenge of navigating the Quasi-War with France, during which he resisted strong domestic pressure to declare a full-scale war. By pursuing negotiation and ultimately achieving the Convention of 1800, Adams preserved American neutrality and avoided a potentially disastrous conflict, reinforcing the principle that prudent diplomacy could safeguard national interests as effectively as military action. His steadfast support for a

---

10 The Alien and Sedition Acts were a series of laws passed in 1798 that strengthened federal authority by allowing the deportation of non-citizens deemed dangerous and criminalizing criticism of the federal government. Enacted amid fears of war with France, the acts were abused and used largely against political opponents and journalists, provoking widespread backlash and shaping longstanding debates over civil liberties and constitutional limits.

strong but balanced federal government and an independent judiciary further shaped the constitutional framework of the young republic.

Yet Adams's legacy is also defined by controversy, particularly the passage of the Alien and Sedition Acts, which damaged his reputation and raised enduring questions about civil liberties during times of perceived national crisis. These laws, aimed at suppressing dissent and controlling foreign influence, appeared to contradict the revolutionary ideals of free expression and fueled partisan divisions that defined the early party system. Nevertheless, Adams's peaceful transfer of power to Thomas Jefferson following the contentious election of 1800 stands as one of his most consequential contributions. By accepting electoral defeat and upholding constitutional processes, Adams helped establish the norm of orderly political transition—an essential precedent for the durability of American democratic governance. Over time, historians have increasingly recognized Adams as a principled, if often austere, statesman whose commitment to republican institutions outweighed his political missteps.

Adams's Views on Slavery. Adams never owned slaves and regarded slavery as incompatible with republican ideals, believing it corrupted both masters and the political system that tolerated it. Adams supported gradual emancipation and legal reforms rather than immediate abolition, arguing that abrupt change could destabilize the fragile union. As a political leader, he avoided making slavery a central national issue, fearing it would fracture cooperation among the states during the Revolution and early republic. His views thus combined personal moral opposition with political caution, illustrating the tension between principle and pragmatism in the founding generation.

Thomas Jefferson (1801–1809)

Early Life and Background

Thomas Jefferson was born on April 13, 1743, at Shadwell, his family's plantation near Charlottesville in the Colony of Virginia. He was the third of ten children born to Peter Jefferson, a successful planter, surveyor, and cartographer, and Jane Randolph Jefferson, who came from one of Virginia's most prominent families. Jefferson thus grew up at the intersection of frontier self-reliance and elite colonial society.

Jefferson's childhood was marked by intellectual discipline. His father, largely self-educated, instilled in him a respect for learning and practical knowledge, while his mother's Randolph lineage exposed him to Virginia's political and social elite. When Jefferson was 14 years old, his father died, leaving him a sizable inheritance, including land and enslaved laborers—an early and lasting contradiction in Jefferson's life.

From a young age, Jefferson showed exceptional academic promise. He received a classical education, studying Latin, Greek, French, mathematics, history, and philosophy. He was also trained in music, becoming an accomplished violinist, and developed lifelong habits of reading, note-taking, and self-directed study. His intellectual curiosity was broad and intense, extending from literature and science to architecture and natural history.

At age 16, Jefferson entered the College of William & Mary, where he studied under Dr. William Small, a Scottish Enlightenment thinker who introduced him to the ideas of John Locke, Francis Bacon, and Isaac Newton. While still young, he also began legal training under George Wythe, one of the most respected legal scholars in the colonies.

Jefferson was admitted to the Virginia bar in 1767 and quickly gained a reputation as a skilled legal thinker and persuasive writer rather than a courtroom orator. His early adulthood was marked by intense intellectual productivity, estate management at Monticello, and growing engagement with colonial politics.

Jefferson entered public life in 1769 as a member of the Virginia House of Burgesses, where he aligned with reform-minded legislators resisting British imperial authority. His political identity took shape around principles of self-government, limits on centralized power, and natural rights, themes that intensified as relations with Britain deteriorated. When the American colonies moved toward independence, Jefferson's greatest early contribution came through his pen rather than his voice.

In 1776, at just 33 years old, Jefferson was selected to draft the Declaration of Independence. Drawing heavily on Enlightenment philosophy—especially the concept of inherent natural rights—he produced a document that articulated the moral and political justification for independence in clear, universal language. This achievement established Jefferson as the Revolution's most eloquent theorist of liberty.

Following independence, Jefferson returned to Virginia politics, serving as Governor of Virginia (1779–1781). His governorship was controversial; British forces invaded Virginia, and Jefferson was criticized for administrative weaknesses.

Jefferson's stature recovered and expanded through diplomacy. From 1785 to 1789, he served as U.S. Minister to France, succeeding Benjamin Franklin. Living in Paris during the early stages of the French Revolution, Jefferson absorbed European political thought while advocating American commercial and diplomatic interests. His time abroad strengthened his belief in republican government, religious freedom, and opposition to hereditary privilege.

Upon returning to the United States, Jefferson became the nation's first Secretary of State (1790–1793) under George Washington. In this role, he emerged as the intellectual leader of what became the Democratic-Republican Party, opposing Alexander Hamilton's vision of a strong centralized government, national bank, and maintaining ties to Britain. Jefferson instead favored states' rights, agrarian republicanism, and sympathy toward revolutionary France.

Jefferson resigned from Washington's cabinet in 1793 but remained deeply engaged in national politics. He was elected Vice President in 1796, serving under political rival John Adams. This uneasy partnership sharpened partisan divisions, particularly over foreign policy and civil liberties. Jefferson strongly opposed the Alien and Sedition Acts, viewing this as unconstitutional threats to free speech and republican governance.

In the bitterly contested election of 1800, Jefferson ran against Adams once more. After a tied electoral vote and a prolonged decision in the House of Representatives, Jefferson emerged victorious. His inauguration in 1801 marked what he famously called the "Revolution of 1800"—the first peaceful transfer of power between opposing political parties in U.S. history.

Domestic Life

Jefferson's family life was centered around Monticello, the plantation home he designed and refined atop a hill near Charlottesville, Virginia. More than a residence, Monticello functioned as a working estate, intellectual retreat, and architectural experiment.

Jefferson married Martha Wayles Skelton in 1772. Their marriage was reportedly affectionate and intellectually compatible, though marked by repeated tragedy. Martha endured difficult pregnancies, and six children were born. However, only two daughters—Martha ("Patsy") and Mary ("Polly")—survived to adulthood. Martha Jefferson died in 1782 at age 33, deeply affecting Jefferson. He never remarried and largely withdrew emotionally, later writing that the loss left him permanently altered.

As a widower, Jefferson devoted himself to his children and grandchildren, maintaining a close and instructive relationship. He emphasized education, languages, music, and moral reasoning, especially for his daughters. Jefferson was a hands-on father in intellectual matters, though much of the daily labor of household management was carried out by others.

Music and learning were central to Jefferson's home life. He was an accomplished violinist, often playing several hours a day in his younger years. His personal library—eventually numbering in the thousands—was one of the finest in America and later formed the foundation of the Library of Congress after the War of 1812. Monticello also served as a place of constant hospitality, with Jefferson entertaining an ongoing stream of guests, foreign visitors, and political allies.

Despite Jefferson's public commitment to liberty, his domestic life was inseparable from slavery. Monticello relied on the labor of hundreds of enslaved people, whose work sustained the household, agriculture, and Jefferson's lifestyle. Jefferson acknowledged slavery as morally troubling but failed to free most of those he enslaved, remaining financially dependent on the system throughout his life. This contradiction stands as one of the most enduring and difficult aspects of his legacy.

Financial strain was a persistent feature of Jefferson's private life. Poor agricultural returns, inherited debts, and an expensive lifestyle left him chronically in debt, forcing the sale of property and enslaved people to meet obligations.

POLITICAL AFFILIATION AND GOVERNING STYLE

As leader of the Democratic-Republican Party, Jefferson came to office committed to limited federal authority, strict constitutional adherence, and opposition to financial centralization. He viewed the Federalist vision as dangerously elitist and corrosive to republican virtue.

In office, Jefferson governed pragmatically. He relied heavily on trusted advisers, particularly James Madison, and conducted much of his leadership through informal channels. While he publicly emphasized restraint and decentralization, Jefferson was willing to stretch constitutional interpretation when he believed national interest required it. His presidency thus revealed the tension between constitutional faithfulness and executive responsibility.

Accomplishments and Vision

During his first term, Jefferson focused on stabilizing the republic after a bitter partisan decade and demonstrating that a Democratic-Republican administration could govern without dismantling federal institutions. His most consequential achievement, the Louisiana Purchase (Figure 5), dramatically expanded the nation's territory, secured control of the Mississippi River, and removed France as a continental rival. Closely linked to this expansion was the Lewis and Clark expedition[11] (1804–1806), which Jefferson authorized to explore the newly acquired lands, assess commercial potential, and establish an American presence in the trans-Mississippi West. While framed publicly as a scientific mission, the expedition served strategic and diplomatic purposes, strengthening U.S. claims to the region and providing invaluable geographic, ethnographic, and scientific knowledge. Together, these actions reshaped the nation's physical and strategic horizon while reinforcing executive flexibility exercised within constitutional bounds.

Jefferson's second term was dominated by foreign policy crisis and exposed the limits of executive power deployed through economic means. The Embargo Act of 1807 represented his most ambitious legislative initiative, using federal authority to restrict American trade to avoid war with Britain and France. Constitutionally enacted but unevenly enforced, the embargo inflicted significant domestic economic harm while failing to coerce European powers.

Criticisms and Controversies

The Embargo Act of 1807 stands as Jefferson's most consequential failure. Intended to coerce Britain and France into respecting American neutrality, the embargo devastated American commerce, particularly in New England, while failing to alter European policy. The episode

---

11 Commissioned by Jefferson after the Louisiana Purchase, the Corps of Discovery—led by Meriwether Lewis and William Clark—was tasked with mapping the new western territories, establishing relations with Native American tribes, and finding a practical route to the Pacific Ocean.

revealed the limits of economic coercion (at least in the nascent republic) and exposed internal divisions within Jefferson's own coalition.

Jefferson's constitutional inconsistency remains a common critique. His strict constructionist philosophy yielded to expansive interpretation when executing the Louisiana Purchase, undermining the fidelity of his stated principles. His presidency also failed to confront slavery or Indigenous displacement, allowing moral and humanitarian crises to deepen under the banner of limited government.

LEGACY

Jefferson's most lasting contribution is his authorship of the Declaration of Independence, which articulated the principles of natural rights, equality, and government by consent in language. These ideas became foundational not only to American constitutional culture but also to democratic movements worldwide. Jefferson helped define what the United States claimed to stand for, even when practice fell short of principle.

As president, Jefferson reshaped the nation's future through the Louisiana Purchase, which doubled the country's size, secured control of the Mississippi River, and set the United States on a path toward continental expansion. Though the acquisition stretched his strict interpretation of constitutional authority, it reflected Jefferson's pragmatic judgment that national survival and opportunity sometimes required flexibility in governance.

Jefferson's vision of government emphasized limited federal power, civil liberties, religious freedom, and an educated citizenry. His advocacy for the separation of church and state and his support for public education—including the founding of the University of Virginia—reinforced his belief that democracy depended on informed, independent thinkers rather than inherited privilege or centralized authority.

Jefferson and Slavery. At the same time, Jefferson's legacy is inseparable from his failure to reconcile his ideals with slavery. While he publicly condemned slavery as incompatible with liberty, he remained personally and economically dependent on enslaved labor. This contradiction has made Jefferson a central figure in modern discussions about the gap between America's founding principles and its historical realities.

Sally Hemings. For more than two centuries, claims that Jefferson fathered children with Hemings were disputed or dismissed.

In 1998, DNA testing[12] provided strong evidence that a male in Jefferson's paternal line fathered Eston Hemings, Sally Hemings's youngest son. Combined with extensive documentary and contextual evidence, the historical consensus today holds that Jefferson himself was the most likely father of Hemings's children, a conclusion endorsed by institutions such as Monticello and by most modern historians.

Sally Hemings had six known children, four of whom survived to adulthood. Unlike most people Jefferson enslaved, these children received unusual treatment: they were trained in skilled trades, allowed greater mobility, and eventually gained freedom—some informally during Jefferson's lifetime and others through his will. Sally Hemings herself was never formally freed but lived the final years of her life in Charlottesville with her sons.

---

12 Foster, E. A., et al., "Jefferson Fathered Slave's Last Child," Nature 396 (1998): 27–28; Thomas Jefferson Foundation, Report of the Research Committee on Thomas Jefferson and Sally Hemings (2000).

James   Madison   (1809-1817)

Early Life and Background

James Madison was born on March 16, 1751, at Belle Grove plantation in Port Conway, Virginia, and grew up primarily at his family's estate, Montpelier, in Orange County. He was the eldest of twelve children in a well-established Virginia planter family; his father, James Madison Sr., managed extensive agricultural lands worked by enslaved laborers, placing young Madison within the social and economic world of the colonial gentry.

Madison was a small, physically frail child, prone to recurring illnesses that kept him close to home. This fragility likely shaped his temperament—quiet, introspective, and intensely studious—and encouraged long hours of reading rather than the outdoor field life typical of many peers.

His early education was unusually rigorous. Taught first by private tutors, Madison studied Latin, Greek, mathematics, history, and moral philosophy. In his teens he attended a boarding school run by Donald Robertson, a Scottish educator whose Enlightenment outlook left a lasting impression. Madison developed an early fascination with ancient republics, law, and political theory, interests that would later inform his constitutional thinking.

Religiously, Madison grew up in the Anglican tradition but became sensitive to issues of religious liberty, witnessing persecution of dissenting sects such as Baptists in Virginia. These experiences planted early convictions about freedom of conscience and limits on government power over religion.

After completing his education at the College of New Jersey (Princeton) in 1771, James Madison returned to Virginia. He briefly considered the ministry or law but soon gravitated toward public service, driven by a conviction that stable republican government required careful design and informed leadership.

Madison's political career began during the American Revolution. In his mid-twenties, he served on Virginia's Committee of Safety and later in the Virginia House of Delegates, where he worked closely with Thomas Jefferson. One of Madison's earliest legislative achievements was helping Jefferson secure passage of the Virginia Statute for Religious Freedom, cementing his long-held belief in freedom of conscience.

From 1780 to 1783, Madison served in the Continental Congress, where he confronted firsthand the weaknesses of the Articles of Confederation—especially Congress's inability to tax, regulate commerce, or enforce national decisions.

Madison emerged as a central figure at the Constitutional Convention of 1787. He proposed the Virginia Plan, which became the framework for the final document. Although compromises altered his original vision, Madison's role in shaping the structure of the federal government earned him lasting recognition as the "Father of the Constitution."

Following the convention, Madison became one of the Constitution's most effective public defender. Alongside Alexander Hamilton and John Jay, he co-authored The Federalist Papers, articulating the logic of federalism, separation of powers, and checks and balances. His essays remain foundational texts in political theory.

Madison served in the U.S. House of Representatives from 1789 to 1797, where he played a key role in drafting the Bill of Rights, translating constitutional principles into enforceable protections. During this period, he gradually broke with Hamilton over the scope of federal power, aligning with Jefferson in what became the Democratic-Republican Party.

When Jefferson assumed the presidency in 1801, Madison became Secretary of State, serving for eight years. In this role, he helped manage major foreign policy challenges, including the Louisiana Purchase and escalating tensions with Britain and France.

DOMESTIC LIFE

In 1794, at age 43, Madison married Dolley Madison, a 26-year-old widow whose warmth, and social intelligence complemented his reserved and scholarly temperament.

The Madisons had no biological children, but James adopted Dolley's son, John Payne Todd, from her first marriage. Todd's life-long struggles with alcoholism, debt, and recklessness became a persistent emotional and financial burden on the Madisons, requiring repeated interventions and draining their limited resources.

At home, Madison preferred reading, correspondence, and structured conversation to leisure. Dolley, by contrast, excelled in the social sphere, acting as both hostess and political facilitator. Their relationship functioned as a public–private partnership: Madison supplied ideas and policy; Dolley managed relationships, softened political tensions, and humanized the presidency.

As First Lady, Dolley transformed the White House into a center of inclusive republican sociability, hosting gatherings that bridged partisan divides. Madison relied heavily on her political instincts and social memory, particularly given his quiet demeanor and aversion to personal confrontation.

The Madisons divided their time between public service in Philadelphia and Washington and private life at Montpelier, the Virginia plantation Madison inherited from his father. Like other members of the Virginia gentry, Madison lived within and benefited from the system of enslavement, owning enslaved people throughout his life. While he expressed moral unease about slavery in theory, he never freed his enslaved laborers during his lifetime, a central contradiction between his principles and practice.

Political Affiliation and Governing Style

As a Democratic-Republican, Madison entered the presidency committed to limited federal power, strict constitutional guidance, and legislative primacy. Yet he governed during a period of escalating international pressure that tested these commitments. His early governing style emphasized consultation, constitutional process, and deference to Congress rather than executive assertion.

Madison was reluctant to centralize authority or impose decisive control over military and administrative institutions. This restraint reflected his principle and temperament, but it also exposed weaknesses associated with an intentionally restrained executive approach during crisis. His presidency also highlighted the challenges of translating constitutional design into effective governance under external threat.

Accomplishments and Vision

Madison's accomplishments evolved over the course of his presidency as external pressures forced adaptation beyond his initial commitment to restrain executive authority.

During his first term, Madison emphasized constitutional process and legislative primacy, relying on economic pressure and diplomatic negotiation to defend American neutrality. This approach reflected his long-standing belief that republican government required limited executive assertion. However, the failure of these measures and escalating conflict with Britain culminated in the War of 1812 (Figure 6) exposing deficiencies in military preparedness, finance, and administrative coordination. The early conduct of the war revealed the limits of decentralized governance and underscored the gap between constitutional design and operational capacity in moments of crisis.

Madison's second term marked a pragmatic shift toward institutional strengthening in response to wartime experience. Following the burning of Washington, he supported measures that expanded federal capacity, including the rechartering of the Bank of the United States, improvements in national finance, and more coordinated military administration. While Madison remained philosophically cautious about concentrated power, his acceptance of these reforms reflected recognition that constitutional durability required functional institutions capable of sustaining national defense and economic stability. The long-term impact of his presidency lies less in battlefield outcomes than in this evolution: Madison demonstrated that constitutional fidelity could coexist with adaptive governance, laying groundwork for a stronger federal framework without abandoning the principle of civilian control or legislative oversight.

CRITICISMS AND CONTROVERSIES

Madison's presidency faced significant criticism for its management of foreign policy and the nation's preparedness for war. His decision to lead the United States into the War of 1812 against Great Britain was controversial, particularly among New England Federalists who opposed the conflict on economic and political grounds. Critics argued that Madison had inadequately prepared the nation militarily and financially, resulting in early American setbacks, including failed invasions of Canada and the British burning of Washington, D.C., in 1814. His reliance on state militias rather than a strong standing army exposed weaknesses in national defense and raised questions about the effectiveness of Jeffersonian policies that had reduced military expenditures prior to the war.

Madison also encountered domestic opposition tied to economic disruption and constitutional debates. The war severely strained American commerce, especially in maritime regions, and contributed to rising sectional tensions. Federalists convened the Hartford Convention (1814–1815), where some delegates discussed constitutional amendments and, controversially, the possibility of regional resistance to federal authority—developments that underscored deep dissatisfaction with Madison's leadership. Additionally, Madison's eventual support for measures such as a national bank and protective tariffs after the war drew criticism from strict constructionists who saw these policies as inconsistent with his earlier constitutional positions. While his presidency ultimately concluded with a surge of nationalism following the war's end, Madison's wartime leadership and policy reversals remained subjects of debate among historians.

LEGACY

Madison is remembered foremost as the principal architect of the U.S. Constitution. His preparation for the 1787 Constitutional Convention, authorship of the Virginia Plan, and detailed notes of the debates established the framework for a federal government strong enough to govern yet constrained enough to protect liberty. His thinking on separation of powers, checks and balances, and federalism remains the foundation of American governance.

Equally important was his role in drafting the Bill of Rights. Although initially skeptical that amendments were necessary, Madison came to see them as essential to public trust and individual liberty. The first ten amendments are among the most revered elements of American law.

Madison's essays in The Federalist Papers[13] elevated him from statesman to revered political theorist.

As president, Madison's legacy is more complex. The War of 1812 exposed weaknesses in American military preparedness and governance, yet its outcome helped confirm U.S. independence and national credibility. While not remembered as a commanding executive, Madison's presidency demonstrated constitutional restraint—a deliberate avoidance of personal power in favor of institutional authority.

Madison's legacy also includes unresolved contradictions. Despite championing liberty and equality in theory, he lived as a slaveholder and failed to translate his constitutional ideals into decisive action against slavery. His cautious temperament and fear of national fracture limited his willingness to confront the institution directly, a hesitation that later generations would judge harshly.

Madison's ultimate legacy is that he did not seek popular acclaim, military glory, or personal dominance. Instead, he gave the United States something rarer: a durable constitutional framework capable of self-correction. In that sense, Madison remains the nation's quiet guardian—the mind behind the machinery of American democracy, still shaping how power is exercised, limited, and justified more than two centuries later.

---

13 The Federalist Papers (1787–1788) remain among the most important sources for understanding the framers' intent regarding the Constitution, republican government, separation of powers, and federalism; see Alexander Hamilton, James Madison, and John Jay, The Federalist Papers, ed. Clinton Rossiter (New York: Signet Classics, 2003).

JAMES MONROE (1817–1825)

EARLY LIFE AND BACKGROUND

James Monroe was born on April 28, 1758, in Westmoreland County, Virginia, into a family of modest means. His father, Spence Monroe, was a small planter and carpenter; his mother, Elizabeth Jones Monroe, came from a locally established Virginia family. Monroe grew up in the tidewater plantation culture of colonial Virginia, where landownership, Anglican religious life, and local civic duty shaped everyday expectations.

Monroe's early education began at home and continued at Campbelltown Academy, a respected local school. His childhood was disrupted by tragedy when both parents died while he was still a teenager, leaving him and his siblings orphaned. Responsibility came early: Monroe inherited property and relied on the guidance of relatives—particularly his uncle, Joseph Jones, a well-connected patriot who would later influence Monroe's political path.

At 16, Monroe entered the College of William & Mary, where he was exposed to Enlightenment ideas and revolutionary sentiment. In 1776, Monroe left college to join the Continental Army, effectively ending his formal schooling but launching a lifelong commitment to public service.

He served with distinction in the Continental Army, famously being wounded at the Battle of Trenton while leading an advance against Hessian forces. His courage earned him respect among Revolutionary leaders, but persistent injuries ended his active military career.

After the war, Monroe studied law under Thomas Jefferson, forging one of the most consequential mentor–protégé relationships of the early republic. He quickly entered public life, serving in the Virginia legislature and then the Continental Congress, where he advocated for a stronger national government—an evolution from his earlier suspicion of centralized power. This pragmatic shift reflected Monroe's growing belief that the fragile republic required unity and institutional strength.

Monroe's ascent accelerated through executive and diplomatic roles. He served as U.S. Senator from Virginia, then as Governor of Virginia. Internationally, Monroe proved especially valuable: he was appointed minister to France, where he helped negotiate the Louisiana Purchase, and later served as minister to Great Britain and Spain, gaining deep experience in European power politics.

His national stature peaked during the Madison administration, when Monroe held the rare dual role of Secretary of State and Secretary of War during the closing phase of the War of 1812. He reorganized the War Department after early failures and helped stabilize the nation's defense and diplomacy.

By 1816, Monroe was widely viewed as the natural successor to James Madison and won the presidency decisively.

DOMESTIC LIFE

In 1786 Monroe married Elizabeth Kortright Monroe, a New Yorker from a well-connected merchant family. Their marriage was close and enduring, though notably private. Elizabeth suffered from fragile health for much of her adult life, which limited her public appearances and shaped the couple's social life. Elizabeth avoided frequent entertaining and preferred a small, controlled household environment.

The Monroe's had three children, though only two daughters—Eliza and Maria—survived to adulthood. Family life was often disrupted by Monroe's long absences in military, diplomatic, and political service, particularly during extended postings in Europe. Elizabeth nevertheless played a quiet but influential role, most famously intervening in France to help secure the release of Madame Lafayette during the French Revolution.

As president, Monroe maintained residences at the White House and at Highland, his Virginia estate. Their home life emphasized dignity over warmth—formal dinners rather than convivial salons. Elizabeth established stricter social protocols than her predecessor, earning her the nickname "the Presidentess" in Washington society. Together, the Monroe's prioritized family loyalty, personal honor, and public duty over personal display.

POLITICAL AFFILIATION AND GOVERNING STYLE

A Democratic-Republican, Monroe governed during the so-called "Era of Good Feelings," a period marked by the temporary collapse of organized Federalist opposition. His governing style emphasized conciliation, geographic balance in appointments (frequently employed in subsequent presidencies), and avoidance of overt partisan conflict. Monroe believed that national unity was essential to institutional compliance after decades of revolutionary and wartime disruption.

Monroe relied heavily on experienced advisers and cabinet consensus. Rather than asserting executive dominance, he positioned the presidency as a stabilizing force, coordinating between regional interests and congressional factions. While partisan competition did not disappear, Monroe successfully lowered political temperature and reduced the visibility of factional struggle at the national level.

ACCOMPLISHMENTS AND VISION

James Monroe's accomplishments reflected a progression from domestic consolidation to enduring strategic doctrine. During his first term, Monroe focused on stabilizing national institutions in the aftermath of the War of 1812. His administration emphasized geographic balance in appointments, administrative normalization, and public reassurance during a period of economic volatility following the Panic of 1819[14]. While legislative innovation was limited, Monroe's extensive national tours and cautious governing style reinforced federal legitimacy across regions, helping to restore public confidence in national authority and easing partisan tension during the so-called Era of Good Feelings.

Monroe's second term produced his most lasting impact through articulation of the Monroe Doctrine[15], which asserted opposition to further European intervention in the Western Hemisphere. Although initially dependent on British naval power for enforcement, the doctrine established a durable principle that framed U.S. foreign policy for generations and elevated the presidency's role in defining strategic national interests. Domestically, Monroe presided over continued territorial consolidation and administrative continuity, while the Missouri Compromise temporarily managed sectional conflict over slavery. Monroe also oversaw acquisition of Florida from Spain, eliminating a lingering source of instability in the Southeast and strengthening national security. Collectively, these outcomes illustrate Monroe's contribution not through dramatic executive action, but through institutional consolidation and strategic clarity—strengthening national cohesion while deferring unresolved moral and political conflicts to the future.

CRITICISMS AND CONTROVERSIES

The Missouri Compromise of 1820 temporarily resolved sectional conflict over slavery's expansion by balancing free and slave state admissions[16]. While politically expedient, the compro-

---

14 The Panic of 1819 was the first major nationwide economic depression, triggered by post–War of 1812 financial contraction, a collapse in agricultural prices, and tight credit policies by the Second Bank of the United States. The crisis exposed weaknesses in the young nation's financial system and fueled popular distrust of banks and paper money.

15 Articulated by President Monroe in his annual message to Congress on December 2, 1823, the Monroe Doctrine declared that any attempt by European powers to extend their political systems into the Americas would be viewed as a hostile act against the United States. The doctrine became a foundational principle of American foreign policy.

16 The Missouri Compromise of 1820 was a legislative agreement designed to preserve the balance between free and slave states as the United States expanded westward. It admitted Missouri to the Union as a slave state and Maine as a free state, maintaining numerical parity in the Senate, and prohibited slavery in the remainder of the Louisiana Purchase territory north of latitude 36°30 (Mason-Dixon line) Missouri's southern boundary. Engineered

mise institutionalized geographic division and conceded slavery via a national fault line. Critics argue Monroe missed an opportunity to confront the long-term destabilizing consequences of slavery expansion, opting instead for short-term political accommodation.

The Panic of 1819 exposed structural weaknesses in the postwar economy and revealed the limited capacity of federal institutions to manage systemic financial disruption. Although Monroe bore little direct responsibility, the crisis undermined public confidence in the presidency and intensified regional resentment.

Legacy

Monroe's legacy rests on his role as a stabilizer and consolidator of the early American republic. His presidency coincided with the so-called Era of Good Feelings, a period marked by diminished partisan conflict and a broad desire for national unity after the War of 1812. Monroe emphasized competent governance and reconciliation helping the United States mature from a fragile post-revolutionary experiment into a more confident nation-state. His extensive tours of the country symbolized this unity and reinforced the legitimacy of the federal government across regions.

Internationally, Monroe's enduring imprint is the Monroe Doctrine. While initially more aspirational than enforceable, the doctrine became a cornerstone of American foreign policy, shaping U.S. relations with Europe and Latin America for generations. Domestically, Monroe's legacy is more mixed: he presided over westward expansion and economic growth but also over unresolved contradictions—most notably the Missouri Compromise, which temporarily managed sectional conflict over slavery while underscoring how deeply entrenched the issue had become.

Monroe was the last president of the Revolutionary generation, bridging the founding era and the more contentious age that followed. His legacy is one of quiet durability—a presidency that strengthened national identity and foreign-policy principles, even as it deferred the hardest moral and political conflicts to future generations.

---

largely by Speaker of the House Henry Clay, the compromise temporarily eased sectional tensions over slavery but implicitly acknowledged its centrality to national politics. The settlement was later undermined by the Kansas–Nebraska Act of 1854, which repealed the 36°30 restriction and contributed to rising sectional conflict leading to the Civil War.

JOHN QUINCY ADAMS (1825–1829)

EARLY LIFE AND BACKGROUND

John Quincy Adams was born on July 11, 1767, in Braintree (now Quincy), Massachusetts. He was the eldest son of John Adams and Abigail Adams, and from an early age he lived at the intersection of family life and national history.

His childhood unfolded during the American Revolution. As a boy, he witnessed pivotal events firsthand—most famously the Battle of Bunker Hill, which he observed from a nearby hill. With his father frequently away on diplomatic and political duties, John Quincy was raised largely under his mother's guidance. Abigail Adams was a rigorous educator, emphasizing discipline, moral reasoning, reading, and writing—habits that shaped her son's lifelong intellectual seriousness.

Unlike most American children of the era, John Quincy spent much of his youth abroad. Beginning at age 10, he accompanied his father on diplomatic missions to Europe, living in France, the Netherlands, and later Russia. These years exposed him to multiple languages, cultures, and political systems. He became fluent in French and Dutch and developed a precocious understanding of international affairs.

By his early teens, Adams was already serving in quasi-official roles, acting as a secretary and translator on diplomatic missions. He attended schools in Europe and briefly studied at Leiden University, experiences that gave him a cosmopolitan education that was rare among early American leaders.

This demanding, often isolated childhood produced a young man who was intellectually formidable, emotionally reserved, and deeply conscientious. The combination of revolutionary-era hardship, strict parental expectations, and early exposure to global diplomacy laid the foundation for John Quincy Adams's later career as one of the most learned and principled figures in American public life.

After returning to the United States, he graduated from Harvard College in 1787 and briefly practiced law, but public service quickly became his calling. His intellect, fluency in multiple languages, and deep familiarity with European politics made him a natural diplomat in the young republic.

In his late twenties and thirties, Adams built a formidable diplomatic resume. He served successively as U.S. minister to the Netherlands, Prussia, Russia, and Great Britain. As minister to Russia under James Madison, he strengthened American commercial ties during the Napoleonic era. He later played a central role in negotiating the Treaty of Ghent, which ended the War of 1812.

Adams's ascent accelerated after the war. As James Monroe's Secretary of State, he became one of the most influential diplomats in U.S. history. He negotiated key agreements expanding American borders and authored the principles behind what became known as the Monroe Doctrine. These accomplishments established him as a leading statesman of the era.

The presidential election of 1824 marked his transition from diplomat to national political figure. Running against Andrew Jackson, William H. Crawford, and Henry Clay, Adams finished second in the popular and electoral vote. Because no candidate won a majority, the election was decided by the House of Representatives, as provided by the Constitution. With Clay's support, Adams was chosen president.

Domestic Life

Adams married Louisa Catherine Adams, a well-educated, musically gifted woman born in London to an American father and English mother. Their marriage was affectionate but strained by long separations, Adams's demanding career, and differences in temperament.

The couple had four children, though only one—Charles Francis Adams—survived into old age. The deaths of two sons in young adulthood and the lifelong struggles of another weighed heavily on Adams and contributed to his somber outlook. He carried a deep sense of personal responsibility for his children's difficulties, reflecting his austere moral standards and high expectations.

Louisa Adams struggled with frequent illness and bouts of depression, made worse by years of isolation while her husband served abroad. Despite this, she proved resilient and capable, famously traveling across war-torn Europe to reunite with Adams in Russia during the War of 1812. As First Lady, she hosted social events competently but never comfortably, finding Washington society taxing and superficial.

Adams himself lived simply, even ascetically. He rose early, maintained meticulous diaries throughout his life, and avoided ostentation. As president, he famously swam naked in the Potomac River for exercise, cared little for fashionable dress, and resisted the social rituals expected of a national leader. He viewed public office as a moral obligation, not a path to status or pleasure.

While not a warm or charismatic family man by modern standards, he was deeply conscientious, loyal, and guided by an unwavering sense of principle that defined both his private and public lives.

Political Affiliation and Governing Style

Although aligned with National Republican principles, Adams resisted strict party identification and distrusted partisan politicians. He believed the presidency should be guided by merit, expertise, and national interest rather than partisan loyalty or popular appeal. His governing style was technocratic and programmatic, emphasizing long-term development over short-term political accomplishments.

Adams underestimated the growing power of party organization and electoral mobilization. He governed without a reliable political coalition, relying instead on constitutional authority and policy persuasion. This approach left him politically isolated in an era when the presidency was becoming increasingly dependent on popular mandate and party discipline.

ACCOMPLISHMENTS AND VISION

Quincy Adams's presidency was marked by an ambitious but often obstructed domestic agenda that emphasized national development and intellectual advancement. He advocated for federally funded internal improvements—including roads, canals, and harbor facilities—to promote economic growth and national cohesion. Adams also proposed the creation of a national university, a naval academy, and a network of astronomical observatories, reflecting his belief that government should support scientific and educational progress. While many of these proposals were ahead of their time and met resistance from Congress, they foreshadowed later federal initiatives and underscored his forward-looking vision of an active national government.

In foreign policy, Adams built on his earlier achievements as Secretary of State by maintaining stable international relations and promoting American commercial interests abroad. He secured favorable trade agreements and upheld the principles of the Monroe Doctrine, helping to solidify U.S. influence in the Western Hemisphere. Though his presidency was politically contentious and many initiatives stalled, Adams's commitment to modernization, education, and national infrastructure left a lasting intellectual and policy legacy that later administrations would adopt and expand.

CRITICISMS AND CONTROVERSIES

Adams' presidency was overshadowed by the disputed election of 1824 and persistent accusations of a "corrupt bargain" following his appointment of Henry Clay as Secretary of State[17]. Although

---

17 In the United States presidential election of 1824, four Democratic-Republican candidates (Andrew Jackson, John Quincy Adams, William H. Crawford, and Henry Clay) split the vote

no evidence substantiated claims of explicit quid pro quo, the perception of illegitimacy undermined Adams' political authority.

His inability—or unwillingness—to engage in mass political mobilization allowed opponents, particularly Andrew Jackson, to frame him as an elitist and disconnected from democratic sentiment.

Legacy

John Quincy Adams's legacy is defined less by his single presidential term than by a lifetime of principled public service.

His greatest historical impact came after the presidency. Adams is the only former president to serve an extended and consequential career in the U.S. House of Representatives. There, he became a relentless opponent of slavery, earning the nickname "Old Man Eloquent." He led the fight against the House "gag rule," which suppressed anti-slavery petitions, ultimately securing its repeal and establishing an important precedent for free speech and the right to petition.

Adams also left a lasting mark on American law and diplomacy. In 1841, he argued before the Supreme Court in the Amistad case, successfully defending the freedom of enslaved Africans who had rebelled against their captors. The case became a landmark moment in the legal and moral struggle against slavery.

As a statesman, Adams helped shape the nation's continental and international outlook. His diplomatic work cemented the United States' role as a sovereign power in the Western Hemisphere. His meticulous diaries, kept for nearly seven decades, remain one of the richest firsthand records of early American political life.

---

such that no candidate received a majority of the electoral votes. Although Andrew Jackson won both the popular and electoral votes, the Twelfth Amendment required a contingent election in the House of Representatives among the top three electoral vote-getters. On February 9, 1825, the House elected John Quincy Adams as president, a result widely criticized by Jackson's supporters as a "corrupt bargain" after Adams appointed Henry Clay as his Secretary of State. This marked the only presidential election in U.S. history where the candidate with the most electoral votes did not become president under the Twelfth Amendment procedures.

POPULISM AND ANTEBELLUM AMERICA
1829-1861

The Antebellum era marked a fundamental transformation in American political life. The presidency shifted from an office defined by restraint and elite consensus to one grounded in popular mobilization and management of the electoral system. Party organizations expanded dramatically and political participation widened. White male suffrage increased, while Native Americans, women, and enslaved people were still excluded from political life.

Presidential authority during this era became increasingly populist and symbolic. Leaders claimed direct representation of "the people," often dodging traditional power structures such as Congress, courts, and party elites. The modern presidency—characterized by appeals to popular mandate and executive assertiveness—emerged in this period, even as formal constitutional limits remained unchanged.

Economic transformation accelerated alongside political change. Market capitalism expanded westward, transportation networks reshaped regional economies, and financial speculation increased vulnerability to economic downfall. The role of the federal government in banking, tariffs, and internal improvements became a defining partisan battleground. Presidents were increasingly expected to take positions on economic development rather than merely administer inherited frameworks.

At the same time, sectional conflict intensified. The expansion of slavery into new territories destabilized earlier compromises and forced moral questions into the center of national politics. Each territorial acquisition reopened disputes over the balance between free and slave states, gradually eroding the ability of political institutions to contain conflict.

Presidents of the antebellum period governed amid shrinking space for moderation. Party systems became more disciplined yet more polarized, and political rhetoric increasingly framed compromise as betrayal (not unlike our current party system). The presidency alternated between strong individual leadership and administrative submissiveness. Executive authority grounded in popular appeal gradually eroded institutional consensus.

By the late 1850s, the mechanisms that had previously managed division—sectional compromise, and congressional negotiation—had largely failed. The presidency, though more visible and symbolically powerful than in the founding era, lacked the capacity to resolve conflicts rooted in incompatible social and economic systems. This era thus concludes not with institutional consolidation, but with fragmentation, crisis, and the collapse of political order that would culminate in civil war.

The population of the United States grew from roughly four million in 1789 to over thirty million on the eve of the Civil War, enabling populism to supplant elite governance as the dominant political force.

ANDREW JACKSON (1829–1837)

EARLY LIFE AND BACKGROUND

Andrew Jackson was born on March 15, 1767, in the Waxhaws region along the border of North and South Carolina. This region was a rough frontier area marked by poverty, violence, and instability. His parents were recent immigrants from Ireland, and his father died just weeks before Andrew was born, leaving the family struggling financially. Jackson's childhood was shaped by hardship from the very beginning, with little formal education and few social advantages.

During the American Revolutionary War, the Waxhaws became a battleground, and Jackson's family was drawn directly into the conflict. As a teenager, he served as a courier for local Patriot forces. At age 13, he was captured by British troops and famously slashed with a sword after refusing to clean an officer's boots—an incident that left both physical scars and a lifelong hatred of the British. Shortly after his release, Jackson lost his two brothers to war-related causes, and his mother died of disease while nursing American prisoners. By age 14, he was an orphan.

These early experiences—violence, loss, and self-reliance—deeply influenced Jackson's personality. His childhood fostered a fierce independence, intense personal pride, and a tendency toward emotional outbursts that would later define both his personal life and political career. Jackson often portrayed himself as a man shaped by the frontier and by suffering. This narrative resonated strongly with many ordinary Americans and became central to his political identity as a champion of the "common man."

After a harsh and unsettled childhood, Jackson remade himself through ambition, resilience, and a willingness to take risks. In his late teens and early twenties, he studied law in North Carolina and was admitted to the bar in 1787. Jackson moved west to the Tennessee frontier, where opportunity was greater and social hierarchies were less rigid. There he worked as a lawyer, land speculator, and merchant, gradually acquiring property, enslaved laborers, and social standing. His marriage to Rachel Donelson—though loving—was shadowed by controversy over the legality of her divorce, a personal matter that later became a political weapon against him.

Jackson's rise accelerated through military and political service. He became Tennessee's first U.S. congressman in 1796 and later served briefly as a U.S. senator, though he found legislative life tedious. His real ascent came through the militia and the U.S. Army. During the War of 1812, Jackson emerged as a national hero after leading American forces to a stunning victory over the British at the Battle of New Orleans in 1815. The victory made him famous nationwide and cemented his reputation as a tough, decisive leader. Subsequent campaigns against Native American nations in the Southeast further enhanced his standing among white frontier settlers.

By the 1820s, Jackson had become a symbol of frontier toughness and populist appeal. He ran for president in 1824 and won the most popular and electoral votes but fell short of a majority, sending the election to the House of Representatives. When John Quincy Adams was chosen president after what Jackson's supporters called a "corrupt bargain," Jackson spent the next four years building a powerful political movement. In 1828, presenting himself as a self-made man and defender of ordinary Americans, Jackson won a decisive victory. His ascent marked a turning point in American politics, ushering in the era of mass democracy and strong presidential leadership often referred to as the Jacksonian era.

DOMESTIC LIFE

Andrew Jackson's domestic life was deeply shaped by his marriage to Rachel Donelson Jackson and by the plantation world of early Tennessee. Jackson married Rachel in the 1790s after a complicated courtship that later became a painful and personal aspect of his private life. Due to confusion over the finalization of Rachel's earlier divorce, the legality of their marriage was questioned. Despite this, their relationship was widely described as affectionate and emotionally close, with Jackson relying heavily on Rachel for stability and counsel.

The Jacksons made their home at The Hermitage, a plantation near Nashville, Tennessee. Although they had no biological children, they adopted and raised several relatives and dependents, including Andrew Jackson Jr., whom they raised as their own. The household was large and complex, reflecting both frontier hospitality and plantation hierarchy, with extended family members, guests, and enslaved workers forming part of daily life.

Like many Southern planters of his era, Jackson was a slaveholder, and enslaved labor was essential to the operation of The Hermitage. While Jackson portrayed himself as a paternalistic master, slavery at the plantation was marked by forced labor, discipline, and the denial of freedom—realities that stand in stark contrast to his public image as a champion of the "common man." This contradiction remains a central tension in assessments of his private life and moral legacy.

Rachel Jackson's death in late 1828, just weeks before Jackson's inauguration, was a devastating personal blow. Jackson blamed political attacks on her character for hastening her death and carried this grief into the presidency. Widowed for the remainder of his life, he relied on family members to serve as White House hostesses. Jackson's domestic life shaped his fierce defensiveness, personal honor culture, and deep sense of grievance, all of which carried over into his public leadership style.

POLITICAL AFFILIATION AND GOVERNING STYLE

As leader of the Democratic Party, Jackson embraced popular democracy and expanded political participation for white men while rejecting entrenched elites and institutional intermediaries. He viewed the presidency as the embodiment of popular sovereignty and asserted executive authority accordingly.

Jackson's governing style was personal, confrontational, and decisive. He relied heavily on loyal advisers and family rather than formal cabinet structures ("the kitchen cabinet") and used the veto power aggressively, transforming it from a constitutional safeguard into a policy instrument. Jackson believed that the president was not merely an executor of congressional will, but an independent representative of the people with authority equal to that of the legislature.

ACCOMPLISHMENTS AND VISION

Andrew Jackson's accomplishments differed in emphasis between his first and second terms, reflecting a progression from consolidation of popular authority to aggressive institutional confrontation. During his first term, Jackson focused on redefining the presidency as a direct representative of the electorate. He expanded use of the presidential veto beyond constitutional objections to include policy disagreement, thereby transforming it into a central instrument of executive power. His handling of the Nullification Crisis[18] marked a critical assertion of federal supremacy: by threatening force while supporting a negotiated tariff compromise, Jackson reinforced the principle that states could not unilaterally defy federal law. These actions strengthened the presidency as an independent branch while affirming the permanence of the Union.

Jackson's second term concentrated presidential power more directly against existing institutions, producing consequences that proved both enduring and destabilizing. His veto of the recharter of the Second

---

18 The Nullification Crisis (1832–1833) arose from South Carolina's claim that a state could declare a federal law unconstitutional and refuse its enforcement, specifically in response to the protective Tariffs of 1828 and 1832. Led intellectually by Vice President John C. Calhoun, the doctrine of nullification asserted that the Constitution was a compact among sovereign states. President Andrew Jackson rejected this view. The crisis ended with Henry Clay's Compromise Tariff of 1833, which gradually reduced rates, prompting South Carolina to repeal its nullification ordinance while symbolically nullifying the Force Bill.

Bank of the United States and subsequent removal of federal deposits represented the most consequential assertion of executive authority over economic policy to that date. While Jackson framed the Bank as incompatible with democratic governance, dismantling it altered the nation's financial structure without establishing a durable alternative, contributing to increased volatility in credit and currency markets. At the same time, Jackson's expansion of patronage and party discipline institutionalized the modern party system, embedding electoral mobilization (e.g., using direct contact such as door-to-door canvassing) and loyalty as defining features of American politics. Taken together, Jackson's two terms reshaped the presidency into a populist, assertive office—capable of decisive action independent of Congress—while demonstrating the long-term costs of executive power exercised primarily through personal authority rather than institutional consensus.

CRITICISMS AND CONTROVERSIES

Jackson's presidency is inseparable from profound moral and humanitarian failures. His enforcement of the Indian Removal Act led to the forced displacement of Native American nations and the deaths of thousands during the Trail of Tears[19]. Jackson's defiance of the Supreme Court (most closely associated with his response to Worcester v. Georgia, in which the Court ruled that the state of Georgia lacked authority to enforce its laws within Cherokee territory) allowed the displacement of Native Americans to proceed. This non-enforcement reflected his view that Indian affairs were primarily a matter for the political branches rather than the judiciary.

His economic policies, particularly the dissolution of the national bank and issuance of the Specie Circular, contributed to finan-

---

19 The Trail of Tears refers to the forced removal, between 1830 and 1850, of Native American nations—most notably the Cherokee, Creek (Muscogee), Choctaw, Chickasaw, and Seminole—from their ancestral lands in the southeastern United States to designated Indian Territory west of the Mississippi River (present-day Oklahoma). Authorized by the Indian Removal Act of 1830 under President Andrew Jackson and enforced despite legal resistance, the removals were conducted under harsh conditions marked by inadequate supplies, disease, and exposure. An estimated 60,000 Native Americans were displaced, and approximately 4,000 Cherokee alone died during their 1838–1839 removal, making the Trail of Tears a defining stain on U.S. expansion.

cial instability and set conditions for the Panic of 1837[20]. Critics argue that Jackson's suspicion of centralized authority and reliance on personal judgment undermined long-term economic stability.

Jackson's use of patronage expanded the spoils system, prioritizing loyalty over competence. While framed as democratic rotation, the practice weakened institutional proficiency and professional norms.

LEGACY

Andrew Jackson's legacy is complex and contested. He is often remembered as the president who reshaped the office itself, strengthening executive power and redefining the relationship between the federal government and the American people. Jackson presented himself as a representative of the "common man," challenging entrenched political and economic elites and helping to expand political participation among white male voters. In this sense, his presidency marked a decisive shift toward mass democracy and a more populist political culture.

Jackson fundamentally altered the balance of power within the federal government. Through frequent use of the presidential veto, he asserted that the president could act as a direct representative of the people rather than merely an executor of congressional will. His opposition to the Second Bank of the United States reinforced his image as a defender of ordinary Americans against concentrated financial power, though critics argue that his economic policies contributed to long-term financial instability and helped set the stage for the Panic of 1837.

At the same time, Jackson's legacy is inseparable from policies that caused profound human suffering. His support for Indian removal led to the forced displacement of Native American nations from the Southeast, culminating in the Trail of Tears, during which thousands died from disease, exposure, and starvation. This policy, carried out under federal authority, remains one of the darkest chapters in U.S. history and overshadows many of Jackson's political achievements in modern assessments.

---

20 The Panic of 1837 was a severe financial crisis that triggered an economic depression in the United States lasting into the mid-1840s. It was precipitated by a speculative bubble in land and commodities, restrictive credit policies by British banks, and domestic monetary decisions—most notably President Andrew Jackson's dismantling of the Second Bank of the United States and the 1836 Specie Circular, which required payment for public lands in gold or silver.

Historically, Jackson has been both celebrated and condemned. To supporters, he embodied toughness, independence, and democratic energy at a formative moment in the nation's growth. To critics, he represents the dangers of unchecked executive power, majoritarian politics, and moral blind spots regarding race and human rights. For a modern reader, Jackson's legacy is best understood as a paradox: a president who expanded democracy for some while denying liberty and justice to others, leaving a lasting imprint that continues to provoke debate.

MARTIN VAN BUREN (1837–1841)

EARLY LIFE AND BACKGROUND

Martin Van Buren was born on December 5, 1782, in Kinderhook, New York, a small Hudson River village with strong Dutch cultural roots. He was the first U.S. president born after American independence, and his early life reflected the social and linguistic diversity of post-Revolutionary America.

Van Buren grew up in a large, modest household; he was the third of five children born to Abraham Van Buren, a farmer and tavern keeper, and Maria Hoes Van Buren. The family tavern served as a local gathering place for farmers, merchants, lawyers, and political figures. As a boy, Van Buren listened closely to adult conversations about law, elections, and public affairs—an informal but influential political education that sharpened his observational skills and social instincts.

Dutch was Van Buren's first language, and he did not learn English fluently until later childhood. This bilingual upbringing made him culturally distinctive among American presidents and likely contributed to his adaptability and sensitivity to different constituencies.

His formal schooling was limited by modern standards. Rather than attending college, Van Buren was apprenticed at age 14 to a local attorney, marking the beginning of his legal and political training. His childhood environment helped shape a leader who rose through organization, negotiation, and coalition-building rather than elite pedigree or oratory.

After completing his legal apprenticeship, Van Buren was admitted to the New York bar and quickly established himself as a capable and disciplined attorney. He began practicing law in Kinderhook and later in Albany, where his talents for organization, negotiation, and party management became evident. Unlike many contemporaries who relied on family pedigree or military fame, Van Buren advanced through methodical coalition-building and legal-political skill.

During the 1810s, Van Buren entered New York politics, serving in the New York State Senate and later as New York Attorney General. His most lasting contribution during this period was his role in creating the Albany Regency, one of the first highly disciplined political organizations in American history. This group pioneered the use of party loyalty, patronage, and coordinated messaging—techniques that helped transform American politics from elite-led factions into mass-based political parties.

Van Buren's growing national influence led to his election to the U.S. Senate in 1821, where he aligned himself with Andrew Jackson's populist vision. He became one of Jackson's most trusted advisers and intellectual architects of Jacksonian Democracy, emphasizing limited government, states' rights, and opposition to entrenched economic privilege.

In 1829, Van Buren resigned from the Senate to serve as Secretary of State under Jackson. In this role, he strengthened U.S. relations with Britain and avoided foreign entanglements, reinforcing Jackson's domestic priorities. Although Van Buren was temporarily sidelined during the

Eaton Affair [21], Jackson ultimately repaid his steadfast loyalty by backing his successful bid for the vice presidency in 1832. By the mid-1830s, Van Buren was widely recognized as Jackson's political heir. Benefiting from Jackson's popularity and the organizational strength of the Democratic Party he had helped build, Van Buren won the presidential election of 1836.

DOMESTIC LIFE

In 1807, Van Buren married Hannah Hoes, a distant cousin and childhood acquaintance from Kinderhook. Their marriage was stable and affectionate, and together they had four sons. Hannah's death from tuberculosis in 1819, when Van Buren was only 36, profoundly shaped his private life. He never remarried, making him the only U.S. president to serve as a widower throughout his political rise and presidency.

After Hannah's death, Van Buren relied heavily on his extended family, particularly his sons, several of whom became his close companions and political aides. His son John Van Buren later emerged as a prominent lawyer and political figure in New York, while other sons assisted with correspondence and household management. This family-centered arrangement provided emotional stability amid an otherwise demanding public career.

Personally, Van Buren was private and socially reserved. He avoided public displays of emotion and cultivated a polished, controlled demeanor that contrasted with the more boisterous style of Andrew Jackson. He did not drink excessively and preferred conversation and reading to social spectacle. While not remembered for warmth or charisma, he was widely regarded as courteous, attentive, and proper in domestic settings.

As president, Van Buren fulfilled social obligations at the White House but delegated much of the ceremonial hosting to female relatives, including his daughter-in-law, who acted as informal hostess. His domestic life thus remained quiet and orderly.

---

21 The Eaton Affair was a cabinet crisis in the administration of Andrew Jackson, triggered by the controversial marriage of Secretary of War John Eaton and his wife Peggy, and it indirectly advanced the career of Martin Van Buren. As Secretary of State, Van Buren supported Jackson and the Eatons while carefully avoiding the social conflicts that divided other cabinet members. When the scandal led to mass cabinet resignations in 1831, Jackson reorganized his administration, sidelined Vice President John C. Calhoun, and elevated Van Buren as his most trusted political ally—clearing the path to the vice presidency and, ultimately, the presidency.

Political Affiliation and Governing Style

A committed Democrat and loyal successor to Andrew Jackson, Van Buren inherited the strengths and liabilities of Jacksonian governance. His governing style was cautious, methodical, and procedural—markedly different from Jackson's confrontational leadership. Van Buren favored institutional stability and political order over personal conflict.

As president, he emphasized party discipline and constitutional restraint. He resisted calls for dramatic executive intervention, particularly during economic crisis, believing that excessive presidential action would undermine republican norms. This restraint, while principled, left him politically vulnerable amid public demand for decisive leadership.

Accomplishments and Vision

Van Buren's most significant policy achievement was establishment of the Independent Treasury system[22], designed to separate federal finances from private banking institutions. The system reflected Jacksonian distrust of centralized finance while offering a more structured alternative to state banks. Though initially controversial, the Independent Treasury became a durable feature of federal financial management.

One of Van Buren's most underappreciated accomplishments was his success in keeping the United States out of war during a volatile and economically fragile period. When he became president in 1837, the nation was reeling from a severe financial crisis, and military conflict would likely have worsened economic hardship and political instability.

The greatest danger came from tensions with Great Britain, especially along the U.S.–Canadian border. A rebellion in Upper Canada (modern Ontario) against British rule sparked sympathy among some Americans, particularly in border states. Volunteers crossed into Canada, arms were smuggled, and clashes threatened to escalate into a broader conflict between the two nations. Many Americans called for a tough response or even open support for the rebels.

---

22 The Independent Treasury System, championed by Van Buren, separated federal funds from private banks by requiring government revenues to be held in Treasury vaults rather than deposited in state or commercial banks. Proposed in response to the Panic of 1837, the system aimed to reduce speculation and strengthen federal financial discipline. Enacted in 1840, repealed by the Whigs in 1841, and permanently restored in 1846, it marked an important step toward modern federal fiscal management.

Van Buren firmly resisted these pressures. He enforced U.S. neutrality laws, ordered federal troops to prevent American citizens from launching private military expeditions into Canada, and made clear that the United States would not risk war over unofficial actions. This stance was unpopular in some quarters, as it required restraining American citizens rather than confronting a foreign power, but it helped prevent a repeat of the War of 1812.

At the same time, Van Buren used diplomacy rather than force to manage disputes with Britain over trade, boundaries, and maritime issues. He instructed U.S. diplomats to calm tensions and seek negotiated solutions, recognizing that peaceful relations with the world's leading naval power were essential for American commerce and security.

By prioritizing restraint and diplomacy, Van Buren preserved peace at a moment when war might have seemed politically attractive but strategically disastrous.

CRITICISMS AND CONTROVERSIES

Van Buren's presidency was dominated by the Panic of 1837, a severe economic downturn triggered by speculative collapse, banking instability, and structural weaknesses inherited from the Jackson era. Van Buren's refusal to intervene aggressively—particularly his opposition to direct federal relief—reinforced perceptions of ineffectiveness and detachment.

Critics argued that his commitment to Jacksonian orthodoxy prevented effective response to crisis. While Van Buren did not cause the panic, his policies failed to alleviate widespread hardship, contributing to his defeat by Harrison. In addition, his support of Indian removal policies also perpetuated humanitarian injustices initiated under Jackson.

LEGACY

Van Buren's most enduring contribution was helping to create the modern political party system. Van Buren believed that organized parties, competing openly for public support, were essential to a stable republic. By turning loose political factions into disciplined, nationwide organizations, he helped normalize peaceful political competition and reduce the risk that personal rivalries or regional tensions would fracture the nation. This framework—still in place today—stands as his greatest historical achievement.

As president, Van Buren also reinforced the idea of constitutional restraint. During a severe economic depression and multiple foreign crises, he resisted calls to expand presidential power, intervene aggressively in markets, or rush into war. His emphasis on limits, process, and legality helped preserve institutional stability during a vulnerable period in the nation's development.

In later years, Van Buren's moral stance against the expansion of slavery into new territories—most notably his involvement with the Free-Soil movement—added a principled dimension to his post-presidential reputation, even as it distanced him from the Democratic Party he helped build.

WILLIAM HENRY HARRISON (1841)

EARLY LIFE AND BACKGROUND

William Henry Harrison was born on February 9, 1773, at Berkeley Plantation along the James River in Charles City County, Virginia, into one of the colony's most prominent families. He was the youngest of seven children of Benjamin Harrison V, a wealthy planter, political leader, and signer of the Declaration of Independence, and Elizabeth Bassett Harrison. Harrison's childhood unfolded during the American Revolutionary era, exposing him early to political discussion, revolutionary ideals, and elite Virginia society.

Growing up on a large plantation, Harrison experienced both the privileges of the Tidewater gentry and the realities of an economy dependent on enslaved labor. His household frequently hosted influential figures of the Revolution, and the expectations for public service were strong. His father served as Governor of Virginia, reinforcing the family's political standing and shaping Harrison's sense of civic duty.

Harrison received a classical education typical of elite Virginia boys, initially through private tutors. At age 14, he was sent to Hampden–Sydney College, where he studied Latin, Greek, history, and philosophy. Following his father's wishes, he later pursued medical studies at the University of Pennsylvania, then one of the leading medical schools in the young republic. However, Benjamin Harrison's death in 1791 left the family finances strained, forcing the younger Harrison to abandon medicine.

After abandoning medical Harrison moved west to seek opportunity on the American frontier. He joined the U.S. Army and quickly distinguished himself during the Northwest Indian War, serving as an aide to General Anthony Wayne. Harrison gained valuable military experience and visibility, particularly at the Battle of Fallen Timbers, which helped secure U.S. control of the Ohio Valley.

Harrison's frontier reputation led to rapid advancement. In 1798 he became Secretary of the Northwest Territory, and in 1801 President Thomas Jefferson appointed him Governor of the Indiana Territory. In this role, Harrison combined civil administration with military authority, negotiating multiple treaties with Native American tribes to open millions of acres to American settlement. His governorship placed him at the center of U.S. westward expansion and Native American resistance.

Harrison achieved national fame in 1811 at the Battle of Tippecanoe[23], where U.S. forces clashed with the Shawnee leader Tecumseh. Although the battle was militarily inconclusive, it was widely portrayed as a U.S. victory and elevated Harrison's public standing. His reputation was cemented during the War of 1812, when

---

23 Fought on November 7, 1811, near the Tippecanoe River in present-day Indiana, the Battle of Tippecanoe pitted U.S. territorial forces under Harrison against a Native American confederation associated with Shawnee leaders Tecumseh and his brother Tenskwatawa (aka "the Prophet"). While Tecumseh was absent seeking wider tribal support, Tenskwatawa authorized a pre-dawn attack on Harrison's encampment at Prophetstown. Although militarily indecisive, the battle disrupted Tecumseh's confederation, and deepened American fears of British involvement with Native resistance, contributing to the War of 1812.

he led American forces to a decisive victory over British and Native forces at the Battle of the Thames, where Tecumseh was killed. This victory made Harrison one of the war's most celebrated generals.

Following the war, Harrison transitioned fully into politics. He served in the U.S. House of Representatives, the U.S. Senate, and later as Minister to Gran Colombia, building a resume that blended military heroism with national political experience. Though he failed in an early presidential bid in 1836, his stature as a war hero endured.

In 1840, the Whig Party capitalized on Harrison's frontier image, nominating him for president against incumbent Martin Van Buren. The campaign famously portrayed Harrison as a humble "log cabin" man—despite his elite Virginia background—and emphasized his identity as the hero of Tippecanoe. The strategy proved highly effective. Harrison won a sweeping electoral victory, completing one of the most successful image-driven ascents to the presidency in early American history.

Domestic Life

Harrison married Anna Tuthill Symmes in 1795. She was the well-educated daughter of Judge John Cleves Symmes, a prominent Ohio landowner. The marriage was affectionate and durable, lasting more than four decades—though it required Anna to manage the household largely on her own while Harrison pursued military and political service.

The Harrison's had ten children, several of whom later became prominent in public life, most notably John Scott Harrison, a U.S. congressman, and Benjamin Harrison, who became the 23rd president of the United States. Family life was often demanding, marked by frequent relocations, financial uncertainty, and the dangers of frontier living. Anna endured long separations while Harrison served as a territorial governor, military commander, and later a national political figure.

Their primary home for many years was North Bend, Ohio, a modest estate along the Ohio River. There, Harrison was known as a devoted father and a courteous, soft-spoken patriarch rather than a dominating presence. Despite his elite Virginia upbringing, his household reflected a comparatively simple frontier lifestyle, shaped by limited resources and practical necessity rather than aristocratic display.

Anna Harrison did not travel to Washington for her husband's inauguration in 1841, remaining in Ohio due to illness. She would have become First Lady only weeks later, but Harrison's death just 31 days into his presidency cut that chapter short. Nonetheless, their marriage and family legacy endured, uniquely linking two generations of the Harrison family to the presidency and underscoring the central role domestic stability played in William Henry Harrison's public life.

POLITICAL AFFILIATION AND GOVERNING STYLE

A Whig, Harrison's election in 1840 represented a rejection of Jacksonian Democratic dominance and the rise of mass campaign spectacle[24]. The "Log Cabin and Hard Cider" campaign emphasized popular imagery over policy detail, signaling a new phase in electoral politics.

Harrison's governing intentions aligned with Whig priorities, including congressional leadership over the executive, support for internal improvements, and restoration of a national bank. However, his governing style and policy agenda remained untested due to the brevity of his term.

ACCOMPLISHMENTS AND VISION

Harrison's presidency produced no substantive policy achievements. He did, however, symbolize the consolidation of mass electoral politics and the maturation of national party voter mobilization. His inauguration marked the first peaceful transfer of power between parties following a sustained period of Democratic control.

CRITICISMS AND CONTROVERSIES

Harrison's presidency is often remembered primarily for its brevity. His death from illness just one month after taking office created immediate constitutional uncertainty regarding presidential succession.

---

24 Mass campaign spectacle refers to the strategic use of large-scale, highly choreographed political events and media performances—such as rallies, conventions, and staged appearances—to mobilize supporters, convey symbolic power, and shape public perception, often emphasizing emotional resonance and visual impact over detailed policy deliberation.

LEGACY

William Henry Harrison's presidential legacy is defined less by his actions in office—he served only 31 days in 1841, the shortest tenure in U.S. history—than by the constitutional and political precedents his death established. His sudden passing from illness precipitated the first presidential succession crisis under the Constitution. Vice President John Tyler's insistence on assuming full presidential powers, rather than serving merely as an acting executive, established the "Tyler precedent," later codified in the Twenty-Fifth Amendment. This clarification of executive continuity proved a lasting institutional contribution, reinforcing stability in moments of national uncertainty.

Beyond the presidency, Harrison's broader historical legacy rests on his earlier career as a military commander and frontier political figure. Celebrated for his role in the Battle of Tippecanoe and the War of 1812, Harrison became a symbol of westward expansion and popular democracy during the era of Jacksonian politics. His 1840 election campaign—emphasizing the "log cabin and hard cider" imagery—helped pioneer modern mass campaigning and political branding. While his presidency itself yielded little policy impact, Harrison's life and death shaped executive succession norms and reflected the emerging populist political culture of the early nineteenth century.

John Tyler (1841–1845)

Early Life and Background

John Tyler was born on March 29, 1790, at Greenway Plantation in Charles City County, Virginia, into a prominent and politically connected Virginia family. He grew up in the final years of the colonial-era planter aristocracy, in a household that emphasized classical education, public service, and states' rights—values that would later define his political outlook.

His father, John Tyler Sr., was a respected Virginia jurist and politician who served as governor of Virginia and later as a federal judge. This gave young Tyler early exposure to legal reasoning, constitutional debate, and the responsibilities of governance. His mother, Mary Armistead Tyler, died when he was seven, an event that left a lasting emotional impact and led to a more formal, structured upbringing under tutors and family supervision.

Tyler was educated at home by private tutors before enrolling at the College of William & Mary at just twelve years old. He studied classical subjects such as Latin, Greek, history, and philosophy—an education typical of Virginia's elite but unusually early even by the standards of the time. He graduated at seventeen, demonstrating both intellectual aptitude and the advantages of his social position.

Growing up on a plantation also meant that Tyler was immersed in the slave-holding economy of Virginia from an early age. This environment shaped his lifelong defense of states' rights and strict constitutional interpretation, particularly regarding federal authority over slavery—positions that would later place him at odds with emerging national trends.

After graduating from the College of William & Mary, he studied law under his father and was admitted to the Virginia bar at just nineteen. He quickly established a legal practice and, consistent with Virginia's planter elite, combined law with plantation management.

Tyler's political career began early. He was elected to the Virginia House of Delegates at age twenty-one and soon became known as a principled advocate of states' rights and strict constitutional interpretation. His views aligned with the Jeffersonian Republican tradition, emphasizing limited federal power and suspicion of centralized authority. These beliefs guided his steady rise through public office.

In 1816, Tyler was elected to the U.S. House of Representatives, where he opposed measures to expand federal authority beyond constitutional limits. His willingness to resign on principle—most notably leaving the House rather than support policies he opposed—earned him a reputation for personal integrity, though it also limited his political flexibility. He later served as Governor of Virginia and then as U.S. Senator, where he continued to resist nationalist policies such as the Bank of the United States and protective tariffs.

By the late 1830s, Tyler found himself politically homeless. He broke with Andrew Jackson over executive power but also distrusted Henry Clay's strong nationalist Whig agenda. Nevertheless, in the 1840 election, the Whig Party selected Tyler as William Henry Harrison's vice-presidential running mate. Tyler was chosen less for ideological compatibility than for geographic balance and his appeal to states' rights voters in the South.

The Whig victory in 1840 unexpectedly placed Tyler one heartbeat from the presidency. When President Harrison died just one month after taking office in April 1841, Tyler asserted—decisively and controversially—that the vice president became the full president, not merely an "acting" executive[25]. His firm stance set a critical constitutional precedent, though it alienated much of the Whig leadership.

DOMESTIC LIFE

Tyler's presidency was deeply affected by personal loss. He was widowed early in his term after the death of his first wife, Letitia Christian Tyler. She died in the White House in September 1842, after suffering a debilitating stroke in 1839. She was the first First Lady to die while her husband was in office. The couple had eight children, several of whom lived with Tyler in Washington during his presidency.

Tyler remarried Julia Gardiner in 1844. She was thirty years his junior and the daughter of a wealthy New York family. Tyler and Julia had seven additional children, bringing his total to fifteen, the most of any U.S. president. Remarkably, because Tyler fathered children late in life, two of his grandsons were still alive into the 21st century, an often-cited historical curiosity. Julia embraced public ceremony and symbolism with enthusiasm, actively cultivating her husband's image at a time when Tyler's political legitimacy was fragile.

Family identity and loyalty mattered deeply to Tyler. He viewed himself first as a Virginian patriarch, and his devotion to family and state reinforced one another. This outlook later influenced his controversial allegiance to Virginia and the Confederacy during the Civil War.

---

25 Following the death of President William Henry Harrison in April 1841, Vice President John Tyler asserted that he became President in full rather than serving merely as "Acting President," despite constitutional ambiguity in Article II regarding whether presidential powers devolved temporarily or permanently. Tyler took the presidential oath, assumed the title and authority of the office, and served the remainder of the term, establishing what became known as the "Tyler Precedent." This practice was subsequently followed in every instance of presidential death in office and was formally codified by the Twenty-Fifth Amendment to the Constitution in 1967.

Political Affiliation and Governing Style

Though elected as a Whig, Tyler quickly clashed with party leadership. He rejected Whig priorities such as reestablishing a national bank and expanding federal involvement in economic growth. His repeated vetoes of Whig legislation shattered party unity and led to his expulsion from the party, leaving him politically unaffiliated for most of his presidency.

Tyler governed assertively but without institutional support. He defended executive independence against congressional dominance, arguing that the president was not obligated to act as an instrument of party will. While consistent with Jacksonian governance, this stance rendered his administration largely ineffective legislatively because the Whigs controlled congress.

Accomplishments and Vision

John Tyler's presidency is most notable for establishing key constitutional precedents and pursuing an assertive, expansion-oriented foreign policy despite deep political isolation. Ascending to office after William Henry Harrison's death, Tyler firmly asserted that he was not merely an "acting" president but the full chief executive with all associated powers. This precedent—sometimes called the "Tyler Doctrine"—settled constitutional ambiguity about presidential succession and has guided every subsequent transfer of power following a president's death or incapacity. In domestic affairs, Tyler opposed much of the Whig Party's economic program, vetoing bills to reestablish a national bank and resisting high protective tariffs, actions that cost him party support but reflected his commitment to limited federal power and strict constitutional interpretation.

Tyler's most enduring accomplishments came in foreign policy and territorial expansion. His administration negotiated the Webster–Ashburton Treaty with Great Britain, peacefully resolving longstanding boundary disputes between Maine and Canada and improving Anglo-American relations. Even more consequential was the annexation of Texas. Although controversial and achieved through a joint congressional resolution late in his term, Tyler's persistent advocacy for annexation set the stage for the United States' continued westward expansion and reshaped the nation's political and geographic trajectory. Together, these actions ensured that Tyler's presidency—often viewed as politically turbulent—nonetheless had lasting constitutional and territorial impact.

CRITICISMS AND CONTROVERSIES

John Tyler's presidency drew intense criticism from both contemporaries and later historians, largely because of his break with the Whig Party and his rigid adherence to states' rights principles. Elevated unexpectedly after William Henry Harrison's death in 1841, Tyler quickly vetoed core elements of the Whig legislative agenda, including bills to reestablish a national bank and implement protective tariffs favored by Henry Clay and congressional Whigs. These vetoes led to an unprecedented rupture: nearly his entire cabinet resigned, and the Whig Party formally expelled him. Lacking party support and a stable political coalition, Tyler's administration struggled to enact domestic legislation, earning him the derisive nickname "His Accidency" and leaving him politically isolated for much of his term.

Tyler also faced enduring criticism for his strong defense of slavery and states' rights, positions that placed him increasingly at odds with growing Northern antislavery sentiment. His support for the annexation of Texas—achieved through a controversial joint resolution rather than a treaty—heightened sectional tensions and accelerated the expansion of slavery into new territories. In retirement, Tyler's decision to side with the Confederacy during the Civil War, even serving in the Confederate Congress, further tarnished his historical reputation. Many historians therefore view Tyler as a president whose constitutional assertiveness strengthened executive authority in the short term but whose policies and loyalties deepened the sectional divisions that would culminate in national conflict.

LEGACY

John Tyler occupies a unique place in presidential history. Though largely ineffective as a policymaker, his insistence on full presidential authority upon succession permanently clarified constitutional practice. This precedent has proven indispensable during subsequent presidential deaths.

In foreign affairs, Tyler's administration achieved a notable success with the Webster–Ashburton Treaty. He also laid the groundwork for the annexation of Texas, an issue that would have enormous consequences for slavery, sectional conflict, and the coming Civil War. While annexation was completed just after he left office, Tyler's role in advancing it is central to his historical evaluation.

JAMES K. POLK (1845–1849)

EARLY LIFE AND BACKGROUND

James Knox Polk was born on November 2, 1795, in rural Mecklenburg County, North Carolina, into a large, hardworking family of Scotch-Irish descent. He was the eldest of ten children. His father, Samuel Polk, was a successful farmer, land surveyor, and local political figure, while his mother, Jane Knox Polk, was deeply religious and emphasized discipline, moral rectitude, and education.

When Polk was about ten years old, the family moved west to the Tennessee frontier near what is now Columbia, Tennessee. Life there was demanding and shaped by the realities of frontier farming—long hours, physical labor, and limited access to formal schooling. Polk was a frail child and suffered from recurring health problems, including severe kidney stones. At age seventeen, he underwent a risky and painful surgery without anesthesia, an experience that altered him physically and psychologically.

Because of his health, Polk's early education was irregular and largely conducted at home by tutors and family members. Despite these limitations, he showed strong intellectual ability and an unusual level of self-discipline. In his late teens, once his health improved, he pursued formal education, eventually enrolling at the University of North Carolina at Chapel Hill, where he excelled academically.

Polk's childhood helped shape the traits that later defined his presidency: personal austerity, relentless work ethic, emotional restraint, and an unwavering focus on clearly defined goals.

Polk graduated first in his class from the University of North Carolina at Chapel Hill in 1818. Returning to Tennessee, Polk studied law under the mentorship of Andrew Jackson's circle, was admitted to the bar in 1820, and quickly established a successful legal practice in Columbia, Tennessee.

Polk's political rise was closely tied to Andrew Jackson, whose populist, expansionist vision strongly shaped Polk's worldview. In 1825, Polk was elected to the U.S. House of Representatives, where he served for fourteen years. He gained a reputation as a tireless worker, skilled parliamentarian, and unwavering Jackson loyalist. His diligence and mastery of procedure led to his election as Speaker of the House in 1835—the only future president to have held that position. As Speaker, Polk was notably partisan and effective, firmly advancing Jacksonian Democratic priorities.

In 1839, Polk resigned from Congress to run for governor of Tennessee. He won once but lost reelection twice, temporarily appearing politically sidelined. These setbacks, however, enhanced his image as a loyal party man willing to sacrifice personal advancement for Democratic principles rather than personal ambition.

Polk's path to the presidency culminated unexpectedly at the 1844 Democratic National Convention. Deeply divided between factions, the party deadlocked between major candidates. Polk emerged as a compromise—later known as the first true "dark horse" presidential nominee. He campaigned on a clear, expansionist platform advocating U.S. territorial growth, including the annexation of Texas and American claims to Oregon.

Polk narrowly won the 1844 election, defeating Henry Clay. His ascent reflected not charisma or celebrity, but a career built on discipline, loyalty, ideological clarity, and procedural skill—qualities that would define his unusually focused and consequential presidency.

Domestic Life

James K. Polk married Sarah Childress Polk in 1824, forming one of the most politically consequential marriages in presidential history. The couple had no children, possibly due to Polk's earlier kidney issues, and their relationship centered less on family life and more on shared discipline, ambition, and public service.

Sarah Polk was exceptionally well educated for her time, having attended the Moravian Female Academy in North Carolina. She was deeply religious, highly intelligent, and politically astute. Far from a passive spouse, she served as Polk's closest confidante, editor, and adviser—reviewing his speeches, correspondence, and political strategies. Polk relied heavily on her judgment, particularly during his presidency.

The Polk's household was marked by austerity and moral rigor. Sarah enforced strict Sabbath observance and banned dancing, card playing, and alcohol at White House events, giving their administration a sober social tone. While this earned criticism from Washington's social elite, it reinforced Polk's image as disciplined, serious, and focused entirely on governance.

Emotionally reserved, Polk devoted nearly all his energy to work. He kept detailed diaries and adhered to punishing schedules, often working from early morning until late at night. Their marriage functioned as a professional partnership rather than a traditional domestic one, with Sarah effectively acting as chief of staff in social and personal matters.

Political Affiliation and Governing Style

A committed Democrat, Polk governed as a strong executive with a clear sense of purpose. He entered the presidency with explicitly stated objectives. Polk approached the presidency as a finite duty, pledging to serve a single term and concentrate on a limited set of national goals.

His governing style was centralized, demanding, and highly structured. Polk maintained tight control over his cabinet, closely monitored departmental performance, and personally directed policy execution. Unlike Jackson, whose leadership was driven by personality, Polk's authority rested on planning and follow-through.

Accomplishments and Vision

James K. Polk's presidency is defined by an unprecedented level of campaign pledge completion. Entering office in 1845, he laid out a short, explicit agenda centered on territorial expansion and economic reform—and then pursued it with relentless discipline. Through negotiation with Great Britain, Polk secured U.S. control of the Oregon Territory south of the 49th parallel, avoiding war while delivering on a major campaign promise. This settlement brought the Pacific Northwest firmly into the United States and completed the nation's northern continental boundary. At the same time, Polk resolved the long-running Texas question by fully incorporating the republic into the Union and asserting the Rio Grande as its southern border.

Polk's most consequential achievement came through the Mexican–American War (Figure 7). Exercising close civilian control, he directed a successful military campaign that ended with the Treaty of Guadalupe Hidalgo in 1848. The resulting Mexican Cession transferred California and much of the Southwest to the United States, expanding the nation to the Pacific and transforming it into a continental power. These acquisitions accelerated economic growth, trade, and westward settlement. However, they also intensified national debates over slavery. Polk regarded these outcomes as essential to national security and prosperity, even as critics questioned the war's justification.

Beyond territorial gains, Polk achieved lasting structural reforms at home. He lowered tariffs through the Walker Tariff of 1846, reflecting Democratic free-trade principles, and restored the Independent Treasury System to separate federal finances from private banks after years of instability. He also signed legislation establishing the Smithsonian Institution, signaling a federal commitment to science, education, and public knowledge. By the time Polk left office in 1849, the United States had acquired its continental shape and a reformed economic framework—making his presidency one of the most consequential single terms in American history.

Criticisms and Controversies

The Mexican–American War remains Polk's most enduring controversy (Figure 8). Critics then and since have argued that Polk provoked the conflict to advance territorial ambitions, misleading Congress and the public regarding its origins. The war resulted in significant loss of life and intensified sectional conflict over the expansion of slavery.

Polk's concentration of executive authority and limited tolerance for dissent raised concerns about transparency and accountability. His relentless pursuit of objectives left little room for moral reflection or political compromise, contributing to ongoing national divisions.

Legacy

Polk's presidential legacy is defined by extraordinary effectiveness. Few presidents entered office with such a clear agenda—and fewer still completed it so fully. In a single four-year term, Polk oversaw the expansion of the United States to the Pacific, settled major territorial disputes, reinvigorated federal economic policy, and voluntarily stepped aside after one term, honoring his campaign pledge. For historians, this combination of clarity, execution, and restraint places Polk among the most successful "results-oriented" presidents in American history.

At the same time, Polk's legacy is inseparable from the moral and political consequences of his achievements. The vast lands acquired during his presidency intensified the national struggle over slavery, accelerating sectional tensions that ultimately led to the Civil War. The Mexican–American War, though militarily successful, has been criticized as aggressive and ethically questionable, particularly by contemporaries such as Abraham Lincoln and Ulysses S. Grant. These criticisms complicate Polk's reputation, raising enduring questions about the costs of expansion and the use of executive power.

ZACHARY TAYLOR (1849–1850)

EARLY LIFE AND BACKGROUND

Zachary Taylor was born on November 24, 1784, in Orange County, Virginia, the third of nine children in a family molded by the aftermath of the American Revolution. His father, Richard Taylor, had served as an officer under George Washington and later moved the family west in search of opportunity.

When Taylor was still young, the family relocated to Kentucky, settling near Louisville on a plantation known as Springfield. Life there was rugged and practical rather than refined. Kentucky in the late 18th century was still a frontier society, with sparse infrastructure and the lingering threat of conflict. Taylor grew up accustomed to physical labor, self-reliance, and outdoor life—traits that would later define his military career.

Taylor received little formal education compared with many future presidents. His schooling was irregular and largely home-based, supplemented by tutors when available. He never developed a reputation as a scholar or intellectual, but he gained a strong working knowledge of practical matters and leadership through experience rather than study. This lack of polish would later contribute to his image as a blunt, plain-spoken soldier.

In 1808, at age 23, he received a commission in the U.S. Army, beginning a career that would span more than four decades. His early years were spent at isolated frontier posts, where discipline, logistics, and endurance mattered more than theory. Taylor steadily advanced through the ranks, earning a reputation as a dependable officer who shared hardships with his troops.

Taylor distinguished himself during the War of 1812, defending frontier settlements against British forces and their Native American allies. Though the war produced no single moment of national fame for him, it reinforced his image as a steady, resilient commander. In the decades that followed, he served across the expanding American frontier—in the Black Hawk War, the Second Seminole War, and other postings—gaining deep experience in warfare and command under difficult conditions.

His national prominence came during the Mexican–American War. Commanding U.S. forces in northern Mexico, Taylor won decisive victories at Palo Alto, Resaca de la Palma, and most famously Buena Vista, where his smaller army repelled a much larger Mexican force led by Santa Anna. These victories established Taylor as a national hero. He was celebrated for personal courage, calm under pressure, and his unpretentious style—earning him the enduring nickname "Old Rough and Ready."

Despite his fame, Taylor had no prior political experience and expressed little interest in partisan ideology. His popularity, however, made him irresistible to the Whig Party, which sought a war hero with broad appeal. Taylor accepted the nomination in 1848, carefully maintaining an image of independence from party politics and avoiding detailed policy commitments.

Taylor won the presidency in 1848, defeating Democratic candidate Lewis Cass. His ascent was thus unusual: a lifelong professional soldier, largely apolitical, propelled to the presidency by military success and public trust rather than legislative or executive experience. This background would shape both the strengths and limitations of his brief presidency.

Domestic Life

Taylor married Margaret "Peggy" Mackall Smith in 1810, a woman from a respected Maryland family. Their marriage lasted nearly four decades. Margaret followed him to some posts early on but later chose stability for their children, often living apart while Taylor served.

The Taylors had six children, though only four survived to adulthood. Family life was grounded in Southern planter culture, particularly at their Kentucky home, Springfield, where the Taylors owned enslaved people. Taylor accepted slavery as part of the existing social and economic system but was not known as an ideological defender of it—a distinction that later influenced perceptions of his presidency.

Margaret Taylor was deeply private and religious, uncomfortable with public attention. She reportedly vowed to withdraw from social life if her husband survived the Mexican–American War, a promise she largely kept. As First Lady, she rarely appeared in public, delegated most social duties to their daughter Sarah Knox Taylor (before her early death) and later other female relatives, and avoided political engagement altogether.

Taylor himself was a devoted but emotionally reserved family man. He preferred simple routines, modest dress, and informal surroundings—traits consistent with his military persona. Even as president, he resisted the ceremonial aspects of elite Washington society and remained more comfortable in small, personal settings than in formal social life.

Political Affiliation and Governing Style

Elected as a Whig, Taylor was an unconventional choice for the party. He did not share the Whigs' enthusiasm for congressional dominance or economic nationalism and resisted strict party discipline. Taylor approached the presidency with a soldier's pragmatism rather than a politician's cunning.

As president, Taylor emphasized national unity and adherence to law over sectional or party loyalty. He relied on common sense judgment rather than ideological agendas and demonstrated a surprising independence from Southern political pressure despite being a slaveholder himself.

Accomplishments and Vision

Zachary Taylor's presidency, though brief (lasting only 16 months[26]), was defined by his unexpectedly firm stance on the nation's most divisive issue: the expansion of slavery. Despite being a Southern slaveholder, Taylor opposed extending slavery into the territories acquired from Mexico, arguing that Congress should not impose the institution where it was economically or socially impractical. He strongly supported the immediate admission of California as a free state and encouraged New Mexico to form a civilian government without congressional direction on slavery. This approach sought to bypass prolonged sectional debate and reflected Taylor's belief that stability and constitutional order were best preserved by limiting federal interference in territorial issues.

Equally significant was Taylor's assertive defense of the Union and the authority of the presidency. He rejected legislative compromises that, in his view, rewarded threats of secession and made clear that preserving the Union took precedence over sectional interests. Taylor signaled—privately and publicly—that he would enforce federal law and resist disunion by force if necessary. While he left little legislative legacy, his presidency established an important precedent: a chief executive willing to act independently of party pressures and to place national unity above political expediency during a period of mounting crisis.

Criticisms and Controversies

Taylor's presidency was marked by limited legislative accomplishment due to its brevity. Critics questioned his lack of political experience and administrative depth, and his independent stance alienated both Whig leadership and Southern allies.

His sudden death in office curtailed potential confrontation over slavery and left unresolved questions about how far he would have gone to enforce federal authority against secessionist threats. As a result, his presidency remains partly speculative in historical assessment.

---

26 Zachary Taylor, died on July 9, 1850, after a brief illness that began following Independence Day celebrations, during which he reportedly consumed iced milk and cherries in extreme heat. Contemporary accounts attributed his death to acute gastroenteritis, then commonly termed "cholera morbus." Although later speculation suggested possible poisoning because of his opposition to the expansion of slavery. A 1991 forensic analysis of his remains found no evidence of arsenic or other toxins, supporting the conclusion that his death was due to natural causes.

LEGACY

Zachary Taylor's presidential legacy is defined by his moderate but consequential stance on the expansion of slavery into the territories acquired after the Mexican–American War. A national war hero with limited political experience, Taylor entered office in 1849 as a Southern slaveholder who nonetheless prioritized preservation of the Union over sectional demands. He opposed the extension of slavery into the Mexican Cession and supported the immediate admission of California as a free state, positions that angered many Southern leaders. Taylor's willingness to confront secessionist threats and his preference for bypassing prolonged territorial debates by advancing statehood for California and New Mexico reflected a pragmatic effort to defuse sectional tensions during a volatile period.

Taylor's sudden death in 1850 curtailed what might have become a pivotal presidency in the escalating conflict over slavery. His passing elevated Vice President Millard Fillmore, whose support for the Compromise of 1850 altered the administration's direction and temporarily eased sectional discord. Although Taylor left few lasting legislative achievements, historians often credit him with a firm pro-Union stance at a moment when compromise and confrontation were both possible paths. His brief presidency thus represents a transitional moment in the antebellum era, highlighting the fragile balance between national unity and sectional division in the decade preceding the Civil War.

MILLARD FILLMORE (1850–1853)

EARLY LIFE AND BACKGROUND

Millard Fillmore was born on January 7, 1800, in a log cabin in the Finger Lakes region of western New York, then a sparsely settled frontier. He was the second of nine children in a poor farming family, and his early years were shaped by hard labor, limited schooling, and economic insecurity. Formal education was sporadic; young Fillmore spent much of his childhood working on the family farm and later apprenticing as a cloth dresser, a trade he disliked and found intellectually stifling.

Despite these constraints, Fillmore developed a strong appetite for self-improvement. He read extensively by borrowed candlelight and sought out mentors who recognized his intellect. His determination eventually led him to study law, first informally and then through more structured training. This combination of frontier hardship, self-education, and social mobility profoundly influenced Fillmore's lifelong respect for order, legal process, and upward advancement through discipline.

After teaching himself law, he was admitted to the New York bar in the 1820s and established a successful practice in Buffalo, then a rapidly growing commercial hub on the Great Lakes. Fillmore became active in civic life, helping found educational and cultural institutions, including what became the University at Buffalo. His reputation as a careful lawyer and principled Whig reformer propelled him into politics: first the New York State Assembly, then the U.S. House of Representatives, where he served multiple terms in the 1830s and 1840s and became known for his attention to fiscal matters and legislative procedure.

Fillmore's ascent accelerated after he withdrew temporarily from Congress and returned to public service at the national level. Elected New York comptroller, he gained executive experience managing state finances, which strengthened his standing within the Whig Party. In 1848, seeking regional balance and administrative competence, the Whigs selected Fillmore as the vice-presidential running mate of Zachary Taylor. The ticket won narrowly, and Fillmore assumed the vice presidency in March 1849. Barely sixteen months later, Taylor's sudden death elevated Fillmore to the presidency, making him the last Whig to hold the office.

Domestic Life

Fillmore's domestic life reflected his modest origins and his respect for education, order, and personal discipline. In 1826 he married Abigail Powers Fillmore, a former schoolteacher who had encouraged his intellectual development when he was a young man of limited means. Their marriage was a partnership grounded in learning rather than social display. They raised two children, Millard Powers Fillmore and Mary Abigail Fillmore, and maintained a household that emphasized reading, moral instruction, and self-improvement. Abigail, though often in fragile health, was deeply influential—most notably in helping establish the White House's first permanent library, reflecting the couple's shared belief in education as a civic virtue.

Abigail Fillmore's death in 1853, shortly after leaving the White House, was a severe personal blow. Several years later, Fillmore remarried Caroline Carmichael McIntosh Fillmore, a wealthy widow who brought social polish and financial comfort into his later life. The second marriage, while stable, lacked the formative intellectual bond of his first. In retirement, Fillmore lived quietly in Buffalo, remaining active in civic, charitable, and cultural institutions but avoiding overt political involvement. His domestic life mirrored the cautious, orderly temperament that defined both his personal conduct and his presidency.

POLITICAL AFFILIATION AND GOVERNING STYLE

A Whig, Fillmore assumed the presidency following Zachary Taylor's death amid mounting sectional crisis. Unlike Taylor, Fillmore aligned closely with Whig congressional leadership and prioritized compromise over confrontation. His governing style was conciliatory, cautious, and oriented toward preserving short-term national stability.

Fillmore viewed the office as a means of mediating sectional conflict, enforcing the law as written, and preserving institutional balance within the framework of the Constitution. Rather than using presidential authority to advance moral causes, he emphasized order, legality, and compromise, believing that national stability depended on restraint and adherence to established constitutional processes.

ACCOMPLISHMENTS AND VISION

Fillmore's presidency is most closely associated with his support for the Compromise of 1850, a series of legislative measures designed to ease sectional tensions between free and slave states and preserve the Union. After assuming the presidency upon Zachary Taylor's death, Fillmore endorsed the compromise and worked with congressional leaders such as Henry Clay and Stephen Douglas to secure its passage. The measures admitted California as a free state, established territorial governments in Utah and New Mexico with the possibility of popular sovereignty on slavery, settled the Texas–New Mexico boundary dispute, abolished the slave trade (though not slavery itself) in Washington, D.C., and enacted a stricter Fugitive Slave Act. While controversial—especially the enforcement of the Fugitive Slave Law—Fillmore viewed the compromise as essential to maintaining national stability during a volatile period.

Fillmore also pursued a pragmatic and forward-looking domestic and foreign policy agenda. He supported federal investment in infrastructure and commercial expansion, including early efforts toward a transcontinental railroad and the development of American trade in the Pacific. His administration played a key role in opening Japan to Western commerce through Commodore Matthew Perry's expedition (launched late in Fillmore's term), laying groundwork for the Treaty of Kanagawa in 1854 under his successor. Fillmore strengthened the U.S. Navy, promoted commercial growth, and encouraged technological and economic development, reflecting a generally nationalist and modernization-oriented vision for the country even as sectional conflict increasingly dominated national politics.

CRITICISMS AND CONTROVERSIES

The Compromise of 1850 carried profound moral and political costs. Most controversially, Fillmore enforced the Fugitive Slave Act[27], which required federal authorities to assist in the capture and return of escaped enslaved people. The law outraged Northern opinion, undermined states' rights in free states, and deepened moral opposition to slavery.

Critics argue that Fillmore's commitment to compromise postponed conflict at the cost of justice. Rather than resolving sectional division, his policies intensified polarization and radicalized public sentiment.

LEGACY

Millard Fillmore occupies an uneasy and often understated place in presidential history. He is most closely associated with the Compromise of 1850, which temporarily eased sectional tensions between free and slave states and helped avert immediate civil conflict. Supporters credit

---

27 The Fugitive Slave Act originated with the Fugitive Slave Clause of the U.S. Constitution (Art. IV, §2) and was first implemented by federal statute in 1793, requiring the return of enslaved persons who escaped to free states. Enforcement proved weak and inconsistent, leading Congress to enact a far more stringent Fugitive Slave Act in 1850. The 1850 law created federal commissioners with authority to issue warrants and return alleged fugitives without jury trials, imposed heavy penalties on individuals who aided escapes or obstructed enforcement, and compelled citizens to assist in captures when called upon. The statute provoked intense resistance in the North and became one of the most polarizing measures of the antebellum era.

Fillmore with prioritizing Union over party and recognizing the fragility of the nation at mid-century. Critics, however, argue that the compromise—especially his enforcement of the Fugitive Slave Act—strengthened pro-slavery interests, inflamed Northern resistance, and delayed rather than resolved the moral and constitutional crisis of slavery. As a result, his presidency is often judged as cautious and procedural rather than visionary, emphasizing stability and legal order over transformative leadership.

Beyond the slavery question, Fillmore's legacy is shaped by what he was not: a partisan ideologue, a charismatic figure, or a long-term political force. He was the last Whig president, and his administration marked the effective collapse of that party as a national institution. Historically, he is remembered as a self-made man who rose from frontier poverty through education and discipline, embodying 19th-century ideals of upward mobility and civic responsibility. Yet in the broader arc of American history, Fillmore is often viewed as an interim figure—competent, earnest, and well-intentioned, but ultimately unable to redirect the nation away from the sectional path that led to the Civil War.

FRANKLIN PIERCE (1853–1857)

EARLY LIFE AND BACKGROUND

Pierce was born on November 23, 1804, in Hillsborough, New Hampshire, the fifth of eight children in a farming family. His father, Benjamin Pierce, was a veteran of the American Revolution and a rising figure in New Hampshire politics, eventually serving multiple terms as governor. This placed young Franklin in a household where public service and loyalty to the Union were regularly discussed, even as the family lived without great wealth. Franklin Pierce's childhood demeanor was marked by sensitivity, sociability, and an early desire for approval rather than by assertiveness or discipline.

Despite early academic difficulties, Pierce matured intellectually during adolescence. With encouragement from his parents, he prepared for college and entered Bowdoin College in Maine in 1820. There, he developed close friendships (including a lifelong relationship with Nathaniel Hawthorne) and grew into a capable student and gifted speaker, laying the foundation for his later political career.

After graduating from Bowdoin College and reading law, Pierce established a successful legal practice in New Hampshire, quickly gaining a reputation as a capable advocate and a genial, conciliatory figure. His political ascent came through the Democratic Party, which valued his loyalty, organizational skills, and ability to bridge factions. Pierce served successively in the New Hampshire legislature, the U.S. House of Representatives, and the U.S. Senate, though he never became a national leader in Congress. He was personally more comfortable behind the scenes than at the rostrum, often emphasizing party unity and compromise rather than ideological crusades. After resigning from the Senate in the early 1840s, he returned to private law practice, remaining active in Democratic politics at the state level while cultivating relationships that would later prove decisive.

Pierce's unexpected rise to the presidency came during a period of intense sectional tension within the Democratic Party. By 1852, party leaders sought a nominee who was acceptable to both Northern and Southern wings and untainted by polarizing positions on slavery. Pierce, largely unknown on the national stage, emerged as a compromise—or "dark horse"—candidate after numerous deadlocked convention ballots. His prior military service as a brigadier general during the Mexican–American War helped bolster his national credentials and appeal to patriotic sentiment. Once nominated, Pierce ran on a platform emphasizing strict constitutionalism, respect for states' rights, and national harmony. He won the general election decisively, defeating the divided Whig Party and becoming, at age 48, one of the youngest men ever elected president.

DOMESTIC LIFE

Pierce's domestic life was marked far more by personal tragedy than by the social warmth. He married Jane Means Appleton Pierce in 1834. Jane Pierce was deeply religious, reserved, and emotionally fragile, traits that contrasted sharply with her husband's sociable and affable temperament. She disliked politics, distrusted Washington society, and viewed public life as morally corrosive. The couple shared genuine affection, but their marriage was strained by Franklin's political ambitions and by repeated personal losses that profoundly shaped their home life.

The Pierces suffered the devastating deaths of all three of their children, none of whom survived to adulthood. Their final and most traumatic loss occurred in January 1853, just weeks before Pierce's inauguration, when their only surviving son, Benjamin ("Benny"), was killed in a horrific train accident witnessed by both parents. Jane Pierce interpreted the tragedy as divine punishment for her husband's political career, withdrawing almost entirely from public life. As First Lady, she rarely appeared at social events, avoided entertaining, and spent long periods in mourning and isolation. Pierce, deeply devoted to his wife, adapted the White House's social life to her reclusiveness, resulting in a notably subdued presidential household.

These domestic burdens weighed heavily on Pierce throughout his presidency. Personally inclined toward warmth, conviviality, and alcohol-fueled camaraderie, he instead lived in an atmosphere of grief and emotional strain. His private life offered little refuge from the pressures of office, and contemporaries often noted that the tragedies of his family life seemed to drain his resilience and confidence. In contrast to presidents whose domestic stability reinforced their public leadership, Pierce governed while carrying unresolved personal sorrow—an undercurrent that shaped both his temperament in office and later historical interpretations of his presidency.

POLITICAL AFFILIATION AND GOVERNING STYLE

A fervent Democrat committed to sectional balance, Pierce sought to suppress conflict through strict enforcement of existing constitutional law and avoidance of moral confrontation. He believed that adherence to constitutional process—particularly compromise—could preserve national unity. Politically, Pierce associated abolitionism with the erosion of party discipline and national cohesion. He blamed antislavery activism—along with emerging Free Soil and later Republican movements—for inflaming sectional tensions and undermining compromise. He regarded them as morally earnest but politically reckless actors whose insistence on immediate justice ignored constitutional constraints and endangered the Union—a judgment that shaped both his policies and his historical reputation.

Accomplishments and Vision

Pierce's presidency was marked by territorial expansion and an assertive, expansionist foreign policy. His administration successfully completed the Gadsden Purchase in 1853, acquiring land from Mexico that now forms parts of southern Arizona and New Mexico. This purchase helped finalize the continental boundaries of the United States and facilitated plans for a southern transcontinental railroad. Pierce also supported commercial expansion abroad, strengthening diplomatic and trade ties with Latin America and Asia. His administration continued efforts to open Japan to American commerce following Commodore Matthew Perry's expedition, helping to expand U.S. influence in the Pacific.

Domestically, Pierce presided over a period of economic growth and supported infrastructure development and westward settlement. He reduced federal debt and maintained relatively low tariffs, reflecting Democratic commitments to limited government and free trade. Pierce also reorganized and modernized certain aspects of the military and civil service while promoting territorial organization in the West, including the formal establishment of the Washington Territory. Although overshadowed by rising sectional tensions, his administration's policies contributed to continued continental expansion, commercial growth, and the development of national transportation and trade networks.

Criticisms and Controversies

Franklin Pierce's presidency drew sharp criticism primarily for its handling of sectional conflict over slavery, most notably through his support of the Kansas–Nebraska Act[28]. By endorsing legislation that repealed the Missouri Compromise and opened western territories to slavery under the doctrine of popular sovereignty, Pierce aligned himself with Southern

---

28 The Kansas–Nebraska Act, sponsored by Senator Stephen A. Douglas, organized the territories of Kansas and Nebraska and allowed settlers to determine the status of slavery through popular sovereignty, effectively repealing the Missouri Compromise's restriction on slavery north of 36°30. The act triggered intense sectional conflict, led to violent clashes known as "Bleeding Kansas," fractured existing political parties, and accelerated the formation of the Republican Party, thereby deepening the national crisis that culminated in the Civil War.

Democrats and deeply alienated many in the North. The resulting violence in "Bleeding Kansas," as pro-slavery and anti-slavery settlers clashed, was widely blamed on the administration's failure to maintain neutrality and order. Pierce recognized and supported a pro-slavery territorial government, further intensifying accusations that he used federal power to advance slaveholding interests rather than preserve national stability.

Pierce was also criticized for weak executive leadership and poor judgment in appointments. His cabinet, though composed of prominent Democrats, was factionalized and dominated by strong personalities who often pursued sectional agendas. Critics argued that Pierce deferred excessively to party leaders rather than asserting independent authority, allowing crises to escalate unchecked. Abroad, his administration's association with the Ostend Manifesto—which suggested the United States might seize Cuba if Spain refused to sell it—sparked outrage in the North, where it was seen as an aggressive attempt to expand slavery. Combined with his enforcement of the Fugitive Slave Act, Pierce's actions cemented a reputation as a president who underestimated the moral and political force of the slavery issue. By the end of his term, divisions within the Democratic Party were so severe that he became the first elected president denied renomination by his own party.

Legacy

Franklin Pierce governed when the slavery question could no longer be managed by silence. His administration actively endorsed sectional compromise as national policy, most notably through strong support of the Kansas–Nebraska Act. By accepting—and enforcing—the principle of popular sovereignty, Pierce effectively dismantled the Missouri Compromise and legitimized the expansion of slavery into territories previously closed to it. His willingness to recognize the pro-slavery government in Kansas, despite widespread fraud and violence, aligned the federal executive with Southern interests and discredited the idea that the presidency could serve as an impartial arbiter.

His personal decency, loyalty, and devotion to duty are acknowledged by historians, as is the burden of profound private tragedy that shadowed his presidency. Yet his reluctance to confront the slavery issue decisively and his tendency to side with Southern interests left him isolated in retirement and largely discredited in Northern memory.

JAMES BUCHANAN (1857–1861)

EARLY LIFE AND BACKGROUND

James Buchanan was born on April 23, 1791, in a log cabin near Cove Gap in the Allegheny Mountains of Pennsylvania. He was the second of eleven children in a Scots-Irish Presbyterian family. His father, James Buchanan Sr., was an ambitious immigrant merchant and farmer, while his mother, Elizabeth Speer Buchanan, emphasized discipline, piety, and education. The family moved to the small frontier town of Mercersburg when Buchanan was a young boy, where his father became a prosperous storekeeper, giving the family relative financial stability by early-19th-century standards.

Buchanan was a serious, intellectually inclined child who showed early aptitude for reading and classical studies. He attended local schools before enrolling at the Old Stone Academy in Mercersburg, where he distinguished himself academically but also earned a reputation for stubbornness and a strong temper. These traits followed him to Dickinson College, which he entered at age sixteen. Though briefly expelled for unruly behavior, he was reinstated and graduated with honors in 1809.

After graduating from Dickinson College, he studied law in Lancaster, Pennsylvania, and was admitted to the bar in 1812. He quickly built one of the most successful legal practices in the state. Financially secure at a young age, Buchanan gained a reputation as a meticulous lawyer and skilled negotiator. His early exposure to commerce through his father and his own legal work reinforced his belief in property rights, values that remained central throughout his career.

Buchanan's political ascent began in earnest after service in the Pennsylvania legislature, followed by election to the U.S. House of Representatives in 1820 as a nationalist who later aligned with Andrew Jackson's Democratic coalition. Over the next three decades, he became one of the most experienced public servants of his generation. He served five terms in Congress, then as U.S. minister to Russia, where he helped negotiate a commercial treaty. Returning home, he was elected to the U.S. Senate and later served as Secretary of State under James K. Polk, playing a major role in territorial expansion during the Mexican–American War, Oregon and the Southwest.

Buchanan's most consequential pre-presidential role was as U.S. minister to Great Britain. This post proved politically advantageous: by being abroad, he avoided taking public positions on the Kansas–Nebraska Act and the violent sectional conflict it unleashed. When the Democratic Party fractured along sectional lines in 1860, Buchanan emerged as a compromise nominee—experienced, nationally known, and not directly entangled in divisive domestic controversies. He won the presidency largely because he was viewed as a steady, orthodox Democrat capable of preserving the Union.

Domestic Life

James Buchanan led an unconventional domestic life by presidential standards. He never married and had no children, making him the only lifelong bachelor to serve as president. In his early thirties, Buchanan was briefly engaged to Ann Coleman, the daughter of a wealthy Pennsylvania industrialist. Her sudden death in 1819 ended any prospect of marriage. He never spoke publicly about the episode, but contemporaries noted that it deeply affected him and reinforced a private, emotionally guarded temperament.

Buchanan's household life centered on extended family rather than a spouse. His beloved niece, Harriet Lane, became the most important personal figure in his adult domestic world. When Buchanan entered the White House, Harriet Lane assumed the role of First Lady, serving as official hostess and social coordinator. Educated, poised, and politically astute, she managed White House social life with considerable skill, helping Buchanan navigate Washington's rigid social hierarchy. Their relationship was warm and mutually supportive, and Buchanan relied heavily on her companionship and judgment in social matters.

Outside Washington, Buchanan's domestic retreat was his estate, Wheatland, near Lancaster, Pennsylvania. There he lived a quiet life marked by reading and reflection. Visitors described him as formal, courteous, and somewhat distant, but attentive to guests and deeply attached to his home. His insular bachelor life mirrored his broader personality: reserved, disciplined, and inclined toward stability and tradition.

Political Affiliation and Governing Style

A Democrat committed to sectional accommodation, Buchanan sought to remove slavery from national politics by treating it as a settled constitutional issue. His governing style emphasized nonintervention and strict separation of powers. He believed the president lacked authority to interfere in matters he considered reserved to states or courts.

This philosophy produced paralysis. Buchanan deferred excessively to judicial authority, particularly in anticipation of the Supreme Court's decision in Dred Scott v. Sandford[29] and avoided executive leadership when

---

29 In Dred Scott v. Sandford, the U.S. Supreme Court held that African Americans—whether enslaved or free—were not citizens of the United States and therefore lacked standing

decisive action might have constrained extremist behavior. His conception of presidential restraint became indistinguishable from abdication.

ACCOMPLISHMENTS AND VISION

Buchanan's presidency achieved several notable diplomatic and administrative successes despite the intensifying sectional crisis of the late 1850s. His administration helped settle a long-standing boundary dispute with Great Britain through the Pig War negotiations over San Juan Island[30], avoiding armed conflict and demonstrating Buchanan's preference for diplomacy. He also worked to strengthen American commercial and diplomatic influence abroad, particularly in Asia and Latin America, building on earlier efforts to expand trade with China and Japan. Buchanan supported the development of a transcontinental telegraph line and backed federal investment in infrastructure that would improve communication and transportation across the growing nation.

Economically, Buchanan presided over recovery from the Panic of 1857, maintaining relatively stable federal finances and continuing policies that encouraged westward expansion and commercial growth. His administration admitted Minnesota (1858), Oregon (1859), and Kansas (1861) to the Union, extending U.S. governance across the continent and reinforcing the nation's territorial consolidation. Buchanan also supported the expansion of the U.S. Navy and modernization of military defenses, seeking to protect American commerce and coastal security. Though his presidency is often judged in light of the looming Civil War, these accomplishments reflected ongoing efforts to expand, stabilize, and modernize the United States during a period of mounting national strain.

---

to sue in federal court. Writing for the majority, Chief Justice Roger B. Taney further ruled that Congress had no authority to prohibit slavery in the federal territories, declaring the Missouri Compromise of 1820 unconstitutional. The decision effectively nationalized the institution of slavery, invalidated longstanding legislative compromises, and intensified sectional tensions. Rather than settling the slavery question, Dred Scott deepened political polarization and is widely regarded as a major catalyst on the path to the Civil War.

30 A boundary dispute between the United States and Great Britain over the San Juan Islands, sparked when an American settler shot a British pig. Both nations briefly deployed troops, but no battle occurred. The conflict was resolved peacefully through international arbitration in 1872, with the islands awarded to the United States.

CRITICISMS AND CONTROVERSIES

Buchanan's handling of the slavery crisis ranks among the most critical failures of presidential leadership. His support for the pro-slavery Lecompton Constitution in Kansas undermined popular sovereignty and alienated Northern Democrats, fracturing his own party.

Most damaging was Buchanan's response to Southern secession following Abraham Lincoln's election. While asserting that secession was illegal, he simultaneously claimed that the federal government lacked authority to prevent it. This contradictory position left the Union leaderless during its gravest crisis and allowed secessionist momentum to proceed unchecked.

LEGACY

James Buchanan is widely regarded as one of the least effective presidents in American history. Buchanan inherited a nation already unraveling and responded with constitutional acceptance. He believed the slavery question lay beyond presidential authority and that the Union could be preserved by strict adherence to legal process. His deference to the Supreme Court in Dred Scott and his refusal to challenge Southern secessionist logic reflected a presidency that saw itself as detached rather than involved. When secession began, Buchanan argued it was illegal yet simultaneously denied that the federal government possessed the power to prevent it. His failure allowed disunion to proceed unchallenged.

Author's Note. Franklin Pierce helped radicalize the conflict by choosing sides under the guise of compromise; Buchanan allowed the conflict to metastasize by refusing to choose at all. Together, they illustrate two different but equally consequential paths by which presidential leadership failed in the final decade before the Civil War.

THE CIVIL WAR AND RECONSTRUCTION
1861-1877

The Civil War (Figure 9) and Reconstruction era constituted the greatest existential test of the American presidency and the constitutional system it defends. Importantly, the survival of the Union depended on whether executive authority could respond decisively to internal rebellion while preserving republican legitimacy. The presidency was forced to evolve rapidly, expanding in scope and power under conditions that made traditional restraint untenable.

Abraham Lincoln inherited a fractured nation, a collapsing federal presence in the South, and a constitution that offered limited guidance for suppressing insurrection on a national scale. His presidency transformed the executive branch from a managing institution into a command authority capable of sustaining civil war. Measures such as suspension of habeas corpus, centralized military mobilization, and direct management of war aims stretched constitutional boundaries.

Yet the Civil War did not solely expand presidential power—it redefined national purpose. The conflict resolved, by force, the question left unanswered since the founding: whether the Union was a voluntary association of states or a unified nation grounded in popular sovereignty. Presidential leadership became inseparable from national survival.

Reconstruction posed a different but equally profound challenge. With the Confederacy defeated, the presidency faced the task of reintegrating rebellious states, redefining citizenship, and enforcing constitutional amendments in the absence of consensus. The Thirteenth, Fourteenth, and Fifteenth Amendments permanently altered the constitutional order, expanding federal responsibility for civil rights and redefining the relationship between the national government and the states.

Andrew Johnson shaped Reconstruction less by building a durable postwar settlement than by provoking a political backlash that shifted authority from the presidency to Congress, leading to the Reconstruction Acts, military oversight of the South, and the Fourteenth and Fifteenth Amendments. Ulysses S. Grant's presidency demonstrated the opposite approach: willingness to use federal authority to protect civil rights amid declining political will.

Ultimately, this era established the modern understanding of presidential responsibility in crisis. It confirmed that executive power may expand dramatically when national survival is at stake, but also that such expansion carries enduring consequences for constitutional balance. Reconstruction's failure to secure authentic racial equality exposed the limits of executive enforcement absent sustained public and institutional support.

ABRAHAM LINCOLN (1861–1865)

EARLY LIFE AND BACKGROUND

Abraham Lincoln's childhood was marked by poverty, instability, and limited formal education, yet it profoundly shaped his character and outlook.

Lincoln was born on February 12, 1809, in a one-room log cabin in Hardin County, Kentucky (now LaRue County). His parents, Thomas Lincoln and Nancy Hanks Lincoln, were frontier farmers of modest means. The family lived a hard scrabble existence, repeatedly uprooted by land disputes, debt, and exhaustion of soil. In 1816, when Abraham was seven, the Lincolns moved to southern Indiana, partly to escape Kentucky's vulnerable land titles and partly to live in a free state.

Tragedy struck early. In 1818, Nancy Hanks Lincoln died from "milk sickness," likely caused by consuming dairy contaminated by poisonous snakeroot plants. Abraham was just nine years old. The loss deeply affected him, leaving a lasting emotional imprint. Two years later, his father remarried Sarah Bush Johnston, a widow who brought stability, warmth, and encouragement to the household, particularly fostering his love of reading and learning.

Formal schooling was sparse—by Lincoln's own estimate, less than a year in total, spread across several short terms with itinerant teachers. Much of his education was self-directed. He read obsessively by firelight, borrowing books when possible. This habit of disciplined self-education honed his language, moral reasoning, and capacity for reflection.

Physically, Lincoln grew tall and strong, performing demanding farm labor such as splitting rails, clearing land, and plowing fields. He disliked manual labor but accepted it as necessary, developing both endurance and empathy for working people. Socially, he was known as thoughtful, humorous, and melancholic—traits that persisted throughout his life.

By his early twenties, Lincoln left the farm for good, carrying with him the formative lessons of his childhood: resilience in the face of hardship, reverence for learning, skepticism of inherited privilege, and a deep sensitivity to human suffering. These early experiences on the frontier would later inform both his moral compass and his political leadership.

DOMESTIC LIFE

Lincoln's Domestic Life was marked by emotional strain, family tragedy, and a complex marriage. In 1842, he married Mary Todd, an intelligent, politically astute woman from a prominent Kentucky family. Their relationship was affectionate but often turbulent, shaped by financial pressures, political ambition, and Mary's volatile temperament. Lincoln relied on her political insight, yet the marriage was strained by differing personalities and recurring stress.

The Lincolns had four sons, but only one—Robert Todd Lincoln—survived to adulthood. The deaths of Edward in 1850 and Willie in 1862 were devastating, particularly Willie's death in the White House, which deeply affected both parents and intensified Mary's emotional instability. Lincoln was a devoted but frequently absent father, especially during his presidency. His Domestic Life, overshadowed by loss and responsibility, contributed to his well-known melancholy and reinforced his capacity for empathy, patience, and emotional strength in both personal and public life.

POLITICAL AFFILIATION AND GOVERNING STYLE

A Republican elected amid national fracture, Lincoln entered office with limited national support and immediate secession by Southern states. His governing style evolved rapidly under pressure. Initially cautious and deferential to constitutional process, Lincoln rapidly embraced broad executive authority as the survival of the Union came into question.

Lincoln governed through persuasion, patience, and adaptability. He tolerated dissent within his cabinet, encouraged debate, and adjusted strategy based on evolving realities. Unlike more doctrinaire leaders, Lincoln demonstrated an exceptional capacity to learn, recalibrate, and balance moral conviction with political necessity. His leadership was neither rigid nor impulsive, but iterative and pragmatic.

From antislavery roots to staunch abolitionist. Lincoln's opposition to slavery developed gradually and pragmatically rather than beginning with radical abolitionism. From early in his life, he regarded slavery as morally wrong, shaped by his upbringing in a free-soil culture and his exposure to slavery in Kentucky and the Deep South. Yet he initially believed the Constitution did not allow the federal government to abolish slavery in states where it already existed. Throughout the 1850s, particularly in response to the Kansas–Nebraska Act, Lincoln argued forcefully against the expansion of slavery, maintaining that it violated the principles of the Declaration of Independence and should be placed on a path toward eventual extinction.

The Civil War (Figure 9) fundamentally altered Lincoln's approach. While he entered the presidency focused on preserving the Union, the realities of war revealed slavery as both the moral core and the practical foundation of the Confederate cause. Emancipation emerged as a military necessity and a moral imperative, culminating in the Emancipation Proclamation. By the war's end, Lincoln fully committed to permanent abolition, actively supporting the Thirteenth Amendment. His evolution reflects a careful balance between moral conviction and constitutional restraint, ultimately making him the central figure in slavery's demise in the United States.

ACCOMPLISHMENTS AND VISION

Lincoln's accomplishments evolved dramatically over the course of his presidency as the demands of civil war reshaped both executive authority and national purpose. During the early phase of the war (1861–1863), Lincoln's primary objective was preservation of the Union rather than immediate social transformation. He exercised emergency powers cautiously but decisively—suspending habeas corpus in limited circumstances, expanding the army and navy without prior congressional authorization, and asserting federal authority over rebellious states. These actions stretched constitutional norms but were grounded in Lincoln's belief that extraordinary measures were justified to preserve constitutional government itself. His leadership during this period focused on maintaining border-state loyalty, holding together a fragile political coalition, and preventing foreign recognition of the Confederacy, all while learning—often through costly trial and error—how to manage large-scale modern warfare.

In the later phase of the war (1863–1865), Lincoln's presidency shifted from crisis management toward redefinition of national meaning and legal structure. The Emancipation Proclamation[31] transformed the war into a struggle against slavery, aligning military necessity with moral purpose and permanently altering the legal status of millions. Lincoln supported passage of the Thirteenth Amendment, ensuring that emancipation rested on constitutional authority rather than wartime decree. At the same time, his leadership in sustaining national mobilization—through conscription, taxation, and industrial coordination—demonstrated the expanded capacity of the federal government under executive direction. Lincoln's most lasting accomplishment was not merely victory in war, but the reassertion of national sovereignty on a new constitutional foundation, preserving the Union while redefining it. His presidency thus illustrates how executive power, when

---

31 Issued by President Abraham Lincoln on January 1, 1863, the Emancipation Proclamation declared that all enslaved persons in states "then in rebellion" against the United States were free. Framed as a war measure under Lincoln's authority as commander in chief, it did not apply to slaveholding border states loyal to the Union or to Confederate states already under Union control. While it did not immediately end slavery nationwide, the proclamation fundamentally transformed the Civil War into a struggle explicitly linked to human freedom, authorized the enlistment of Black soldiers in the Union Army, weakened the Confederate labor system, and made the abolition of slavery a central objective of Union victory.

exercised under existential threat, can permanently reshape both the scope of federal authority and the moral framework of the nation.

CRITICISMS AND CONTROVERSIES

Lincoln exercised extraordinary executive power, including suspension of habeas corpus, military tribunals, and suppression of dissent. Critics then and now argue that these measures violated civil liberties and expanded presidential authority beyond constitutional bounds.

Lincoln also approached emancipation cautiously, delaying action until military and political conditions aligned. His prioritization of Union preservation over immediate abolition frustrated abolitionists and exposed the tension between moral urgency and political feasibility.

These controversies underscore the difficulty of constitutional leadership during existential crisis. Lincoln himself acknowledged the dangers of executive overreach, framing his actions as temporary necessities rather than permanent precedents.

LEGACY

Abraham Lincoln is widely regarded as the most consequential president in American history. He preserved the Union, abolished slavery, and fundamentally redefined the relationship between the presidency, the Constitution, and national purpose. His leadership demonstrated that executive power could expand dramatically without permanently abandoning republican legitimacy.

Lincoln's presidency established the modern model of crisis leadership: decisive yet reflective, moral yet restrained, powerful yet accountable to history. His death prevented him from shaping Reconstruction, leaving unresolved questions about reconciliation and justice.

Historically, Lincoln stands as both a savior of constitutional order and a reminder of its fragility. His presidency revealed that democracy can survive internal collapse only through leadership capable of balancing force, law, and moral vision.

The Lincoln Assassination. Lincoln's assassination in April 1865 magnified the legacy of his presidency and altered the trajectory of Reconstruction. Murdered just days after the Confederate surrender, Lincoln was denied the opportunity to guide Reconstruction with the restraint, moral authority, and political skill that had defined his wartime leadership. His death transformed a moment that demanded reconciliation and constitutional repair into one of uncertainty, bitterness, and institutional conflict. The presidency passed to a successor ill-equipped for the task, and the absence of Lincoln's leadership contributed directly to the failures of Reconstruction that followed.

ANDREW JOHNSON (1865–1869)

EARLY LIFE AND BACKGROUND

Andrew Johnson was born on December 29, 1808, in Raleigh, North Carolina, into deep poverty. His father died when Johnson was three, leaving the family without stable support, and his mother worked as a washerwoman to provide for her children. Johnson received no formal schooling and was apprenticed as a tailor at a young age, a trade that defined his early social identity and lifelong resentment of economic and political elites. Unlike most Southern politicians, he remained loyal to the Union during the Civil War, a stance that elevated him nationally and led to his selection as Lincoln's running mate in 1864.

Johnson's political identity was greatly influenced by personal resentment toward Southern elites and rigid constitutional views rather than commitment to racial equality or institutional reform. His elevation to the presidency following Lincoln's assassination placed immense responsibility on a man ill-suited—by temperament and ideology—for the demands of Reconstruction.

Domestic Life

Andrew Johnson's domestic life reflected his deep insecurity, rigid worldview, and sensitivity to personal status. His wife, Eliza McCardle Johnson, was intellectually influential early in his life, helping him overcome illiteracy and encouraging self-education, but she suffered from chronic illness and withdrew almost entirely from public life during his presidency. As a result, Johnson lacked moderating domestic presence in the White House. His children were politically active but did not soften his confrontational temperament. Johnson's isolation at home mirrored his isolation in office, reinforcing his resentment toward elites and reformers alike. The absence of empathic emotional counsel during Reconstruction amplified his rigidity, contributing to a presidency marked by personal grievance rather than idealistic leadership.

Political Affiliation and Governing Style

Though elected as part of a Republican-led unity ticket, Johnson was not a Republican nor was he aligned with congressional Reconstruction goals. His governing style was combative, inflexible, and deeply personal. Andrew Johnson viewed Southern elite and political leaders after the Civil War with a mixture of resentment and misplaced confidence. A lifelong opponent of the planter aristocracy, he blamed wealthy slaveholders and secessionist politicians—not ordinary white Southerners—for the rebellion, and he believed their power should be curtailed. Yet Johnson simultaneously assumed that many former Confederate leaders could be quickly reconciled to the Union if they pledged loyalty and accepted emancipation. This led him to issue broad pardons and to restore political authority to prewar Southern elites, whom he believed would resume responsible governance. In practice, this leniency allowed many of the same leaders who had encouraged secession to reassert control over Southern governments, undermining Reconstruction and deepening conflicts with Congress.

Johnson resisted congressional authority, vetoed civil rights legislation, and framed opposition as unconstitutional usurpation. Unlike Lincoln, who balanced executive authority with legislative partnership, Johnson treated Congress as an adversary, escalating institutional conflict and paralyzing governance.

ACCOMPLISHMENTS AND VISION

Johnson's presidency was defined largely by the immense challenge of post–Civil War reconstruction and restoring the Union. His principal accomplishment was overseeing the formal reintegration of the former Confederate states into the United States. Johnson quickly implemented a program of Presidential Reconstruction that restored civilian governments across the South, required new state constitutions, and secured ratification of the Thirteenth Amendment, which permanently abolished slavery. Under his administration, most former Confederate states were readmitted to representation in Congress, and the federal government began the complex process of reestablishing national political and economic unity after the Civil War.

Johnson also presided over an important territorial expansion: the 1867 purchase of Alaska from Russia, negotiated by Secretary of State William H. Seward. Initially criticized as "Seward's Folly," the acquisition added vast natural resources and strategic value to the United States and later proved highly beneficial. Additionally, Johnson's administration supported early efforts to build a transcontinental nation, including continued backing for western settlement and infrastructure development following the Civil War. While his presidency remains controversial due to fierce conflicts with Congress over Reconstruction policy, these actions contributed to the restoration and geographic growth of the United States in the immediate postwar era.

CRITICISMS AND CONTROVERSIES

Andrew Johnson's presidency is widely judged among the most damaging in American history because of his handling of Reconstruction. He favored rapid restoration of the former Confederate states with minimal federal oversight, issuing broad pardons and permitting Southern governments to enact restrictive Black Codes. His vetoes of the Civil Rights Act of 1866[32] and the Freedmen's Bureau Act of 1866[33]—both overridden by Congress—along with his opposition to the Fourteenth Amendment to the United States Constitution, placed him in direct conflict with emerging constitutional guarantees of citizenship and equal protection. Critics argue that his leniency toward former Confederates and resistance to federal civil rights enforcement emboldened white supremacist violence and squandered a critical opportunity to secure durable protections for formerly enslaved Americans.

His impeachment in 1868, formally triggered by his alleged violation of the Tenure of Office Act when he attempted to remove Secretary of War Edwin Stanton, reflected a deeper constitutional struggle over executive defiance of congressional Reconstruction policy. Although acquitted by a single Senate vote, Johnson was politically crippled, and the episode clarified that persistent obstruction of duly enacted law could provoke removal proceedings. For many historians, the central criticism of Johnson rests not only on impeachment but on the long-term consequences of his policies: weakened early Reconstruction, intensified sectional conflict, and a delayed realization of civil rights that would not be meaningfully advanced again for nearly a century.

Legacy

Inheriting the office at a moment requiring extraordinary moral clarity and political dexterity, Johnson instead accelerated institutional breakdown

---

32 Enacted over President Johnson's veto, the Civil Rights Act of 1866 was the first federal law to define U.S. citizenship and affirm that all citizens were entitled to equal protection of the law. It declared that all persons born in the United States (except Native Americans not taxed) were citizens and guaranteed fundamental civil rights—including the rights to make contracts, own property, and access the courts—regardless of race. The Act was designed to counter the Black Codes enacted in Southern states after the Civil War and laid the statutory foundation for the Fourteenth Amendment's citizenship and equal protection clauses.

33 The Bureau of Refugees, Freedmen, and Abandoned Lands—commonly known as the Freedmen's Bureau—was established by Congress in March 1865 to assist formerly enslaved people and poor whites in the post–Civil War South. The Bureau provided food, medical care, education, legal assistance, and helped negotiate labor contracts. Although initially intended as a temporary agency, it was fiercely opposed by President Andrew Johnson, who vetoed the 1866 extension bill-Congress overrode the veto. The Bureau was ultimately weakened by political resistance, underfunding, and racial violence, and was dissolved in 1872.

through rigidity and resentment. His inability to build coalitions or adapt to constitutional transformation severely undermined Reconstruction.

Johnson's effect on civil rights during and immediately after the Civil War was overwhelmingly negative and long-lasting. Although he formally supported the abolition of slavery and oversaw the ratification of the Thirteenth Amendment, Johnson opposed nearly every subsequent federal effort to secure civil and political rights for formerly enslaved people. He rejected the idea of Black citizenship and equality, insisting that civil rights were matters best left to the states, particularly the former Confederate states.

Johnson repeatedly vetoed landmark civil rights legislation, including the Civil Rights Act of 1866 and the Freedmen's Bureau bills, arguing that they infringed on states' rights and unfairly favored African Americans. His vetoes were overridden by Congress. Johnson's lenient Reconstruction policies allowed Southern state governments—often dominated by prewar elites—to enact Black Codes that restricted Black mobility, labor rights, and legal protections, effectively preserving a racial hierarchy close to slavery in practice.

By obstructing congressional Reconstruction and signaling tolerance for racial inequality, Johnson emboldened white supremacist resistance and delayed meaningful federal protection of civil rights for nearly a century. His presidency forced Congress to assume leadership on civil rights, setting important constitutional precedents through the Fourteenth Amendment, but at the cost of intensified sectional conflict and the abandonment of millions of formerly enslaved people to discriminatory state regimes.

ULYSSES S. GRANT (1869–1877)

EARLY LIFE AND BACKGROUND

Ulysses S. Grant was born on April 27, 1822, in Point Pleasant, Ohio, and spent most of his childhood in nearby Georgetown. His father, Jesse Root Grant, was a tanner and a strong-willed, outspoken man who valued discipline, industriousness, and education; his mother, Hannah Simpson Grant, was quiet, reserved, and deeply religious. Grant inherited many of his mother's traits—emotional restraint, modesty, and an aversion to self-promotion—qualities that would later define his public demeanor.

As a boy, Grant showed little interest in his father's tannery and disliked the smell and labor associated with it, but he excelled in working with animals, particularly horses. He became known locally for his exceptional ability to ride, train, and manage horses.

Grant graduated from the United States Military Academy at West Point in 1843, ranking 21st in a class of 39. He demonstrated competence, especially in horsemanship and mathematics. Commissioned as a brevet second lieutenant, he served in the Mexican–American War (1846–1848) under Generals Zachary Taylor and Winfield Scott. Although Grant later criticized the war as unjust, he gained invaluable battlefield experience, observing leadership at the highest level and distinguishing himself for bravery in several engagements, including at Molino del Rey and Chapultepec. These experiences shaped his understanding of maneuver warfare, logistics, and the importance of decisive action.

After the Mexican-American war, Grant struggled during a series of isolated frontier postings, separated from his family and dissatisfied with garrison life. In 1854, amid financial hardship and personal discouragement, he resigned from the army. When the Civil War erupted in 1861, Grant reentered service as a volunteer officer, rising rapidly due to his effectiveness and willingness to fight aggressively. He won early Union victories at Forts Henry and Donelson, earning national attention and the nickname "Unconditional Surrender" Grant. Subsequent campaigns—most notably at Shiloh, Vicksburg, and Chattanooga—demonstrated his strategic vision, persistence, and ability to coordinate large-scale operations. In 1864, President Lincoln promoted Grant to lieutenant general and placed him in command of all Union armies. Grant's relentless pressure against Confederate forces, culminating in Robert E. Lee's surrender at Appomattox Court House in April 1865, secured Union victory and established him as one of the most consequential military leaders in American history.

DOMESTIC LIFE

In 1848, he married Julia Dent, the sister of a fellow West Point classmate, whose warmth and sociability complemented Grant's quiet, inward nature. Their marriage was notably affectionate by nineteenth-century standards; Grant relied heavily on Julia for emotional support and expressed a tenderness toward her that contrasted with his stoic public image.

The Grants had four children—Frederick, Ulysses Jr. ("Buck"), Nellie, and Jesse—and Grant was deeply devoted to them, though often absent during their early years. His peacetime struggles after leaving the army in 1854 were especially difficult for the family, as Grant faced repeated business failures and bouts of discouragement, at times relying on Julia's family for financial support. These years reinforced Grant's sense of responsibility and humility, shaping his later aversion to ostentation and debt.

Even at the height of his military fame and later during his presidency, Grant preferred domestic quiet to social display. He was uncomfortable with formal entertaining and depended on Julia to manage household and social obligations. In his final years, as he battled terminal illness and financial ruin following the collapse of an investment firm, Grant's devotion to his family remained paramount. Writing his personal memoirs to secure their financial future, he found solace in domestic life. Grant was defined less by ease or privilege than by perseverance, loyalty, and enduring affection.

POLITICAL AFFILIATION AND GOVERNING STYLE

A Republican aligned with Lincoln's Reconstruction goals, Grant supported federal enforcement of civil rights and constitutional amendments. His governing style was earnest, loyal, and deferential. Grant trusted subordinates deeply—often excessively—and preferred clear lines of authority over political maneuvering.

As president, Grant exercised executive authority to suppress violent resistance to Reconstruction, particularly through the Enforcement Acts and federal intervention against the Ku Klux Klan. These actions marked one of the strongest uses of federal power to protect civil rights in American history.

ACCOMPLISHMENTS AND VISION

Ulysses S. Grant's accomplishments as president were shaped by the challenge of translating military victory into durable civil order. During his first term, Grant prioritized enforcement of Reconstruction and protection of newly won civil rights. His administration supported and implemented the Fifteenth Amendment, extending voting rights to African American men, and aggressively enforced the Enforcement Acts

(1870–1871), including the Ku Klux Klan Act, which authorized federal intervention against domestic terrorism. Grant used federal troops and the Justice Department to suppress Klan violence in the South, marking one of the most forceful assertions of federal authority in defense of civil rights in American history. These measures temporarily restored political participation and public order in several former Confederate states and demonstrated that the federal government possessed both the legal authority and executive will to defend constitutional rights.

Grant's second term was dominated by economic crisis and growing administrative strain. The Panic of 1873[34] shifted national priorities away from Reconstruction toward economic recovery, limiting political support for sustained federal intervention in the South. While Grant remained personally committed to civil rights enforcement, declining public consensus, congressional resistance, and administrative corruption weakened the effectiveness of his agenda. Nevertheless, Grant presided over important institutional developments, including efforts to professionalize the civil service and stabilize postwar finance through the resumption of specie payments (redemption of paper currency in gold/silver). The long-term significance of Grant's presidency lies in its demonstration of both the potential and the limits of executive power in advancing social transformation: his administration established the legal foundations for federal civil rights enforcement, even as the political will to sustain those commitments eroded. Grant's presidency thus illustrates how constitutional authority, once asserted, can outlast the circumstances that first enabled its use—even when immediate outcomes fall short of lasting success.

CRITICISMS AND CONTROVERSIES

Grant's presidency was plagued by corruption scandals involving close associates, including the Crédit Mobilier affair and the Whiskey Ring[35]. Although Grant himself was personally honest, his loyalty to

---

34 The Panic of 1873 was a severe international financial crisis that marked the beginning of a prolonged economic downturn known in the United States as the Long Depression. It was triggered by speculative overinvestment in railroads and the collapse of financial institutions following the Civil War.

35 The Whiskey Ring was a major corruption scandal involving distillers, federal revenue agents, and Treasury officials who conspired to evade federal excise taxes on whiskey. Although President Grant was not implicated, the scandal damaged his administration.

subordinates and reluctance to impose discipline undermined public confidence and damaged the credibility of his presidency. Economic turmoil, including the Panic of 1873, further weakened support for federal intervention in the South. As Northern political will eroded, Reconstruction enforcement declined, allowing white supremacist regimes to regain control in former Confederate states.

A Balanced Account of Grant's Alcohol Consumption. A factual assessment of Grant's purported drinking shows a pattern of intermittent alcohol misuse rather than chronic alcoholism, with evidence concentrated in specific periods and often exaggerated by critics. Contemporary accounts confirm that Grant occasionally drank to excess during his early army career, particularly in the 1850s while stationed at isolated frontier posts and separated from his family. These episodes contributed to his resignation from the army in 1854, though no formal charge of drunkenness was recorded; instead, he was facing financial strain, loneliness, and professional dissatisfaction. Importantly, multiple officers who served with Grant in the Mexican–American War and the Civil War— including William Tecumseh Sherman—stated that Grant drank rarely during active campaigns and never allowed alcohol to interfere with command decisions. During the Civil War, rumors of drinking circulated widely, often fueled by political rivals, but investigations ordered by President Lincoln found no evidence that Grant's performance was impaired. Grant himself acknowledged that he could drink too much if he drank at all and appears to have exercised restraint during periods of responsibility. Modern historians generally conclude that Grant had a vulnerability to alcohol under stress and isolation, not a persistent dependency, and that his military and presidential records do not support claims that drinking materially affected his leadership or judgment.

LEGACY

Grant's historical legacy has undergone one of the most dramatic reassessments of any American president. Once dismissed as a passive executive presiding over corruption, modern scholarship now views Grant as

---

The Crédit Mobilier scandal involved the Union Pacific Railroad and a construction company, Crédit Mobilier of America, which overcharged the federal government for railroad construction and distributed discounted stock to prominent members of Congress. It became a symbol of Gilded Age corporate corruption and legislative bribery.

a committed defender of the Union victory and one of the most consequential champions of civil rights during Reconstruction. As president, he worked vigorously to protect the rights of newly freed African Americans in the South. Grant supported and enforced the Reconstruction Amendments (13th, 14th, and 15th), used federal authority to combat the Ku Klux Klan through the Enforcement Acts, and deployed federal troops and the Justice Department to suppress political violence and protect Black voting rights. His administration marked the high point of federal commitment to civil rights between the Civil War and the 20th century.

Grant also pursued a foreign policy grounded in stability and peaceful arbitration, most notably resolving the Alabama Claims dispute with Great Britain through international arbitration. Domestically, he supported sound money policies and a return to the gold standard, though these positions drew criticism during periods of economic hardship such as the Panic of 1873. Grant backed infrastructure expansion, western development, and attempted—though with mixed success—to pursue a more humane policy toward Native Americans through his "Peace Policy," which sought to reduce corruption and violence on the frontier.

Despite these achievements, Grant's presidency was tarnished by a series of scandals involving members of his administration, including the Crédit Mobilier fallout, the Whiskey Ring, and other instances of corruption. Although Grant himself was personally honest and often acted to prosecute wrongdoing, critics argued he was too loyal to subordinates and slow to recognize abuses. His reputation declined sharply after leaving office, but contemporary historians now emphasize his integrity, his steadfast commitment to preserving the Union's gains, and his central role in advancing civil rights during a fragile and transformative era. Today, Grant is increasingly regarded as a consequential and morally serious president whose leadership helped nurture the post–Civil War United States.

The Gilded Age and Early Industrialization
1877-1901

The Gilded Age marked one of the most remarkable economic trans-formations in American history. In the decades following Reconstruction, the United States evolved from a predominantly agrarian society into the world's leading industrial economy. Railroads, steel, oil, finance, and man-ufacturing expanded at unprecedented scale, generating immense wealth and accelerating urbanization. Yet this growth far outpaced the political and institutional capacity of government to regulate its consequences.

Federal governance during this era remained rooted in nine-teenth-century assumptions of limited state intervention. Constitu-tional interpretation, judicial doctrine, and political culture favored property rights, contractual freedom, and minimal regulation. As a result, corporations expanded rapidly through consolidation, verti-cal integration, and financial coordination. Economic power concen-trated faster than democratic accountability mechanisms could adapt.

Presidential authority during the Gilded Age was institutionally weak. Congress dominated domestic policy, while presidents func-tioned largely as administrators, veto players, and party figures rather than agenda-setting leaders. With few exceptions, executive leadership was cautious, procedurally constrained, and reactive. Patronage—not policy—remained the primary currency of political power, reinforc-ing party loyalty while undermining administrative professionalism.

Labor unrest became a defining feature of the era. Industrial accidents, wage instability, and long working hours produced fre-quent strikes, including violent confrontations such as the Home-stead and Pullman strikes. Federal intervention, when it occurred, generally prioritized restoration of commercial order rather than protection of labor rights. Courts issued injunctions against unions, reinforcing an adversarial industrial relations system.

Early regulatory efforts reflected growing public unease but lacked enforcement strength. The Interstate Commerce Act and the Sher-man Antitrust Act acknowledged the dangers of monopoly power, yet weak statutory design and narrow judicial interpretation rendered them largely symbolic. Courts often treated economic coordination as lawful unless explicitly coercive, delaying meaningful federal regulation until the Industrialization Era redefined administrative authority.

Political parties during this period functioned primarily as patronage networks. Electoral competition was intense, but substantive policy differentiation between Democrats and Republicans was limited, centering on tariffs, currency standards, and access to federal employment. Civil service corruption, machine politics, and electoral manipulation weakened public confidence in democratic governance.

Racial retrenchment accelerated as federal commitment to Reconstruction collapsed. Southern states consolidated systems of segregation, disenfranchisement, and racial violence with minimal national interference. Supreme Court decisions narrowed the scope of Reconstruction amendments, effectively removing federal protection of Black civil rights.

Foreign policy during the Gilded Age remained largely commercial and continental. The United States focused on trade expansion, hemispheric influence, and naval modernization rather than direct imperial control. Nevertheless, growing industrial capacity and financial integration laid the groundwork for overseas engagement by the century's end.

In historical perspective, the Gilded Age represents a prolonged period of institutional lag. Economic scale, corporate power, and social complexity expanded faster than the governing framework available to manage them. The presidency remained subordinate to Congress and private economic forces. The unresolved tensions of this era—inequality, labor conflict, monopoly power, and administrative weakness—directly precipitated the Progressive reforms that followed.

Racial exclusion hardened during this period as Southern states consolidated systems of legal segregation and voter suppression. Supreme Court decisions such as Plessy v. Ferguson[36] constitutionalized separate but equal doctrine, effectively removing federal oversight from everyday civil rights enforcement.

---

36 In Plessy v. Ferguson, 163 U.S. 537 (1896), the Supreme Court upheld a Louisiana law requiring racial segregation in public accommodations, establishing the constitutional doctrine of "separate but equal." The Court ruled that segregation did not violate the Equal Protection Clause of the Fourteenth Amendment so long as the separate facilities were purportedly equal, a standard that in practice sanctioned widespread racial discrimina-

In sum, this era reflects a paradox of extraordinary productive economic growth paired with institutional stagnation. The mismatch between economic scale and political capacity generated social instability that neither patronage politics nor minimal government doctrine could resolve. These unresolved pressures would ultimately drive the Progressive movement.

---

tion. The decision legitimized Jim Crow laws across the South and remained a controlling precedent until it was explicitly overturned by Brown v. Board of Education in 1954.

RUTHERFORD B. HAYES (1877–1881)

EARLY LIFE AND BACKGROUND

Rutherford Birchard Hayes was born on October 4, 1822, in Delaware, Ohio, just months after the death of his father, a frontier businessman of modest means. Raised primarily by his mother, Sophia Birchard Hayes—a well-educated, deeply religious woman with strong Whig and antislavery sympathies—Hayes grew up in a disciplined, morally serious household that emphasized education and self-improvement. He showed early intellectual promise and was prepared for college by his uncle, Sardis Birchard, a successful businessman who became a lifelong mentor and benefactor. Hayes attended Kenyon College, graduating as valedictorian in 1842, and went on to Harvard Law School, where he earned a reputation for diligence rather than brilliance. These formative years instilled in Hayes a strong sense of personal goodness, respect for law, and belief in social order.

Though initially reluctant to seek office, Hayes volunteered for the Union Army in 1861 and rose from major to brevet major general in the Army of the Shenandoah. He was wounded four times, most seriously at the Battle of South Mountain, yet repeatedly returned to duty—earning a reputation for personal courage, discipline, and concern for his men. His battlefield leadership and visible sacrifice made him a credible Union hero.

Hayes entered politics during the war, winning election to the U.S. House of Representatives in 1864 while still in uniform, though he refused to campaign actively. After three terms in Congress, he declined further legislative service and instead served three nonconsecutive terms as governor of Ohio. As governor, Hayes aligned with the reform wing of the Republican Party, advocating civil service reform, fiscal conservatism, and continued support for African American civil rights during Reconstruction. His reputation for integrity and moderation led Republicans to nominate him in 1876 as a compromise candidate capable of appealing to both reformers and party regulars.

DOMESTIC LIFE

Hayes' marriage to Lucy Webb Hayes was unusually influential and morally grounded. Lucy, known for her strong religious convictions and commitment to temperance, shaped the social tone of the White House and reinforced Hayes' personal integrity. The couple had eight children, though only five survived to adulthood—a common but deeply felt tragedy in nineteenth-century Domestic Life. Hayes was a devoted father who took an active interest in his children's education and character, even amid the demands of war and public office. Domestic Life was structured, pious, and intellectually engaged, with reading, discussion, and religious observance central to their daily routine. During Hayes's presidency, Lucy became the first First Lady to hold a college degree and was a visible advocate for temperance and veterans' welfare, reinforcing the image of the Hayes household as earnest, reform-minded, and morally upright rather than socially extravagant.

POLITICAL AFFILIATION AND GOVERNING STYLE

A Republican, Hayes assumed office under extraordinary circumstances. The disputed election of 1876[37].—resolved by a congressional commission—left his legitimacy fragile and his political capital constrained. Hayes governed cautiously, emphasizing legality, moderation, and reconciliation over confrontation.

Hayes believed the presidency should restore confidence in institutions rather than assert dominance over them. This approach reflected both personal conviction and political necessity given the contested nature of his election.

ACCOMPLISHMENTS AND VISION

Hayes's presidency is best known for restoring a measure of stability after the turmoil of Reconstruction and for advancing civil service reform. Entering office following the disputed election of 1876, Hayes helped broker the informal Compromise of 1877, which led to the withdrawal of federal troops from the South and effectively ended Reconstruction. While this decision reduced sectional tensions and allowed for a more unified national government, it also permitted Southern states to curtail many of the civil and political rights of African Americans. Hayes nonetheless consistently supported equal rights in principle, vetoing efforts to restrict Black voting and advocating for federal protection of civil liberties.

Hayes's most lasting domestic achievement was his early push for civil service reform. Determined to curb the patronage-based "spoils system," he issued executive orders barring federal officeholders from being required to make political contributions and sought to appoint qualified individuals based on merit. Although comprehensive reform would come later with the Pendleton Act, Hayes laid important groundwork for a professionalized federal workforce. He also pursued sound currency policies by supporting the resumption

---

37 Democrat Samuel J. Tilden won a majority of the popular vote and led in the electoral count, but disputed returns from Florida, Louisiana, and South Carolina left 19 electoral votes unresolved; amid competing slates of electors and allegations of fraud and intimidation, Congress established a bipartisan Electoral Commission in early 1877 that, by strict party lines, awarded all disputed votes to Republican Rutherford B. Hayes by a one-vote margin (185–184), an outcome which later became known as the Compromise of 1877.

of specie (gold) payments in 1879, which strengthened confidence in the U.S. dollar and helped stabilize the post–Civil War economy.

CRITICISMS AND CONTROVERSIES

Hayes' withdrawal of federal troops enabled the rapid consolidation of segregation, disenfranchisement, and racial violence across the South. Critics argue that his prioritization of sectional harmony over civil rights abandoned formerly enslaved Americans to systematic oppression, with consequences that would endure for generations.

His reform efforts, while sincere, lacked sufficient political support to overcome entrenched interests. Hayes' insistence on integrity over coalition-building limited his ability to institutionalize change during his term.

The Compromise of 1877, which resolved the disputed election and secured Hayes's presidency, was widely perceived as a political bargain that sacrificed federal civil rights enforcement for sectional peace[38].

LEGACY

Rutherford B. Hayes assumed the presidency in 1877 under contentious circumstances following the disputed election of 1876, resolved by the Compromise of 1877. His presidency is most closely associated with the end of Reconstruction. By withdrawing the remaining federal troops from the South, Hayes effectively ended direct federal enforcement of civil rights protections for formerly enslaved people. While this decision helped restore a measure of national political stability and reconciliation between North and South, it also allowed Southern states to impose discriminatory laws and practices that undermined Black civil rights for decades. Hayes believed he could foster a "New South" based on economic development and gradual racial progress, but his policies ultimately marked a turning point away from federal commitment to Reconstruction-era reforms.

---

38 The Compromise of 1877 was an informal political agreement that resolved the disputed presidential election of 1876 between Rutherford B. Hayes and Samuel J. Tilden. In exchange for Democratic acceptance of Hayes's victory, Republicans agreed to withdraw the remaining federal troops from the South, effectively ending Reconstruction. The settlement also included assurances of federal support for internal improvements in the South and the appointment of at least one Southern Democrat to Hayes's cabinet. While it restored home rule to Southern states, the compromise allowed the rapid rise of Jim Crow laws and the systematic disenfranchisement of Black citizens for decades thereafter.

Despite these controversies, Hayes pursued a reform-minded domestic agenda emphasizing civil service reform, fiscal responsibility, and governmental integrity. He worked to reduce corruption in federal offices, challenged the patronage-based spoils system, and supported merit-based appointments, laying groundwork for later civil service reforms such as the Pendleton Act of 1883. Hayes also vetoed efforts to inflate the currency through unlimited silver coinage, favoring sound-money policies and economic stability. Although often overshadowed by the circumstances of his election and the end of Reconstruction, Hayes's presidency contributed to the gradual professionalization of the federal government and reflected the broader political and economic transitions of the post–Civil War United States.

James A. Garfield (1881)

Early Life and Background

James Abram Garfield was born on November 19, 1831, in a modest log cabin in Orange Township, Ohio, to Abram and Eliza Garfield. His father died when James was just two years old, leaving Eliza to raise four children in near poverty and instilling in Garfield a lifelong respect for self-education, discipline, and moral seriousness. As a boy, Garfield worked on the family farm and briefly as a canal boat laborer, an experience that nearly cost him his health but reinforced his determination to pursue schooling. Exceptionally studious, he attended Western Reserve Eclectic Institute (later Hiram College), where he excelled in classical studies and mathematics, then went on to Williams College in Massachusetts, graduating in 1856 as salutatorian. Garfield became a teacher, college president, lawyer, and minister. His intellectual breadth and rhetorical skill distinguished him among Gilded Age politicians.

Garfield served with distinction as a Union Army officer during the Civil War before entering Congress, where he spent nearly two decades. By the time he assumed the presidency, Garfield was one of the most intellectually capable presidents in American history, combining policy knowledge with political experience across military, legislative, and educational spheres.

Domestic Life

Garfield's Domestic Life reflected intellectual partnership and emotional warmth. His wife, Lucretia Garfield, was highly educated and shared his moral seriousness and commitment to self-improvement. Their marriage was affectionate but disciplined, grounded in shared ambition and mutual respect. Garfield was deeply attached to his children and envisioned a presidency that would balance public service with private stability. Lucretia's presence during his prolonged illness after being shot humanized the tragedy and captured public sympathy[39]. Garfield's brief presidency ended before Domestic Life could shape governance, but his domestic relationships reveal a thoughtful, aspirational leader whose promise was cut short.

Political Affiliation and Governing Style

A Republican, Garfield emerged as a compromise nominee between party factions, particularly the Stalwarts[40]. and Half-Breeds. Despite his conciliatory nomination, Garfield entered

---

39 President James A. Garfield was shot on July 2, 1881, at the Baltimore and Potomac Railroad Station in Washington, D.C., by Charles J. Guiteau, a disgruntled office seeker who believed he was owed a political appointment. Although the gunshot wounds were not immediately fatal, Garfield suffered for nearly eleven weeks due to infection and complications exacerbated by unsanitary medical practices and repeated probing of the wounds. He died on September 19, 1881. The assassination directly contributed to the passage of the Pendleton Civil Service Reform Act in 1883, which established merit-based federal employment.

40 The Stalwarts were a faction of the Republican Party in the late 19th century that strongly defended the patronage-based "spoils system" and the power of entrenched party organizations. Led most prominently by Senator Roscoe Conkling of New York, the Stalwart machine used federal appointments and party loyalty to maintain political control, particularly during the Grant and Hayes administrations.

office determined to assert presidential authority over patronage and appointments, challenging entrenched party bosses.

His governing style balanced executive independence and merit-based administration, with constitutional responsibility. Garfield believed the presidency must rise above factional patronage politics and reassert institutional integrity, even at the cost of intra-party conflict.

ACCOMPLISHMENTS AND VISION

James A. Garfield's presidency, though tragically brief, reflected a clear commitment to political reform, national reconciliation, and educational advancement. A former Civil War general and congressman, Garfield entered office determined to confront the entrenched patronage system that dominated federal appointments. He challenged the powerful Stalwart faction of his own Republican Party by asserting presidential authority over civil service appointments, most notably in his dispute with Senator Roscoe Conkling over control of New York's lucrative customs house. Garfield's firm stance signaled an emerging reform movement aimed at replacing the spoils system with merit-based public service, a vision that gained momentum after his assassination and culminated in the Pendleton Civil Service Reform Act of 1883.

Garfield also advocated for national unity and equal rights during the post-Reconstruction era. He supported federal protection of African American voting rights and emphasized education as the foundation of economic opportunity and civic participation for all citizens. A strong proponent of internal improvements and fiscal responsibility, he envisioned a modernizing nation guided by efficient government, sound currency policies, and expanded access to public education. Although his presidency lasted only a few months before his death from an assassin's bullet, Garfield's reformist ideals and moral leadership left an enduring influence on the direction of late nineteenth-century American governance.

CRITICISMS AND CONTROVERSIES

James A. Garfield faced criticism during his brief presidency primarily for the political conflicts that surrounded his administration and for the perception that he struggled to fully control the factionalism within the Republican Party. His appointment of several political allies to federal posts, despite his reformist rhetoric, led some contemporaries to question the consistency of his commitment to civil service reform. The fierce intra-party battle with the Stalwart faction—especially his confrontation with Senator Roscoe Conkling over New York patronage—paralyzed parts of his early administration and exposed the depth of partisan divisions in Washington. Critics argued that Garfield underestimated the intensity of the patronage system and the resistance of entrenched political interests.

Garfield was also criticized by some for his limited executive record, a consequence of his assassination just four months into office. Because his presidency ended before many of his initiatives could be implemented, detractors viewed his administration as politically unsettled and incomplete. Additionally, his strong advocacy for federal protection of African American voting rights and education in the South drew opposition from white Southern leaders and some Northern politicians who favored reconciliation over continued federal involvement. While historians generally view Garfield sympathetically, his presidency was marked by political turbulence and unrealized ambitions that left his leadership open to critique.

Legacy

Garfield's legacy rests less on enacted policy than on the reformist principles he championed and the national response to his assassination. Though his presidency lasted only a few months, Garfield forcefully challenged the entrenched patronage system that dominated federal appointments. His confrontation with powerful party bosses signaled a growing demand for merit-based civil service and a more professional federal bureaucracy. After his death public sympathy and outrage accelerated the movement for reform, culminating in the Pendleton Civil Service Reform Act. In this sense, Garfield's martyrdom became a catalyst for lasting structural change in American governance.

Garfield also left a broader intellectual and moral legacy as one of the most academically accomplished presidents of the nineteenth century. A self-educated scholar, Civil War veteran, and advocate of equal rights and public education, he envisioned a nation strengthened by learning, economic opportunity, and honest government. His support for African American civil rights and national unity during the post-Reconstruction era reflected a forward-looking but largely unrealized agenda.

Although his presidency was tragically brief, Garfield is remembered as a symbol of integrity and reform whose death helped spur meaningful progress toward a more modern and accountable federal government.

CHESTER A. ARTHUR (1881–1885)

EARLY LIFE AND BACKGROUND

Chester A. Arthur was born on October 5, 1829, in Fairfield, Vermont, to William Arthur, an Irish-born Baptist preacher, and Malvina Stone Arthur, an American-born schoolteacher. His childhood was marked by frequent moves across Vermont and upstate New York as his father took on a series of short-term pastorates. He proved academically gifted, attending Union College in Schenectady, New York, where he excelled in rhetoric and debate and graduated in 1848. To support himself, Arthur worked as a schoolteacher before studying law and being admitted to the New York bar in 1854. His early professional life included notable civil rights work, most famously his successful legal challenge to racial segregation on New York City streetcars in the 1850s.

After establishing himself as a capable lawyer, Arthur gravitated toward Republican Party organization work, where advancement depended less on reformist conviction than on loyalty, competence, and personal reliability—traits Arthur had developed through years of adapting to new environments and authority figures. Roscoe Conkling, the dominant leader of New York's Stalwart faction, valued Arthur precisely for these qualities: he was disciplined, discreet, socially adept, and administratively efficient, making him an ideal lieutenant rather than a rival.

Arthur's early exposure to moral argument (via his abolitionist father and his own civil rights cases) did not disappear, but it was subordinate to career survival within a machine-driven system. Serving as Collector of the Port of New York, Arthur learned to operate within Conkling's patronage network, enforcing party loyalty while maintaining a polished public face that reassured elites and moderates alike. In effect, Arthur's upbringing taught him how to navigate power without confronting it directly, allowing him to thrive under Conkling's dominance—until the presidency forced a break between personal loyalty and constitutional responsibility.

Domestic Life

Arthur's domestic life was marked by personal reserve, social polish, and private loss. He married Ellen "Nell" Herndon in 1859; she was cultured, politically connected, and deeply interested in music and the arts. The Arthur's had three children, though only two—Chester Jr. and Ellen ("Nellie")—survived to adulthood. Ellen Arthur died suddenly of pneumonia in 1880, just two years before Arthur became president, a loss that profoundly affected him. Widowed and emotionally private, Arthur never remarried and deliberately avoided bringing a first lady into the White House, instead relying on his sister Mary Arthur McElroy to serve as social hostess. At home, Arthur was known as a meticulous dresser, a gracious host, and a man who prized order, culture, and discretion.

Political Affiliation and Governing Style

Arthur entered the presidency unexpectedly following Garfield's assassination, amid widespread public distrust of patronage politics. Contrary to expectations, he governed with notable independence from his former political allies. Arthur distanced himself from Stalwart leadership and embraced administrative reform, signaling a deliberate break from factional obligation.

His governing style emphasized moderation, professionalism, and institutional mending rather than ideological confrontation. Arthur relied on expert advice, pursued bipartisan cooperation where possible, and avoided the overt personalization of executive authority. This quiet, corrective approach reflected an acute awareness of public disillusionment with party politics.

Accomplishments and Vision

Arthur's presidency is best remembered for advancing civil service reform and helping shift the federal government away from the patronage-heavy spoils system that had dominated 19th-century politics. In response to public outrage following President James Garfield's assassination by a disgruntled office seeker, Arthur supported and signed the Pendleton Civil Service Reform Act. This landmark legislation created a merit-based system for many federal positions, requiring competitive examinations and protecting certain officeholders from political dismissal. Although initially limited in scope, the Pendleton Act laid the institutional foundation for a professional federal bureaucracy and marked a turning point in the modernization of American governance.

Arthur also promoted fiscal restraint and administrative efficiency. He vetoed excessive pork-barrel spending in the Rivers and Harbors Act of 1882, arguing for responsible federal expenditures, and supported efforts to reduce tariff rates, though comprehensive reform remained elusive. In foreign policy and infrastructure, his administration helped modernize the U.S. Navy—beginning the transition from a largely wooden fleet to a more modern steel navy—and approved funding for improvements to ports and coastal defenses. Though often underestimated at the time of his accession, Arthur's presidency is now viewed as competent and reform-minded, contributing to the gradual professionalization and modernization of the federal government.

Criticisms and Controversies

The major criticism of Arthur's presidency is that it was cautious and reactive rather than directly addressing systemic Gilded Age problems. Systemic Gilded Age problems were the entrenched structural flaws of governance and capitalism, in which powerful corporations and monopolies dominated markets and policymaking. Rapid industrialization produced widespread labor exploitation and recurring industrial conflict, while weak federal regulatory capacity left railroads, finance, and industry largely unchecked.

At the same time, policies to protect the interests of immigrants or minority groups, often based on ethnicity, race, religion, or national origin were not enforced. Most notably the Chinese Exclusion Act of 1882—institutionalized these anxieties by using federal law to exclude Chinese immigrants from the labor market.

Legacy

Chester A. Arthur's presidency stands as one of the most unexpected institutional turning points in American executive history. A product of patronage politics who became a reform president, Arthur demonstrated that presidential leadership could evolve in response to national crisis and public expectation.

Historically, Arthur represents the beginning of the end of the spoils system at the federal level. While the Pendleton Act did not eliminate political patronage, it permanently altered norms of public administration and initiated a gradual professionalization of government service. Arthur's legacy lies not in ideological transformation, but in restoring credibility to executive governance during an era of deep institutional cynicism.

GROVER CLEVELAND (1885–1889)

EARLY LIFE AND BACKGROUND

Grover Cleveland was born on March 18, 1837, in Caldwell, New Jersey, the fifth of nine children in a strict and intellectually serious Presbyterian household. His father, Richard Falley Cleveland, was a Presbyterian minister, and the family moved frequently as he accepted new pastorates. When his father died suddenly in 1853, Cleveland—then just sixteen—was forced to abandon formal schooling to help support his family. He worked as a clerk, teacher, and legal apprentice. This early exposure to financial hardship and moral rigor influenced Cleveland's later political identity as a reformer who valued integrity, hard work, and resistance to corruption.

After moving to Buffalo, New York, in the mid-1850s, Cleveland studied law independently while working as a clerk and was admitted to the bar in 1859. He built a successful legal practice known for diligence and an aversion to political favoritism. Cleveland's entrance into public life came through law enforcement. He served as Erie County sheriff (1871–1873), where he personally carried out executions as required by law, reinforcing his image as a man who accepted responsibility rather than delegating unpleasant duties. After returning to private practice, his reputation for honesty led to his election as mayor of Buffalo in 1881, where he earned national attention by vetoing corrupt contracts and resisting machine politics. This reformist stance elevated him to governor of New York (1883–1885), where he continued to oppose patronage and special interests.

DOMESTIC LIFE

A lifelong bachelor until well into his presidency, Cleveland married Frances Folsom in 1886 while serving as president—the only presidential wedding held in the White House. Frances, twenty-seven years his junior and the daughter of Cleveland's former law partner, became an exceptionally popular First Lady, admired for her youth, grace, and discretion. Their marriage softened Cleveland's austere public image and provided a sense of personal stability during his first term.

As a husband and father, Cleveland was devoted but private, preferring family life away from public display. The Cleveland's had five children, one of whom was born during his second term, making Cleveland the only president to have a child born in the White House. Despite his high office, he maintained a relatively simple domestic routine and resisted social excess, consistent with his lifelong values of restraint and propriety. His domestic life, though limited in public visibility, reinforced his broader image as a man of personal honestly and quiet discipline rather than warmth or charisma.

POLITICAL AFFILIATION AND GOVERNING STYLE

A Democrat and the first of his party elected since the Civil War, Cleveland believed deeply in limited government, fiscal restraint, and strict adherence to constitutional authority. Cleveland viewed public office as a fiduciary trust rather than a vehicle for social reform or partisan advantage.

His governing style emphasized executive independence and frequent use of the veto. Cleveland was willing to confront Congress—including members of his own party—when legislation conflicted with his principles. Unlike Arthur's quiet institutional adherence, Cleveland practiced assertive restraint, using presidential authority to limit rather than expand federal action.

ACCOMPLISHMENTS AND VISION

Cleveland established a reputation as a reform-minded, fiscally conservative president committed to limited government and political integrity. He aggressively used the presidential veto to curb what he viewed as wasteful federal spending and private-interest legislation, vetoing hundreds of private pension bills and pork-barrel measures that lacked clear national purpose. Cleveland also signed the Interstate Commerce Act of 1887[41], the first federal law to regulate railroads, which created the Interstate Commerce Commission (ICC) to oversee unfair rates and discriminatory practices—an important early step in federal economic regulation.

Cleveland opposed the annexation of Hawaii, arguing that it violated principles of national self-determination. He also favored arbitration over military confrontation in international disputes. In the U.S.–Canadian fisheries dispute, Cleveland backed firm diplomacy rather than naval coercion, supporting congressional authority to protect American fishing rights while ultimately favoring negotiation with Great Britain. He also upheld strict neutrality laws, refusing to allow U.S. territory to be used as a base for foreign revolutionary movements, particularly in Latin America.

Cleveland also championed civil service reform and merit-based appointments, reinforcing the principles of the Pendleton Civil Service Act by resisting pressure from party patronage networks. On economic policy, he supported tariff reduction to lower consumer costs and reduced federal budget surpluses, arguing that high protective tariffs unfairly favored certain industries. Although Congress ultimately

---

41 The Interstate Commerce Act of 1887 was the first federal law enacted to regulate private industry in the United States, targeting abuses by railroad companies such as discriminatory rates, rebates, and monopolistic practices. It required railroad rates to be "reasonable and just," prohibited rate discrimination, and mandated the public disclosure of shipping rates. The Act also established the Interstate Commerce Commission (ICC), the first independent federal regulatory agency, marking a significant expansion of federal authority over interstate commerce under the Constitution's Commerce Clause.

resisted major tariff reform during his first term, Cleveland's advocacy helped define the Democratic Party's late-19th-century commitment to lower tariffs, fiscal restraint, and governmental reform.

CRITICISMS AND CONTROVERSIES

Cleveland's rigid commitment to limited government generated criticism during periods of economic hardship. His veto of relief measures for drought-stricken Texas farmers reinforced perceptions of executive indifference to social suffering. Critics argued that his constitutional literalism ignored emerging realities of industrial capitalism and social dislocation.

His opposition to protective tariffs placed him at odds with powerful industrial interests and contributed to partisan polarization over trade policy. Cleveland's confrontational style and limited political coalition-building reduced legislative effectiveness despite personal popularity.

Additionally, revelations surrounding his personal life—including acknowledgment of an illegitimate child—became campaign issues, though Cleveland addressed the matter directly and retained public trust.

LEGACY

Cleveland's first term had an important historical impact by restoring executive integrity, fiscal restraint, and constitutional discipline after decades of Gilded Age patronage politics. As the first Democrat elected since the Civil War, Cleveland symbolized a partial political realignment and governed independently of party machines, enforcing civil service reform and using the presidential veto aggressively to block what he viewed as corrupt or unconstitutional spending bills. His actions helped redefine the veto as an active policy instrument and reinforced the principle that the presidency should serve as a check on legislative excess.

Economically, Cleveland championed limited government and sound money, opposing high protective tariffs and inflationary silver policies that he believed distorted markets and created wasteful federal surpluses. Although he failed to enact major tariff reform during his first term, his 1887 message to Congress elevated the issue to national prominence and reshaped political debate heading into the 1888 election. Overall, Cleveland's first presidency is best understood as a corrective administration—not transformative in scope, but influential in reasserting ethical governance and executive restraint during the late Gilded Age.

BENJAMIN HARRISON (1889–1893)

EARLY LIFE AND BACKGROUND

Benjamin Harrison (born August 20, 1833, in North Bend, Ohio) grew up in a politically prominent but disciplined household. He was the second son of John Scott Harrison, a U.S. congressman, and the grandson of William Henry Harrison, the ninth president. Despite this lineage, Harrison's childhood was marked less by privilege than by moral rigor and routine. Raised on a farm along the Ohio River, he was taught habits of self-control, industriousness, and religious devotion, shaped in part by his family's strong Presbyterian faith. His parents emphasized education and character over political ambition, instilling in him a sense of duty rather than entitlement.

Harrison was a quiet, studious child who showed early intellectual promise. He attended local schools before enrolling at Farmer's College near Cincinnati, where his formal education began in earnest. Harrison's professional ascension reflected steady, merit-based advancement rather than reliance on family pedigree. He left Farmer's College and completing his studies at Miami University in 1852. He studied law in Cincinnati and was admitted to the Ohio bar in 1854. Seeking opportunity on the western frontier, he moved to Indianapolis, Indiana, where he established a modest legal practice. His early career was financially precarious, but he gradually earned a reputation for careful preparation, intellectual rigor, and ethical conduct, qualities that distinguished him within Indiana's legal community.

Harrison's rise accelerated during the Civil War. Commissioned as an officer in the Union Army, he served with distinction, eventually attaining the rank of brevet brigadier general. His wartime leadership enhanced his public standing and forged political connections without casting him as a flamboyant figure. After the war, Harrison returned to Indianapolis, where his legal practice flourished and his stature within the Republican Party grew. He served as U.S. senator from Indiana (1881–1887), gaining national recognition for his command of constitutional law and tariff policy. Though initially defeated in a presidential bid in 1888's popular vote, his discipline and party loyalty culminated in election to the presidency in 1889.

Domestic Life

In 1853, shortly after graduating from Miami University, he married Caroline "Carrie" Lavinia Scott, the daughter of a Presbyterian minister. Their marriage was marked by shared religious commitment and mutual support rather than public displays of intimacy. Carrie Harrison played a central role in managing the household and supporting her husband's professional ambitions, particularly during his early, legal career in Indianapolis. The couple had two surviving children, Russell Benjamin Harrison and Mary "Mamie" Harrison McKee.

Tragedy defined much of Harrison's family life. Caroline Harrison suffered from chronic ill health and died of tuberculosis in 1892, while Harrison was serving as president. Her death deeply affected him and contributed to his reputation for emotional distance during his time in office. In the White House, Harrison's daughter Mamie often served as hostess. In 1896, four years after leaving the presidency, Harrison remarried Mary Scott Lord Dimmick, his late wife's niece, a union that drew public criticism but brought him personal companionship in his final years.

POLITICAL AFFILIATION AND GOVERNING STYLE

A Republican aligned with nationalist and pro-business factions; Harrison favored a more active federal role than his immediate predecessor. Unlike Cleveland's philosophy of executive restraint, Harrison viewed government as a legitimate instrument for economic development, veterans' support, and national integration.

His governing style emphasized close collaboration with Congress, particularly during his first two years when Republicans controlled both chambers. Harrison was comfortable with legislative activism and supported an ambitious statutory agenda. However, he lacked the political skills to manage public reaction to expansive policy, allowing Congress to drive initiatives that ultimately proved politically costly.

ACCOMPLISHMENTS AND VISION

Benjamin Harrison's presidency was marked by an unusually active legislative agenda and a significant expansion of federal authority, even though his personal style was restrained and non-theatrical. His accomplishments and vision fall into four broad areas: economic policy, civil rights and elections, foreign policy, and territorial expansion.

Economic and Fiscal Policy. Harrison presided over one of the most productive Congresses in U.S. history. The McKinley Tariff of 1890 raised protective tariffs to historically high levels, reflecting Republican commitments to industrial growth and wage protection. To address the resulting federal surplus and appease western silver interests, Harrison signed the Sherman Silver Purchase Act[42]. Though later contribut-

---

42 The Sherman Silver Purchase Act of 1890 required the U.S. Treasury to purchase approximately 4.5 million ounces of silver per month, and issue Treasury notes redeemable in gold or silver. Enacted to appease silver-mining interests and advocates of bimetallism, the law increased pressure on federal gold reserves as note holders redeemed paper currency for gold. The resulting drain on gold contributed to a loss of confidence in the Treasury and was a significant factor in the Panic of 1893.

ing to economic instability, these measures reflected the era's attempt to balance industrial, agricultural, and monetary interests. He also signed the Sherman Antitrust Act[43], the first federal statute aimed at curbing monopolistic practices. Though initially weakly enforced, it established the constitutional foundation for later regulatory expansion

Expansion of Federal Power and Civil Rights. Harrison strongly supported federal enforcement of Black voting rights in the South. He backed the Federal Elections Bill (aka, the Lodge Bill), which sought to protect African American suffrage through federal oversight of elections. Although the bill failed in the Senate, Harrison's advocacy marked the most serious presidential effort for civil rights since Reconstruction. He also appointed African Americans to federal posts at a level unmatched until the mid-20th century.

Foreign Policy and Naval Modernization. Harrison advanced American international influence. He promoted naval expansion, helping transition the U.S. from a wooden fleet to a modern steel navy. His administration asserted U.S. authority in the Western Hemisphere and laid groundwork for expanded American influence in the Pacific, including Hawaii.

Territorial Expansion and Conservation. Harrison oversaw the admission of six new states—North Dakota, South Dakota, Montana, Washington, Idaho, and Wyoming—more than any president since the Civil War. He also signed landmark conservation legislation, including the Forest Reserve Act of 1891, which authorized the creation of national forest reserves, establishing a foundation for modern federal land conservation.

CRITICISMS AND CONTROVERSIES

The McKinley Tariff raised import duties to historically high levels, protecting domestic industry but sharply increasing consumer prices. Combined with expanded federal spending, it contributed to voter backlash and earned the 51st Congress the derisive label "The Billion-Dollar Congress."

---

43 The Sherman Antitrust Act was the first major federal law aimed at curbing monopolies and restraining anti-competitive business practices. It declared illegal any "contract, combination, or conspiracy in restraint of trade" and prohibited efforts to monopolize interstate commerce. Although initially enforced weakly and sometimes even used against labor unions, the Act established the constitutional basis for federal regulation of large corporations and became a cornerstone of Progressive Era trust-busting under later presidents, notably Theodore Roosevelt and William Howard Taft.

Critics argued that Harrison failed to exercise sufficient executive restraint, allowing Congress to enact politically unsustainable policies. His antitrust enforcement was largely symbolic, reinforcing perceptions that regulation existed more on paper than in practice.

Harrison also struggled to communicate policy to the public. His reserved style and lack of rhetorical expertise left him vulnerable to charges of elitism and fiscal excess, despite genuine reform intent.

LEGACY

Harrison's historical impact lies in the substantive expansion of federal authority during the Gilded Age, despite his restrained personal leadership style. His administration produced major legislation on tariffs, monetary policy, veterans' pensions, conservation, and federal elections. Though some policies—particularly high tariffs and expanded silver purchases—contributed to economic volatility, they reflected a decisive shift toward a more interventionist national government responsive to industrial, agrarian, and labor pressures.

Harrison also left a lasting institutional and geographic legacy. He made the most serious presidential effort since Reconstruction to protect African American voting rights, expanded U.S. influence abroad through naval modernization, and admitted six western states, permanently reshaping the Union. His conservation initiatives established the legal foundation for national forest reserves. Taken together, Harrison's presidency marked a transition from limited post–Civil War governance toward a modern federal state—quiet in tone, but consequential in effect.

Nevertheless, the economic backlash against Harrison's policies paved the way for Cleveland's return.

GROVER CLEVELAND (1893–1897)

EARLY LIFE AND BACKGROUND

Grover Cleveland returned to the presidency in 1893 as the first president in American history to serve non-consecutive terms. Unlike his first term, which unfolded during relative economic stability, Cleveland's second administration began under conditions of severe economic distress. The Panic of 1893, one of the deepest economic depressions of the nineteenth century, erupted shortly after his inauguration, collapsing railroads, triggering widespread bank failures, and producing mass unemployment (estimated at 15-20 percent).

Cleveland entered this crisis with a fully formed and inflexible governing philosophy. Deeply committed to classical liberal economics, he viewed federal restraint not as a preference but as an obligation. His return to office represented not a new mandate, but a restoration of nineteenth-century economic orthodoxy at the very moment it was becoming untenable.

DOMESTIC LIFE

During his second term, Cleveland's Domestic Life was more stable and mature. Frances Cleveland remained a highly visible and effective First Lady, balancing public engagement with private Domestic Life as they raised young children. Cleveland was a devoted but distant father, maintaining emotional separation between family and governance. Domestic stability did not translate into greater empathy for public suffering during the Panic of 1893, highlighting a disconnect between private affection and public policy. His Domestic Life softened his image but did not alter his governing rigidity.

POLITICAL AFFILIATION AND GOVERNING STYLE

A Democrat committed to limited government, Cleveland governed through executive veto, legal argument, and fiscal discipline. He rejected populist appeals, distrusted mass movements, and resisted congressional pressure for interventionist relief. His leadership style during this time was confrontational and uncompromising, particularly toward members of his own party who embraced inflationary or redistributive measures.

Cleveland believed economic downturns, while painful, were part of market correction and should not be mitigated through federal support. This philosophy placed him increasingly at odds with public sentiment, organized labor, and emerging reform movements.

ACCOMPLISHMENTS AND VISION

Cleveland's second term was dominated by severe economic depression and contentious monetary and labor issues. Soon after he took office, the Panic of 1893 triggered a deep national downturn marked by bank failures, railroad bankruptcies, and widespread unemployment. Cleveland responded by defending the gold standard and seeking to stabilize federal finances. He successfully urged Congress to repeal the Sherman Silver Purchase Act (1893), arguing that continued large-scale silver purchases threatened the nation's gold reserves and financial credibility. His commitment to sound currency and fiscal discipline reassured many eastern financial interests but alienated agrarian and silver-supporting Democrats in the South and West, contributing to a major split within his party.

Cleveland also confronted major labor unrest and issues of federal authority. During the Pullman Strike of 1894, he ordered federal troops to ensure delivery of U.S. mail and maintain interstate commerce, asserting federal power to break the strike despite opposition from Illinois Governor John Altgeld and many labor advocates. While the move restored rail operations, it damaged Cleveland's standing among organized labor. In foreign policy, he continued to oppose the annexation of Hawaii after the overthrow of its monarchy and pursued a generally restrained, anti-imperialist approach. Despite limited legislative successes beyond monetary stabilization and tariff reduction through the Wilson–Gorman Tariff (1894), Cleveland's second term reinforced his image as a principled but politically embattled defender of fiscal conservatism and limited government.

CRITICISMS AND CONTROVERSIES

Cleveland's refusal to support federal unemployment relief, public works, or food assistance during the depression fueled widespread suffering and political backlash. His veto of relief legislation—most notably aid for drought-stricken farmers—cemented perceptions of executive indifference to human hardship.

The Pullman Strike intervention alienated labor unions and progressive reformers, who viewed Cleveland as an enforcer of corporate order rather than a neutral arbiter. His reliance on private banking syndicates (JP Morgan) to replenish federal gold reserves further reinforced perceptions of elite alignment, even as it stabilized government finances.

Within his own party, Cleveland's gold standard absolutism fractured Democratic unity and accelerated the rise of populist insurgency, culminating in William Jennings Bryan's 1896 nomination.

LEGACY

Historically, Cleveland stands as a principled but isolated figure whose integrity outpaced his adaptability. His presidency did not fail because of corruption or incompetence, but because it adhered too rigidly to assumptions that no longer matched economic reality. His presidency showed the limits of small, hands-off government. His decision to send federal troops during the Pullman Strike restored order but reinforced the image of a president more concerned with stability than with workers' grievances.

His firm stance on American authority in the Western Hemisphere strengthened the nation's international confidence, while his refusal to annex Hawaii showed that expansion was still morally contested.

Most importantly, his presidency convinced many Americans that the old style of limited government was no longer enough. The political shift that followed paved the way for populist and progressive reforms and a larger federal role in economic and social life.

WILLIAM MCKINLEY (1897–1901)

EARLY LIFE AND BACKGROUND

William McKinley Jr. was born on January 29, 1843, in Niles, Ohio, into a large, close-knit family shaped by modest prosperity and strong moral discipline. His father, William McKinley Sr., was an iron manufacturer and manager whose work exposed the family to the rhythms and uncertainties of early industrial America, while his mother, Nancy Allison McKinley, was deeply religious and instilled in her children's habits of piety, self-control, and earnestness. These values—order, duty, and respectability—became central to McKinley's character and public demeanor.

McKinley's childhood was marked by frequent moves within northeastern Ohio as his father pursued business opportunities, most notably to Poland, Ohio, where McKinley spent much of his youth. He was a diligent student, known for politeness, reliability, and courtesy toward teachers and peers. He showed early intellectual seriousness and a strong sense of obligation to family and community.

The outbreak of the Civil War abruptly ended McKinley's adolescence and formal schooling. At just eighteen, he left home to enlist in the Union Army, an experience that forced an early transition into adult responsibility. He served with distinction as a Union Army officer which reinforced his discipline and respect for institutional authority.

After returning from the war, McKinley studied law in Poland and Canton, Ohio, and quickly became active in local Republican politics. His war record, polished demeanor, and reliability made him attractive to party leaders, and in 1876 he won election to the U.S. House of Representatives. Over the next fourteen years, McKinley built a national reputation as a thoughtful, earnest legislator, particularly as a leading advocate of high protective tariffs. He framed his tariff views as a moral and economic duty to American workers and industry. His authorship of the McKinley Tariff of 1890[44] solidified his standing within the party.

McKinley's relationship with Marcus Alonzo ("Mark") Hanna proved decisive in McKinley's political career. Hanna, a wealthy Cleveland industrialist and master political organizer, met McKinley in the late 1870s and gradually became his closest political ally, strategist, and financial backer. Where McKinley was personally reserved, conciliatory, and principled, Hanna was blunt, transactional, and relentlessly pragmatic. Hanna admired McKinley's integrity and popular appeal, while McKinley relied on Hanna's organizational genius, fundraising ability, and willingness to do the unglamorous work of modern politics.

Their partnership matured during McKinley's tenure as governor of Ohio (1892–1896), where Hanna worked behind the scenes to stabilize party factions, cultivate business support, and protect McKinley from political isolation after the backlash to the tariff. By the time of the 1896

---

44 The McKinley Tariff raised average duties on imported goods to nearly 50 percent, reflecting Republican commitments to industrial protection and wage security. The act contributed to higher consumer prices and provoked strong political backlash. The tariff was a significant factor in the Republican Party's losses in the 1890 midterm elections and briefly interrupted McKinley's congressional career, even as it elevated his national profile as the party's leading tariff advocate.

presidential campaign, Hanna had effectively professionalized national campaign management, raising unprecedented sums from business leaders and orchestrating McKinley's "front porch" campaign. The McKinley–Hanna relationship became symbolic of the Gilded Age transition to modern, organization-driven politics: a fusion of personal decency and managerial power that reshaped how national elections were won.

Domestic Life

McKinley's married Ida Saxton in 1871. Ida was the daughter of a prominent Canton, Ohio, banker. The marriage was affectionate, but it was soon overshadowed by profound personal tragedy. The deaths of their two young daughters—Katherine in 1873 and Ida in 1875—devastated Mrs. McKinley.

Following these losses, Ida McKinley suffered from chronic illness, including what contemporaries described as epilepsy, as well as depression and physical frailty. McKinley responded with extraordinary attentiveness. He structured his daily routines around his wife's needs, insisted she accompany him to social functions, and quietly accommodated her condition even in formal settings, including during his presidency. His public courtesy toward her—such as holding her hand at dinners and shielding her during seizures—became widely noted and reinforced his reputation for gentleness, patience, and personal loyalty.

McKinley's domestic world thus reinforced his political temperament: cautious, empathetic, and deeply attentive to stability and harmony. In both private and public life, he embodied a late-nineteenth-century ideal of moral respectability grounded not in flamboyance, but in faithfulness and care.

Political Affiliation and Governing Style

A Republican aligned with business and industrial interests; McKinley governed as a chief executive rather than an ideological crusader. He believed national prosperity depended on tariff protectionism, monetary stability, and confidence among investors and workers alike. His leadership style emphasized coordination, consultation, and disciplined party organization.

McKinley avoided direct confrontation and public moralizing. Instead, he allowed events and political pressure to mature before committing to executive action. This cautious approach gave him flexibility but also made him appear reactive—particularly in foreign affairs.

Accomplishments and Vision

McKinley presided over the Spanish–American War. The conflict was triggered by public outrage following the sinking of the USS Maine in Havana Harbor and fueled by the Cuban rebellion against Spain. U.S. forces quickly defeated Spain in the Caribbean and the Pacific, notably in Puerto Rico, and the Philippines. Under the Treaty of Paris, Spain relinquished control of Cuba and ceded Puerto Rico, Guam, and the Philippines to the United States. The war signaled the emergence of the United States as a global imperial power, intensified debate over imperialism at home, and laid the groundwork for prolonged U.S. involvement in Caribbean and Pacific affairs, including the Philippine–American War that followed.

The annexation of Hawaii during his term further expanded American presence in the Pacific.

These actions transformed the United States from a continental power into a global imperial power. McKinley accepted territorial acquisition reluctantly but decisively, framing expansion as both a strategic necessity and moral responsibility. The outcome permanently altered American foreign policy and global military presence.

Domestically, McKinley restored economic confidence by reaffirming the gold standard, stabilizing currency and encouraging industrial growth after the depression of the 1890s. Protective tariffs encouraged the growth of manufacturing nationwide and contributed to renewed prosperity.

Criticisms and Controversies

Imperial expansion provoked intense domestic opposition. Critics argued that the control of the Philippines violated republican principles, entangled the nation in colonialism, and contradicted foundational ideals of self-government. The Philippine–American War that followed annexation highlighted the moral and military costs of imperial governance.

McKinley's cautious leadership during the march toward war drew criticism from both hawks and anti-imperialists. Some argued he allowed public sentiment and media pressure to dictate foreign policy rather than exercising decisive restraint.

LEGACY

McKinley's helped transition the United States from an inward-looking republic into a more centralized, industrial, and internationally engaged power. Domestically, his firm support for protective tariffs and the gold standard aligned federal policy with industrial capitalism and restored business confidence after the Panic of 1893.

Politically, his 1896 election marked a realignment that marginalized agrarian Populism and ushered in an era of organization-driven, nationally coordinated campaigns.

In foreign affairs, McKinley presided over the Spanish-American War and the acquisition of overseas territories, setting precedents for American imperialism and a permanent global presence. Although personally cautious and temperamentally conciliatory, his presidency reshaped the scope of federal authority and the nation's international posture, laying essential groundwork for the more assertive executive leadership of the Progressive Era.

His assassination in 1901[45] abruptly transferred power to Theodore Roosevelt, accelerating trends McKinley had cautiously initiated.

---

45 President William McKinley was shot on September 6, 1901, by anarchist Leon Czolgosz while attending a public reception at the Pan-American Exposition in Buffalo, New York. Initially appearing to recover, McKinley developed gangrene due to infection and died eight days later, on September 14. Vice President Theodore Roosevelt was sworn in the same day. The assassination intensified public concern over anarchist movements and led to major reforms in presidential security, including the permanent assignment of the U.S. Secret Service to protect the president.

THE EARLY PROGRESSIVE ERA
1901-1921

The progressive era marks the decisive transformation of the American presidency from a restrained, reactive office into the central engine of national reform and regulatory authority. Limited government and market self-correction—proved inadequate in the face of industrial consolidation, labor unrest, urban poverty, and political corruption. The presidency emerged as the institution most capable of responding to these systemic pressures.

Theodore Roosevelt's accession following McKinley's assassination represented the critical inflection point. Roosevelt articulated the stewardship theory of the presidency, asserting that executive power could be exercised proactively in the public interest unless explicitly prohibited by the Constitution. Action, rather than cautious restraint, became the defining measure of executive power.

Progressive reform expanded government across multiple domains: antitrust enforcement, food and drug safety, labor mediation, environmental conservation, and consumer protection. These reforms were not intrinsically anti-capitalist; rather, they sought to stabilize capitalism by curbing its most destructive excesses. Moreover, presidents increasingly acted as national arbiters between economic power and public welfare.

The Progressive era also institutionalized the modern administrative state. Independent regulatory commissions, professionalized civil service structures, and expert-driven governance reduced reliance on patronage and congressional micromanagement. Presidential leadership shifted from personal intervention toward management of complex bureaucratic systems.

Woodrow Wilson extended Progressive principles into wartime governance. World War I dramatically expanded executive authority over industry, finance, speech, and national mobilization, highlighting both the capacity and danger of centralized power. By 1921, Americans emerged victorious but exhausted, wary of moral crusades and skeptical of permanent executive activism.

The Progressive era concludes not because Progressive ideas failed, but because public tolerance for reformist intensity waned. The institutional architecture of the activist presidency was now established, even as political appetite for its aggressive use temporarily receded.

THEODORE ROOSEVELT (1901–1909)

EARLY LIFE AND BACKGROUND

Born on October 27, 1858, in New York City to a wealthy and socially prominent family, Roosevelt suffered from severe childhood asthma, frequent illnesses, and poor eyesight. These conditions left him physically weak and often confined indoors. Rather than discouraging him, this limitation pushed Roosevelt toward books, keen observation, and structured self-improvement. He became an avid reader of natural history, adventure stories, and classical works. By his early teens he had begun collecting and cataloging insect specimens, laying the groundwork for his lifelong passion for science and conservation.

Roosevelt's father, Theodore Roosevelt Sr., was the dominant moral force in his early life. A philanthropist and reform-minded civic leader, his father impressed upon young Theodore the idea that privilege carried obligations. Most famously, when Theodore was about twelve, his father told him that he had "the mind but not the body," and that it was his duty to build physical strength through discipline and effort. Roosevelt took this lesson seriously, embracing exercise, boxing, and endurance training—an early expression of the self-improvement that later defined his public image.

His mother, Martha "Mittie" Bulloch Roosevelt, came from a Southern, slaveholding family. She brought warmth, charm, and a sense of storytelling into the household. The tension between his father's Unionist views and his mother's Southern loyalties exposed Roosevelt to moral and political complexity.

Educated largely at home until college, Roosevelt grew up in an environment that encouraged curiosity, debate, and moral seriousness. By the time he entered Harvard, he had already internalized the themes that would dominate his life: disciplined self-improvement, moral responsibility, intellectual engagement, and a belief that personal effort could overcome natural limitation.

Roosevelt entered Harvard College in 1876, where he distinguished himself academically while continuing to enhance his physical prowess. He studied history, government, and science, and though he was not at the very top of his class, he was intellectually serious and intensely driven. At Harvard he met figures who shaped his worldview, including historian Henry Adams. Moreover, he began writing his first major work, The Naval War of 1812, which underscored his scholarly commitment. The sudden death of his father in 1878 devastated Roosevelt but also strengthened his sense of duty and self-reliance.

After graduating in 1880, Roosevelt entered New York politics, winning election to the New York State Assembly at just 23. He quickly gained a reputation as an independent reformer willing to challenge party bosses and political corruption. Personal tragedy struck in 1884 when, on the same day, his wife Alice and his mother both died. Grief-stricken and emotionally exhausted, Roosevelt withdrew from politics and headed west.

In the Dakota Badlands, Roosevelt reinvented himself as a rancher and frontiersman. He invested in cattle ranching, endured brutal winters, and lived a physically demanding life that tested the resilience he had spent years cultivating. Though financially unsuccessful, the Badlands experience profoundly shaped his views on masculinity, conservation, and American character. It also cemented his belief that strenuous effort and frontier values were essential antidotes to social and personal decay.

Roosevelt returned to public life in the late 1880s, holding several reform-oriented positions, most notably as President of the New York City Police Commission (1895–1897). As police commissioner, Roosevelt aggressively enforced civil service rules, attacked corruption, and insisted on professional standards. His highly visible night patrols and confrontations with entrenched interests made him both admired and resented, but they reinforced his national reputation as an incorruptible reformer.

In 1897, President William McKinley appointed Roosevelt Assistant Secretary of the Navy. In this role, Roosevelt pressed for naval modernization, expanded shipbuilding, and strategic preparedness, believing conflict with Spain was increasingly likely. When the Spanish-American War broke out in 1898, Roosevelt resigned his post to raise the volunteer cavalry regiment known as the Rough Riders, further enhancing his public stature[46].

Following the war, Roosevelt was elected Governor of New York (1899–1900). As governor, he pursued progressive reforms, including regulation of corporations, labor protections, and conservation measures. His willingness to confront powerful party interests alarmed Republican leaders, who viewed him as politically uncontrollable.

To sideline him, party bosses supported Roosevelt's nomination as Vice President in 1900, placing him in what was generally considered a ceremonial role. The strategy backfired. After McKinley's assassination in September 1901, Roosevelt—at age 42—became the youngest president in American history.

---

46 Roosevelt helped organize the 1st United States Volunteer Cavalry—popularly known as the Rough Riders—for service in the Spanish-American War. The regiment was an unconventional mix of western cowboys, ranch hands, Native Americans, and eastern elites, including Ivy League athletes and society figures, reflecting Roosevelt's belief in uniting social classes through shared national service. Roosevelt served as lieutenant colonel under Leonard Wood but effectively commanded the unit after Wood's promotion. The Rough Riders gained national fame for their role in the Battle of San Juan Heights (including Kettle Hill) near Santiago, Cuba, where Roosevelt led a highly publicized uphill charge under fire. Though militarily limited in scale, the episode proved politically transformative: it elevated Roosevelt to national celebrity status, reinforced his image of "strenuous life" leadership, and directly propelled his election as governor of New York later that year.

DOMESTIC LIFE

Roosevelt married Alice Hathaway Lee in 1880. In 1884, just two days after the birth of their daughter Alice Lee Roosevelt, Alice died of kidney failure on the same day Roosevelt's mother passed away. The double loss devastated him and led to his temporary withdrawal from public life and his retreat to the Dakota Badlands. Roosevelt rarely spoke of Alice, thereafter, marking her death in his diary with a stark black "X,".

In 1886, Roosevelt married Edith Kermit Carow, a childhood acquaintance who became the stabilizing force of his adult life. Their marriage was enduring and loving, resulting in five children—Theodore Jr., Kermit, Ethel, Archibald, and Quentin—who, along with Alice from his first marriage, formed a famously lively household. Edith managed family life with discipline and order, providing structure that complemented Roosevelt's exuberance and intensity.

Roosevelt was an unusually hands-on and emotionally expressive father for his era. He insisted on physical activity, outdoor adventure, and moral courage. Family life at Sagamore Hill in Oyster Bay, New York, was marked by constant motion—pets, games, letters, and lessons—mirroring Roosevelt's belief in the "strenuous life." Even as president, he integrated family into the White House, allowing the children considerable freedom, which contrasted sharply with the more reserved presidential households before and after his tenure.

Roosevelt's domestic life also reflected his values of duty, discipline, and affection. While demanding high standards, he maintained close personal bonds through frequent letters and shared experiences. The deaths of his youngest son, Quentin, during World War I, deeply affected him later in life, underscoring how inseparable his identity as a public figure was from his role as a father.

Overall, Roosevelt's family life was not a retreat from politics but a central expression of his worldview—an arena in which he sought to cultivate character, resilience, and moral responsibility, both in his children and, by extension, in the nation he led.

POLITICAL AFFILIATION AND GOVERNING STYLE

A Republican, Roosevelt assumed the presidency following McKinley's assassination and immediately redefined the office. He rejected the

Gilded Age model of executive restraint and articulated the steward-ship theory of the presidency: that the president may do anything not explicitly forbidden by the Constitution to advance the public good.

The "bully pulpit" was Theodore Roosevelt's term for the presidency itself, and he meant bully in its older sense—excellent or powerful. Under Roosevelt, the bully pulpit became an active instrument of governance. He used speeches, press access, and carefully staged public events to frame political debates in moral terms—casting issues such as corporate power, labor conditions, conservation, and consumer safety as questions of fairness and national character rather than policy disputes. By appealing directly to the public, Roosevelt bypassed entrenched party machines and forced legislators and business leaders to respond to popular pressure.

Roosevelt's energetic, moralizing use of the presidency permanently altered expectations of the office, establishing the modern model of the president as chief national communicator and agenda-setter, not merely a caretaker of existing laws.

Accomplishments and Vision

Roosevelt assumed the presidency after William McKinley's assassination and quickly asserted an energetic, reform-minded leadership style. He embraced the role of "steward of the people," using the presidency as a platform to regulate corporate power and protect consumers. Roosevelt's trust-busting campaign targeted monopolistic practices, most notably in the Northern Securities case, signaling that large corporations would be subject to federal oversight. He also supported the passage of the Elkins Act[47] and strengthened enforcement of the Sherman Antitrust Act to curb railroad rate discrimination and industrial consolidation.

Roosevelt's domestic agenda, known as the Square Deal, emphasized fairness for labor, business, and consumers. He intervened in the 1902 coal strike, pressuring both labor and management to accept arbitration—an unprecedented presidential role as a neutral mediator in labor disputes. His administration also advanced conservation policy, estab-

---

47 Federal legislation signed by President Theodore Roosevelt that strengthened earlier Interstate Commerce Act provisions by prohibiting railroad rebate practices and discriminatory pricing for large shippers. The act made both the railroads and the favored shippers liable for penalties, marking an important early Progressive Era effort to regulate corporate power and promote fair competition in interstate commerce..

lishing national forests, wildlife refuges, and federal oversight of public lands under the guidance of Gifford Pinchot. These initiatives marked the beginning of modern environmental stewardship at the federal level and expanded executive authority in managing natural resources.

Elected to a second term in 1904, Roosevelt expanded his progressive reform agenda. Consumer protection became a centerpiece of his second term, culminating in the Pure Food and Drug Act[48] and Meat Inspection Act[49] of 1906, both designed to ensure food safety and establish federal oversight of food and drug purity. He also pushed for stronger railroad regulation through the Hepburn Act, which empowered the Interstate Commerce Commission to set maximum freight rates and increased federal oversight of transportation networks. These measures significantly broadened federal regulatory power over the national economy.

Roosevelt also achieved major foreign policy successes that enhanced the United States' global standing. He redefined U.S. foreign policy through active diplomacy backed by military strength—summarized in his famous quote, "speak softly and carry a big stick." He oversaw the construction of the Panama Canal, a transformative engineering and strategic achievement that reshaped global trade and American naval power. In Latin America, the Roosevelt Corollary to the Monroe Doctrine asserted the United States' right to intervene to stabilize nations and prevent European involvement, marking a major expansion of U.S. influence in the Western Hemisphere.

On the global stage, Roosevelt elevated American diplomacy. He mediated the end of the Russo-Japanese War, earning the Nobel Peace Prize in 1906—the first awarded to an American. He also strengthened the U.S. Navy, notably sending the Great White Fleet on a world tour to demonstrate American naval strength and global reach.

---

48 Pure Food and Drug Act (1906). Enacted in response to widespread public concern over unsanitary food production and fraudulent patent medicines—the Pure Food and Drug Act prohibited the interstate sale of adulterated or misbranded foods and drugs. The law required accurate labeling of ingredients, particularly for products containing alcohol, opiates, cocaine, and other dangerous substances. It laid the foundation for the modern Food and Drug Administration.

49 The Meat Inspection Act of 1906, enacted during the Progressive Era, established federal oversight of meatpacking plants to ensure sanitary conditions and accurate labeling of meat products sold in interstate commerce. Prompted by public outrage following Upton Sinclair's The Jungle, the law authorized the U.S. Department of Agriculture to conduct continuous inspections of livestock before and after slaughter and to regulate meat processing standards.

CRITICISMS AND CONTROVERSIES

Roosevelt's expansive view of executive power alarmed critics who feared erosion of constitutional balance. His willingness to act without explicit congressional authorization raised enduring concerns about executive overreach and precedent.

Progressive reforms under Roosevelt were uneven. Labor protections remained limited, racial justice was largely neglected, and federal segregation persisted. His moralized rhetoric often exceeded practical outcomes, and his trust-busting targeted only select corporations.

In foreign affairs, Roosevelt's interventionism normalized the use of executive authority in projecting power abroad, with long-term consequences for regional sovereignty and U.S. foreign policy norms.

LEGACY

Theodore Roosevelt's legacy rests on his transformation of the presidency into a modern, activist institution capable of shaping national policy and public opinion. He redefined executive leadership by asserting that the president could act in the public interest unless explicitly forbidden by law—a sharp departure from the more restrained 19th-century model. This expansive view of presidential authority strengthened the federal government's role in regulating the economy, protecting consumers, and managing natural resources, establishing precedents that later reformers and presidents would build upon throughout the Progressive Era and beyond.

Roosevelt is widely regarded as the nation's first modern conservation president. He dramatically expanded the national park and forest systems, set aside millions of acres of public land, and institutionalized federal responsibility for environmental stewardship. His efforts laid the groundwork for future conservation policies and agencies, ensuring that preservation of natural resources became a permanent national priority. At the same time, his advocacy for fair regulation of large corporations and support for labor arbitration helped frame the federal government as a balancing force between competing economic interests.

In foreign policy, Roosevelt elevated the United States to a more prominent global role. His mediation of the Russo-Japanese War, support for construction of the Panama Canal, and articulation of the Roosevelt Corollary signaled a willingness to project American influence abroad while maintaining stability in the Western Hemisphere. Although some critics have viewed his assertive diplomacy as imperialistic, many historians credit Roosevelt with positioning the United States as an emerging world power in the early 20th century. Overall, his presidency left a durable imprint on executive authority, regulatory governance, conservation policy, and America's international posture.

William Howard Taft (1909–1913)

Early Life and Background

William Howard Taft was born on September 15, 1857, in Cincinnati, Ohio, into a prominent, intellectually rigorous family that emphasized education, public service, and moral discipline. His father, Alphonso Taft, was a distinguished lawyer, judge, and cabinet member under Presidents Grant and Hayes. Raised in a structured but supportive household, Taft excelled academically, attending local schools before enrolling at Yale University, where he was known for his diligence, good nature, over ambition or risk-taking. His childhood and youth fostered traits—respect for institutions, devotion to law, and personal steadiness—that would define his lifelong preference for judicial service and constitutional order over political combat.

After graduating first in his class at Yale and earning a law degree from Cincinnati Law School, he entered public service through judicial and administrative roles that highlighted his respect for institutional order and the rule of law. He served successively as an assistant prosecutor, judge of the Ohio Superior Court, U.S. Solicitor General, and judge on the U.S. Court of Appeals, gaining a national reputation for intellectual rigor and fairness. Taft's effectiveness as a colonial administrator in the Philippines further elevated his standing, demonstrating executive skill without demagoguery. His reputation for integrity and administrative competence led Theodore Roosevelt to view him as a natural successor, culminating in Taft's election to the presidency in 1908—an ascent shaped more by duty and opportunity than by a quest for power.

Domestic Life

Taft's domestic life was defined by stability, intellectual companionship, and a genuine affection for family. In 1886 he married Helen "Nellie" Herron Taft, an ambitious, politically astute partner who played a central role in shaping both his career and his public image. Their marriage was a close collaboration: Nellie strongly encouraged Taft's rise in public service and remained an influential adviser throughout his political life, including his presidency.

The Taft's had three children—Robert, Helen, and Charles—and family life was a grounding force for Taft, who was by temperament more comfortable in private settings than in the political spotlight. He was a devoted husband and father, deeply attached to routine, domestic comfort, and the rhythms of family life. Taft enjoyed reading, conversation, and informal gatherings at home. He valued the moral and emotional stability his family provided amid the pressures of public office.

As First Lady, Nellie Taft transformed the White House into an active social and cultural center, most notably championing the planting of the Japanese cherry trees along the Potomac. Taft's domestic life reinforced his reputation as a conscientious, family-oriented figure whose private character emphasized duty, loyalty, and personal restraint.

POLITICAL AFFILIATION AND GOVERNING STYLE

A Republican and Roosevelt's handpicked successor, Taft inherited a presidency dramatically expanded in power and public expectation. Yet Taft rejected the stewardship theory embraced by Roosevelt. He believed the president must act only when authority was clearly granted by statute or the Constitution, not when policy goals seemed morally justified.

Taft's governing style was legalistic, procedural, and deferential to Congress. He favored administrative restraint over public persuasion. While competent and sincere, his reluctance to mobilize public opinion left him politically exposed amid rising Progressive demands.

ACCOMPLISHMENTS AND VISION

Taft's presidency was marked by a vigorous—if less theatrical—continuation of Progressive Era reforms. He pursued antitrust enforcement more aggressively than Roosevelt, filing nearly twice as many antitrust suits and successfully breaking up major monopolies, including Standard Oil and American Tobacco under the Sherman Antitrust Act. Taft also strengthened federal regulatory authority through support of the Interstate Commerce Commission and the Mann–Elkins Act, which expanded federal power over railroads and telecommunications. In conservation, despite controversy surrounding Interior Secretary Richard Ballinger, Taft actually set aside more federal land for conservation than Roosevelt, placing millions of additional acres under federal protection.

Taft also advanced important institutional and administrative reforms that reshaped the modern presidency and federal government. He supported the establishment of a federal income tax (ratified as the 16th Amendment in 1913) and the direct election of senators through the 17th Amendment, both central Progressive goals. His administration created the U.S. Court of Commerce and later helped lay groundwork for the modern federal budget system through the Commission on Economy and Efficiency. In foreign policy, Taft promoted "Dollar Diplomacy," encouraging American investment abroad—particularly in Latin America and East Asia—as a means of extending U.S. influence and stability. Although often overshadowed by Roosevelt and Wilson, Taft's presidency significantly strengthened federal regulatory capacity and the administrative structure of the national government.

CRITICISMS AND CONTROVERSIES

William Howard Taft's presidency was marked by significant political controversies that fractured the Republican Party and weakened his public standing. His support for the Payne–Aldrich Tariff of 1909 disappointed Progressives who had expected meaningful tariff reduction, leading many to view Taft as too aligned with conservative business interests. The Ballinger–Pinchot dispute further damaged his reputation among conservationists and reformers when Taft sided with Interior Secretary Richard Ballinger over Gifford Pinchot, Theodore Roosevelt's ally and chief forester, creating the perception that Taft was retreating from Roosevelt's conservation legacy. These disputes deepened the split between Progressive and conservative Republicans, contributing to the party's division in the 1912 election and Roosevelt's third-party candidacy[50].

Taft's cautious leadership style and reliance on legalistic, methodical governance often contrasted unfavorably with Roosevelt's energetic progressivism, making him appear politically tone-deaf despite substantive policy achievements. His foreign policy of "Dollar Diplomacy," which sought to expand American influence through financial investment abroad, drew criticism for entangling the United States in unstable regions and prioritizing economic interests over democratic principles. Ultimately, Taft's presidency was overshadowed by party division and political miscalculation, culminating in a decisive electoral defeat in 1912 that limited his ability to shape the Progressive agenda and left a mixed contemporary reputation despite later recognition of his institutional accomplishments.

LEGACY

Taft's long-term legacy rests largely on his commitment to strengthening the rule of law, federal regulatory power, and the administrative capacity of the national government. Although often overshadowed by Theodore Roosevelt and Woodrow Wilson, Taft pursued Progres-

---

50 Formed in 1912 after Theodore Roosevelt broke with the Republican Party, the Progressive Party—popularly known as the "Bull Moose" Party—advocated an ambitious reform agenda that included trust-busting, women's suffrage, labor protections, social insurance, and stronger federal regulation of corporations. Roosevelt's candidacy split the Republican vote, enabling Democrat Woodrow Wilson to win the presidency, but the Bull Moose campaign marked a high point of Progressive Era reform politics and reshaped the national debate over the scope of federal power and social justice.

sive reforms through the courts and legal system rather than through public crusades. His vigorous antitrust enforcement reinforced the federal government's role in regulating large corporations and preserving competition, while support for the 16th and 17th Amendments advanced democratic reforms and modernized the nation's fiscal structure. Taft also contributed to the professionalization of the civil service and the development of a more systematic federal budget process, helping to shape the modern administrative state.

Taft's most enduring historical impact came after his presidency when he served as Chief Justice of the United States (1921–1930), the only former president to hold that position. In this role he reorganized and strengthened the federal judiciary, advocated for judicial efficiency, and oversaw construction of the Supreme Court Building, reinforcing the institutional independence of the Court. Today, Taft is remembered as a constitutional conservative and institutional reformer who prioritized legal order, administrative competence, and the steady expansion of federal authority within constitutional boundaries.

Taft and Roosevelt. Taft's relationship with Theodore Roosevelt deteriorated rapidly during Taft's presidency, largely over policy differences and political alliances. Roosevelt grew disillusioned with Taft's support for the Payne–Aldrich Tariff, his handling of conservation issues during the Ballinger–Pinchot controversy, and what Roosevelt saw as Taft's alignment with conservative Republicans. By 1912 the split had become irreparable, prompting Roosevelt to challenge Taft for the Republican nomination and ultimately run as the Progressive ("Bull Moose") Party candidate, dividing the Republican vote and ensuring Woodrow Wilson's victory. Despite this bitter political rupture, Taft and Roosevelt gradually reconciled after leaving office, aided by mutual friends and shared experiences during World War I. By the time of Roosevelt's death in 1919, the two men had largely restored their personal friendship, with Taft expressing deep admiration and respect for his former ally and political patron.

WOODROW WILSON (1913–1921)

EARLY LIFE AND BACKGROUND

Woodrow Wilson was born Thomas Woodrow Wilson on December 28, 1856, in Staunton, Virginia, into a close-knit Presbyterian family. He was the third of four children born to Joseph Ruggles Wilson, a minister and theologian, and Jessie Janet Woodrow. The Wilson household emphasized religious devotion, moral discipline, and intellectual dialogue, with family conversation often centered on theology and public affairs. Growing up in the American South during the Civil War and Reconstruction, Wilson experienced both familial stability and social upheaval. Though he struggled with reading in early childhood—possibly due to undiagnosed dyslexia—he developed strong verbal skills through debate and discussion at home.

After graduating from Princeton University (then the College of New Jersey) in 1879, Wilson studied law, earning a degree from the University of Virginia, before completing a PhD in political science at Johns Hopkins University in 1886—the only U.S. president to hold a doctorate. He built a distinguished academic career at Bryn Mawr, Wesleyan, and most notably Princeton, where he became president of the university in 1902. He pursued ambitious reforms aimed at curbing elite privilege and strengthening merit-based education. His intellectual reputation and reformist instincts brought him to public attention, leading to his election as governor of New Jersey in 1910, where he championed progressive legislation on labor, utilities, and political transparency. Wilson's success as a reform governor propelled him onto the national stage, and in 1912 he won the presidency, presenting himself as a reformer committed to using executive power to promote economic fairness, accountability, and moral purpose in public life.

DOMESTIC LIFE

Wilson married Ellen Louise Axson in 1885. She was an artist and the daughter of a Presbyterian minister, whose intellectual and cultural interests closely matched his own. Their marriage was affectionate and supportive, producing three daughters—Margaret, Jessie, and Eleanor. Ellen played an important role as Wilson's confidante and emotional anchor during his academic and early political career. Her death in 1914, while Wilson was president, devastated him and left him isolated as Europe descended into World War I.

In 1915 Wilson remarried Edith Bolling Galt, a widowed Washington socialite from a prominent Virginia family. Edith proved to be a far more active and politically engaged partner, particularly after Wilson suffered a severe stroke in 1919. During his long recovery, she tightly controlled access to the president and managed the flow of information and routine affairs of the executive branch, a role that later historians have described as unprecedented for a first lady. Across both marriages, Wilson's domestic life reveals a man deeply dependent on close personal relationships, emotionally vulnerable, and increasingly reliant on his wife's support to sustain his public responsibilities.

POLITICAL AFFILIATION AND GOVERNING STYLE

A Democrat elected amid Republican division in 1912, Wilson governed as a moral executive, believing presidential leadership should shape national purpose rather than merely administer policy. He revived presidential engagement with Congress, delivering legislative agendas personally and framing reform as an ethical imperative.

Wilson leadership style favored intellectual coherence and moral clarity over compromise, making him highly effective during periods of alignment—and deeply polarizing when consensus fractured.

ACCOMPLISHMENTS AND VISION

Wilson's first term centered on an ambitious progressive legislative agenda known as the "New Freedom," aimed at tariff reform, banking modernization, and stronger regulation of corporate power. The Underwood Tariff substantially reduced protective tariffs that had long favored American manufacturers and lowered consumer costs; to offset lost revenue, it implemented a graduated federal income tax made possible by the 16th Amendment. Perhaps his most enduring achievement was the Federal Reserve Act, which created a decentralized central banking system with regional Federal Reserve Banks and a governing board.

Wilson also strengthened antitrust enforcement. The Clayton Antitrust Act clarified and expanded earlier antitrust laws by prohibiting practices such as price discrimination, exclusive dealing, and certain types of corporate mergers that reduced competition; it also protected labor unions by declaring that organized labor was not an illegal restraint of trade. Complementing this law was the creation of the Federal Trade Commission, an independent regulatory agency empowered to investigate unfair business practices and enforce consumer protections, thereby institutionalizing ongoing federal oversight of corporate conduct. Additional economic and social reforms included the Federal Farm Loan Act, which established cooperative lending banks to provide affordable credit to farmers and stabilize rural economies, and the

Adamson Act, which mandated an eight-hour workday for interstate railroad workers, marking one of the first major federal labor protections.

In foreign policy, Wilson emphasized neutrality and "moral diplomacy," seeking to promote democratic governance and stability abroad, particularly in Latin America and Mexico. However, escalating tensions with Germany over unrestricted submarine warfare and diplomatic incidents gradually moved the United States toward intervention in World War I (Figure 10 and Figure 11).

Wilson's second term was dominated by World War I and the shaping of the postwar order. After asking Congress for a declaration of war in April 1917, he oversaw the mobilization of the American economy and military. Federal agencies such as the War Industries Board coordinated industrial production, transportation, and resource allocation, enabling the United States to supply and deploy millions of troops to Europe. Wilson framed the war in ideological terms, presenting it as a global effort to defend democracy and establish a just international order.

In January 1918, Wilson outlined his Fourteen Points, a program for a stable and peaceful world that emphasized open diplomacy, freedom of the seas, reduced trade barriers, arms limitations, and national self-determination. Most importantly, he proposed the creation of a League of Nations, an international body designed to resolve disputes and prevent future wars through collective security. At the Paris Peace Conference, Wilson played a leading role in shaping the Treaty of Versailles and secured inclusion of the League covenant. For his efforts to promote international peace, he was awarded the Nobel Peace Prize in 1919. Despite this global influence, Wilson failed to win Senate ratification of the treaty, and the United States never joined the League.

Domestically, his second term coincided with major constitutional changes. The 18th Amendment (Prohibition), ratified in 1919, banned the manufacture and sale of alcoholic beverages, reflecting long-standing temperance activism. The 19th Amendment granted women the right to vote nationwide, marking a significant expansion of American democracy achieved during his presidency. Wilson's final years in office were overshadowed by declining health after a severe stroke in 1919, limiting his ability to govern during the closing phase of his administration.

CRITICISMS AND CONTROVERSIES

Wilson has faced significant criticism for both his domestic racial policies and aspects of his leadership style. Despite his progressive economic reforms, Wilson presided over the resegregation of several federal agencies, reversing gains made during Reconstruction and reinforcing discriminatory employment practices within the federal government. His administration tolerated and, at times, endorsed segregationist policies that marginalized African American civil servants. Wilson's views on race—including his screening of The Birth of a Nation at the White House and his support for states' rights on racial matters—have drawn strong condemnation from many modern historians, who view his record as a significant moral failing that complicated his progressive reputation.

Wilson was also criticized for his handling of civil liberties and executive leadership, particularly during and after World War I. The Espionage Act and Sedition Act led to prosecutions of dissenters and restrictions on free speech. His determined but inflexible advocacy for U.S. entry into the League of Nations contributed to the Senate's rejection of the Treaty of Versailles when he refused key compromises. In October 1919, Wilson suffered a severe stroke that left him partially incapacitated for the remainder of his presidency. The extent of his disability was not fully disclosed to the public, and his wife, Edith Wilson, along with close advisers, managed access to the president and many executive matters. While intended to preserve governmental continuity, this arrangement raised concerns among contemporaries and later scholars about transparency, executive capacity, and the effective exercise of presidential leadership during the final months of his administration.

LEGACY

Wilson's legacy is defined by his transformative domestic reforms and ambitious, though only partially realized, international vision. At home, he helped reshape the modern American state by strengthening federal regulatory authority and stabilizing the national economy. The Federal Reserve System, Federal Trade Commission, and strengthened antitrust framework became permanent pillars of the U.S. financial and regulatory structure. His support for tariff reduction, banking reform, and labor protections reflected the progressive movement's effort to adapt American capitalism to an industrial, national economy.

Internationally, Wilson is remembered as the leading American architect of twentieth-century liberal internationalism. His wartime leadership and the Fourteen Points articulated a vision of diplomacy grounded in collective security, self-determination, and international cooperation. Although the United States never joined his proposed League of Nations, the concept influenced later institutions, particularly the United Nations and other multilateral alliances that shaped the post–World War II order. At the same time, Wilson's legacy remains contested. His presidency saw significant restrictions on civil liberties during World War I, including prosecutions under the Espionage and Sedition Acts, and his administration tolerated or reinforced racial segregation within the federal government. As a result, historians continue to view Wilson as a consequential but complex figure whose achievements in economic reform and international idealism were accompanied by notable limitations and enduring controversies.

Market Autonomy
1921-1929

This era represents a retreat from Progressive-era activism without dismantling the institutional framework it created. Following World War I, American voters demanded normalcy, stability, and economic growth rather than moral reform or regulatory expansion.

Republican administrations during this era emphasized fiscal restraint, tax reduction, business growth, and limited regulatory control. Presidential leadership favored efficiency, predictability, and deference to economic expertise over reformist intervention.

Importantly, this era did not restore nineteenth-century governance. Progressive institutions—regulatory agencies, professional civil service, and expanded executive capacity—remained intact. What changed was philosophy, not structure. Presidents now believed that restraint, rather than action, best served national interest.

This era also witnessed the normalization of close relationships between government and business. Administrative agencies often cooperated with industry rather than regulate it aggressively. Labor protections stagnated, and economic inequality widened beneath general prosperity.

The apparent success of the 1920s reinforced confidence in market self-regulation and limited government. That confidence would prove fragile. The onset of the Great Depression would expose the inadequacy of this approach, forcing a dramatic redefinition of presidential responsibility in the next era.

WARREN G. HARDING (1921–1923)

EARLY LIFE AND BACKGROUND

Warren Gamaliel Harding was born on November 2, 1865, in Blooming Grove, Ohio, and grew up in a modest, rural setting shaped by small-town Midwestern values. His parents, George Tryon Harding and Phoebe Dickerson Harding, were both physicians. The family later settled in the village of Caledonia. As a boy, he was known as affable and sociable rather than academically driven, developing an early talent for public speaking and a strong interest in newspapers and politics. Harding attended Ohio Central College (later Ohio Wesleyan University), where he studied journalism and honed his rhetorical skills, experiences that laid the foundation for his later career as a newspaper publisher and, eventually, a politician. His appeal rested heavily on personal charm and an ability to connect with ordinary voters.

After purchasing the Marion Daily Star in 1884, Harding used the newspaper to build name recognition, cultivate relationships with Ohio Republicans, and establish himself as a reliable party man. His affable temperament, talent for speaking, and ability to avoid conflict made him attractive to party leaders seeking unity. Harding served in the Ohio Senate (1899–1903), where he gained experience and visibility, followed by terms as Ohio lieutenant governor (1904–1906). Though he lost races for governor in 1910 and U.S. senator in 1914, these defeats increased his statewide profile. He was ultimately elected to the U.S. Senate in 1914, taking office in 1915. By 1920, Harding's reputation as a conciliatory, non-threatening figure positioned him as a compromise candidate at a deadlocked Republican National Convention.

Domestic Life

Harding's domestic life was complex and often troubled, standing in contrast to the genial public image he projected. In 1891 he married Florence Kling DeWolfe, an older, strong-willed divorcée who played a significant role in managing the Marion Daily Star and advancing Harding's political career. Their marriage was childless and marked by periods of emotional distance, shaped in part by Florence's dominance in both domestic and professional matters. Harding also engaged in extramarital relationships, most notably with Nan Britton, who later claimed he fathered her child—an allegation long controversial but supported by modern DNA evidence. As president, Harding relied heavily on Florence to manage access to him and to protect his health, as he suffered from chronic fatigue and cardiovascular problems. Privately, he sought companionship and escape from the pressures of office, revealing a domestic life characterized by personal vulnerability.

Political Affiliation and Governing Style

A Republican elected in a landslide; Harding campaigned on a promise of "normalcy"—a return to stability after the disruptions of World War I and Progressive reform. His governing style emphasized delegation, consensus, and avoidance of confrontation. Harding believed the presidency should soothe rather than direct national life.

He relied heavily on advisors and cabinet officials, granting them wide autonomy. While this approach reduced executive activism, it also weakened accountability and oversight. Harding's preference for personal loyalty over administrative rigor created ripe conditions for misconduct within his administration.

ACCOMPLISHMENTS AND VISION

Harding's presidency achieved notable success in foreign policy. The Washington Naval Conference (1921–1922) produced landmark arms limitation agreements, reducing naval competition among major powers and demonstrating that international cooperation could serve American interests without permanent alliances.

Domestically, Harding supported tax reductions, deregulation, and budgetary restraint, aligning federal policy with business confidence and economic recovery. He also endorsed the creation of the Bureau of the Budget[51], strengthening executive fiscal management and institutionalizing budgetary oversight.

Harding issued pardons and commutations for individuals convicted under wartime speech restrictions, signaling retreat from Wilson-era repression and restoring civil liberties.

CRITICISMS AND CONTROVERSIES

Harding's presidency is most notorious for corruption scandals that emerged after his death, particularly the Teapot Dome scandal, in which senior officials accepted bribes in exchange for access to federal oil reserves. While Harding was not personally implicated, his failure to supervise appointments and enforce ethical standards damaged public trust. Personal scandals, including extramarital relationships, further complicated his legacy.

---

51 The Bureau of the Budget, established by the Budget and Accounting Act of 1921 during Harding's administration, created for the first time a centralized executive mechanism for preparing the federal budget, strengthening presidential control over fiscal policy by shifting budget formulation from Congress to the executive branch; in 1970 it was reorganized and renamed the Office of Management and Budget (OMB), which continues to perform these functions today while also overseeing regulatory review and executive-branch management.

Critics argue that Harding's passive leadership enabled corruption and signaled executive abdication rather than principled restraint.

LEGACY

Harding's legacy is defined by a sharp contrast between a brief period of post–World War I stabilization and the profound damage caused by scandals within his administration. Elected in 1920 on a promise of a "return to normalcy," Harding oversaw policies that favored economic expansion, lower taxes, and reduced federal regulation. His administration supported business growth, raised protective tariffs, and helped guide the nation through a short but severe postwar recession into the more prosperous early 1920s. He also signed the Budget and Accounting Act of 1921, which modernized federal budgeting and strengthened executive oversight of government finances.

However, Harding's historical reputation has been overshadowed by corruption among several trusted appointees. The most infamous episode, the Teapot Dome scandal—exposed after his death in 1923—involved the secret leasing of federal oil reserves by Interior Secretary Albert B. Fall in exchange for bribes, becoming one of the largest political scandals of the early twentieth century. Additional controversies in the Veterans Bureau and Justice Department reinforced perceptions of weak leadership and poor judgment in choosing associates. While Harding himself was not directly implicated in criminal wrongdoing, his administrative laxity and reliance on compromised advisers have led historians to view his presidency as a cautionary example of the importance of executive oversight and ethical governance.

Harding's death[52] elevated Calvin Coolidge, whose philosophy of restraint was matched by personal discipline and administrative control—producing a markedly different outcome.

---

52 Harding died suddenly on August 2, 1923, while on a cross-country speaking tour known as the "Voyage of Understanding." He collapsed in San Francisco after weeks of fatigue and abdominal distress and was pronounced dead at the Palace Hotel. No autopsy was performed at the request of First Lady Florence Harding. His vice president, Calvin Coolidge, was sworn in as president later that night.

CALVIN COOLIDGE (1923–1929)

EARLY LIFE AND BACKGROUND

Calvin Coolidge was born on July 4, 1872, in the small village of Plymouth Notch, Vermont, into a family shaped by rural New England values of frugality, self-reliance, and civic duty. His father, John Calvin Coolidge Sr., was a storekeeper, farmer, and local public official who served in roles ranging from town clerk to state legislator. Coolidge's childhood was marked by emotional reserve and personal loss—his mother died when he was twelve and his younger sister several years later. These events likely reinforced his quiet demeanor and habit of introspection. Growing up in a sparse, disciplined environment with few comforts, Coolidge developed the self-control, austerity, and moral seriousness that later defined both his personal character and his restrained approach to political leadership.

After graduating from Amherst College in 1895, he studied law in Northampton, Massachusetts, entered local politics, and rose methodically through municipal and state offices—city councilor, mayor of Northampton, state legislator, lieutenant governor, and governor of Massachusetts. His decisive but legally grounded response to the 1919 Boston Police Strike, in which he asserted that "there is no right to strike against the public safety by anybody, anywhere, any time," propelled him onto the national stage as a figure of order amid postwar unrest. This reputation led to his selection as Warren G. Harding's vice president in 1920; upon Harding's sudden death in 1923, Coolidge assumed the presidency, carrying into the White House the same restrained, law-centered style that had defined his ascent.

Domestic Life

Coolidge's domestic life was defined by a strong partnership with his wife, Grace Goodhue Coolidge. Grace, a teacher of the deaf with a warm and outgoing personality, complemented Coolidge's reserved nature and served as an effective social presence in both the Massachusetts State House and the White House. The couple had two sons, John and Calvin Jr., and maintained a family life that emphasized privacy, routine, and moral discipline. Their household was deeply affected by the sudden death of Calvin Jr. in 1924 from blood poisoning following a minor injury. The tragedy profoundly affected the president and cast a long shadow over his remaining years in office. Despite public perceptions of Coolidge as emotionally distant, his private writings suggest a man deeply attached to family, who viewed domestic stability and personal self-control as essential foundations of character and public service.

Political Affiliation and Governing Style

A Republican, Coolidge governed as a committed advocate of limited government and market autonomy. Unlike Harding's passive delegation, Coolidge's restraint was deliberate and controlled. He believed that the federal government should interfere as little as possible in economic and social life, allowing private enterprise and local institutions to function freely.

Coolidge exercised executive authority primarily through veto, appointment discipline, and rhetorical restraint. He resisted pressure for agricultural subsidies, labor intervention, and regulatory expansion, arguing that long-term prosperity depended on fiscal discipline and constitutional restraint.

ACCOMPLISHMENTS AND VISION

Under Coolidge, the Roaring Twenties reached an apex, characterized by rapid economic expansion, consumer optimism, and a federal government committed to limited intervention. Coolidge embraced a pro-business philosophy, supporting significant tax reductions under Treasury Secretary Andrew Mellon, restraining federal spending, and promoting regulatory stability, all of which encouraged investment, industrial growth, and rising consumer credit. Mass production—especially automobiles, household appliances, and radios—transformed daily life, while urbanization and stock market speculation symbolized widespread confidence in continued prosperity. At the same time, the era exposed structural weaknesses: agricultural sectors lagged, income inequality widened, and financial speculation went largely unchecked. Coolidge viewed these developments as the natural outcomes of individual initiative rather than problems requiring federal correction.

Administratively, Coolidge strengthened fiscal oversight through support of the Bureau of the Budget and reinforced civil service professionalism. In foreign policy, he maintained diplomatic stability, supported international arbitration, and continued arms limitation efforts initiated under Harding.

Coolidge also signed the Immigration Act of 1924, which sharply restricted immigration and reflected the era's nativist sentiments, and approved the Indian Citizenship Act of 1924, granting U.S. citizenship to all Native Americans born in the United States.

Coolidge restored public confidence in executive integrity following the scandals of the Harding administration.

CRITICISMS AND CONTROVERSIES

Critics argue that Coolidge's administration failed to regulate financial markets adequately, allowing excessive speculation and credit expansion that contributed to the conditions leading to the Great Depression. Coolidge also opposed federal relief for struggling farmers, repeatedly vetoing the McNary–Haugen bills, a stance seen as indifference to farmers. His support for restrictive immigration laws is viewed as morally and socially regressive. More broadly, historians fault Coolidge for treating economic inequality, corporate consolidation, and labor tensions as private matters rather than public responsibilities, leaving the federal government ill-prepared to respond when the economic boom collapsed at the decade's end.

Additionally, Coolidge's limited engagement with social reform left racial and labor inequalities largely untouched, reflecting the narrow scope of federal responsibility during the era.

Legacy

Calvin Coolidge's legacy rests largely on his advocacy of limited government, fiscal restraint, and pro-business economic policy during the prosperous 1920s. As president, he emphasized balanced budgets, reduced federal spending, and significant tax cuts, reflecting his belief that economic growth was best achieved through private enterprise rather than government intervention. His administration oversaw a period of strong industrial expansion, rising consumerism, and relative domestic stability. Coolidge also supported regulatory restraint and business-friendly policies that many contemporaries credited with sustaining the decade's economic boom.

At the same time, historians often debate whether Coolidge's commitment to minimal federal oversight contributed indirectly to structural weaknesses that culminated in the Great Depression shortly after he left office. His cautious approach to farm relief, financial regulation, and economic intervention reflected his philosophy but left certain systemic risks unaddressed. Nonetheless, Coolidge is remembered as a symbol of small-government conservatism, personal integrity, and administrative efficiency, with a reputation for restoring public confidence in the presidency following the scandals of the Harding era.

THE NEW DEAL AND WORLD WAR

1929-1945

This era represents the most profound transformation of American governance since the Civil War. Triggered by the collapse of the global economy in 1929, this era forced a fundamental reassessment of the relationship between citizens, markets, and the federal government. The assumptions underlying both Gilded Age laissez-faire and 1920s retrenchment proved incapable of addressing systemic economic failure. In their place emerged a new governing consensus: that national stability required active federal intervention and sustained executive leadership.

The Great Depression was not merely an economic downturn but a legitimacy crisis. Mass unemployment, bank failures, and social dislocation threatened democratic institutions worldwide. In many nations, economic collapse led to authoritarianism. In the United States, the crisis instead produced an unprecedented expansion of democratic government, centered on the presidency.

Franklin D. Roosevelt's election in 1932 marked a decisive break with prior models of restraint. The New Deal redefined federal responsibility for economic security, labor relations, banking stability, and social welfare. Through emergency legislation, regulatory agencies, and direct relief programs, the federal government assumed roles previously considered incompatible with American traditions. The presidency became the primary engine of national response, coordinating legislative action, administrative implementation, and public confidence.

This era also reshaped constitutional interpretation. Judicial resistance to early New Deal programs gave way to acceptance of broad federal authority under the Commerce Clause and the General Welfare Clause. The balance between state and federal power shifted permanently, and the administrative state became an enduring feature of governance rather than a temporary expedient.

World War II completed the transformation. World war required full national mobilization—economic, industrial, scientific, and human. Executive authority expanded dramatically as the president coordinated production, managed alliances, directed military strategy, and framed national purpose. Unlike World War I, this expansion proved durable. The scale and success of wartime mobilization validated the enlarged role of the federal government and the presidency in the eyes of the public.

By 1945, the United States emerged as the world's dominant economic and military power. More importantly, democratic governance had survived simultaneous economic collapse and global war—an outcome far from guaranteed in 1929. The presidency stood at the center of this achievement, no longer merely a constitutional officer, but the institutional embodiment of national leadership in crisis.

This era thus marks the birth of the modern American state. The federal government's responsibility for economic stability, social welfare, and global engagement became accepted rather than exceptional. Future debates would concern the limits of this power—not its legitimacy.

HERBERT HOOVER (1929–1933)

EARLY LIFE AND BACKGROUND

Herbert Clark Hoover was born on August 10, 1874, in West Branch, Iowa, into a modest Quaker family that emphasized hard work, personal integrity, and self-reliance. His father, Jesse Hoover, a blacksmith and farm equipment dealer, died when Herbert was six, and his mother, Hulda Minthorn Hoover, a devout Quaker and community organizer, died four years later, leaving him orphaned by age nine. Hoover was subsequently raised by relatives, first in Iowa and then in Oregon, where he lived with his uncle, Dr. Henry Minthorn, a stern but influential figure who instilled discipline and responsibility. These early experiences of loss, economic insecurity, and moral rigor shaped Hoover's lifelong belief in individual initiative and voluntary cooperation—principles that later defined both his humanitarian work and his presidency.

Hoover's rise to national prominence was unconventional and rooted not in electoral politics but in engineering, management, and humanitarian service. After graduating from Stanford University in 1895, Hoover built a highly successful international career as a mining engineer and executive. He amassed significant wealth and acquired a reputation for organizational efficiency. His global stature expanded dramatically during World War I, when he led the Commission for Relief in Belgium, coordinating massive private and governmental efforts to prevent famine in German-occupied Europe. Hoover later served as head of the U.S. Food Administration, where he promoted voluntary conservation and efficient resource management. These achievements made him one of the most admired public servants in the world and propelled him into Republican Party leadership. Appointed Secretary of Commerce under Presidents Harding and Coolidge, Hoover transformed the department into a central hub for economic data collection, standardization, and industrial coordination. By the late 1920s, his technocratic competence, international prestige, and association with the prosperity of the Coolidge years positioned him as the logical Republican nominee which led to his overwhelming victory in the 1928 presidential election.

Domestic Life

In 1899 Hoover married Lou Henry, a fellow Stanford graduate and trained geologist, who became his closest confidante and collaborator. The Hoovers' marriage was notably modern for its time: Lou Henry was fluent in multiple languages, managed many household and travel logistics during Herbert's international engineering work, and played an active advisory role in his humanitarian and governmental endeavors. They had two sons, Herbert Jr. and Allan, but family life was often disrupted by Hoover's extensive travel and public responsibilities. As First Lady, Lou Henry Hoover emphasized efficiency, youth organizations (notably the Girl Scouts), and historical preservation, while maintaining a low public profile consistent with her husband's temperament. Personally, Hoover was uncomfortable with political socializing and deeply private.

POLITICAL AFFILIATION AND GOVERNING STYLE

A Republican, Hoover assumed the presidency amid widespread optimism and economic confidence. His governing philosophy blended Progressive-era administrative expertise with Coolidge-era skepticism of direct federal intervention. Hoover believed the federal government should coordinate, encourage, and stabilize, but not directly manage markets or provide large-scale relief.

Hoover favored voluntary cooperation between government, business, and labor. He relied heavily on conferences, moral persuasion, and expert planning. These traits reflected a belief that economic crises could be mitigated through careful planning and individual initiative rather than large-scale governmental intervention.

ACCOMPLISHMENTS AND VISION

Hoover entered the presidency with a reputation as an accomplished engineer, humanitarian, and progressive-minded administrator. Before and during World War I, he gained international recognition for organizing large-scale relief efforts that fed millions in war-torn Europe, demonstrating his belief in efficient, technocratic governance and voluntary cooperation between government and private institutions. As president, Hoover promoted what he called "associationalism," encouraging collaboration among business, labor, and government to stabilize and modernize the economy. He supported infrastructure development such as the Boulder (Hoover) Dam, expanded federal involvement in flood control and public works, and signed the Smoot–Hawley Tariff—intended to protect American industries—reflecting his commitment to economic nationalism and domestic stability.

Hoover's broader vision emphasized limited but active government working in partnership with private enterprise and local institutions to promote prosperity and social welfare. In response to the early years of the Great Depression[53], he increased federal spending on public works, established the Reconstruction Finance Corpora-

---

53 The Great Depression was triggered by the stock market crash of October 1929. The real GDP fell by roughly 30 percent, industrial production collapsed, and unemployment peaked near 25 percent by 1933. The crisis spread internationally through trade contraction, debt deflation, and adherence to the gold standard, deepening and prolonging the downturn. Recovery began unevenly after 1933 with New Deal reforms—bank sta-

tion to provide emergency loans to banks and key industries, and supported efforts to stabilize agriculture and housing markets. Although many of these initiatives were later overshadowed by the depth of the economic crisis, Hoover's approach represented an important transitional phase between the more limited federal role of the 1920s and the expanded interventionism of the New Deal. His presidency reflected a belief in managerial expertise, humanitarian responsibility, and the capacity of coordinated voluntary action to address national challenges.

CRITICISMS AND CONTROVERSIES

Herbert Hoover's presidency drew intense criticism for its handling of the Great Depression, which began shortly after he took office and deepened throughout his term. Although Hoover implemented a number of relief and recovery measures—including public works spending and creation of the Reconstruction Finance Corporation—many Americans viewed his response as too cautious and reliant on voluntary cooperation rather than direct federal aid to individuals. His belief in limited government intervention and balanced budgets led critics to argue that he underestimated the severity of the economic collapse and acted too slowly to provide widespread relief. The Smoot–Hawley Tariff of 1930, intended to protect American industries, was widely blamed for worsening the global economic downturn by provoking retaliatory tariffs and constricting international trade.

Hoover also faced significant public backlash over social unrest and unemployment during the Depression. The dispersal of the "Bonus Army" in 1932—when federal troops removed World War I veterans who had gathered in Washington, D.C., to demand early payment of promised bonuses—damaged his public image and reinforced perceptions of an administration out of touch with the struggles of ordinary Americans. Critics portrayed Hoover as overly committed to individualism and insufficiently responsive to widespread hardship, contributing to his decisive defeat in the 1932 election. While many historians now recognize that Hoover pursued more active federal measures than earlier presidents had in economic crises, his leader-

---

bilization, public works, and social insurance—but full economic recovery in the U.S. is generally dated to the mobilization and demand surge associated with World War II.

ship remains closely associated with the nation's most severe economic downturn and the limitations of pre–New Deal policy approaches.

Legacy

Hoover's legacy is defined by a stark contrast between his distinguished pre-presidential humanitarian achievements and the perceived failures of his presidency during the onset of the Great Depression. Before taking office, Hoover had earned global acclaim as a mining engineer, international relief organizer, and Secretary of Commerce. He coordinated massive food relief efforts in Europe during and after World War I, helping feed millions and earning a reputation for administrative brilliance and humanitarian commitment. As commerce secretary in the 1920s, he promoted standardization, infrastructure development, and business cooperation with government—an early model of technocratic, data-driven governance.

His presidency, however, was overshadowed by the catastrophic economic collapse following the stock market crash of 1929. Hoover believed strongly in voluntary cooperation between government, business, and labor rather than direct federal intervention. He supported public works spending, the Reconstruction Finance Corporation (RFC) to stabilize banks and industry, and limited relief measures, but resisted large-scale federal welfare programs, fearing they would undermine local responsibility and individual initiative. To many Americans suffering mass unemployment and bank failures, these responses appeared inadequate and overly cautious.

In historical perspective, Hoover's legacy has been reassessed with greater nuance. Many policies later expanded under Franklin Roosevelt had roots in Hoover's initiatives. Hoover is thus remembered as a capable administrator and humanitarian whose presidency was overwhelmed by economic forces and whose policy philosophy proved ill-suited to the demands of the Great Depression.

FRANKLIN D. ROOSEVELT (1933–1945)

EARLY LIFE AND BACKGROUND

Franklin Delano Roosevelt was born in 1882 at the Roosevelt family estate in Hyde Park, New York. He was the only child of James Roosevelt Sr. and Sara Delano Roosevelt, members of old, affluent families with deep ties to New York society. FDR grew up in a sheltered, highly cultivated environment—tutored at home until age 14, and surrounded by books, music, and adults rather than peers.

His parents, particularly his mother, fostered confidence, emotional resilience, and a sense of noblesse oblige. Frequent travel to Europe exposed young Franklin to languages, diplomacy, and international culture, while summers at Campobello Island in New Brunswick nurtured his love of sailing and the sea.

Educated at Groton School, Roosevelt absorbed Endicott Peabody's ethic of Christian duty and public service, reinforcing a belief that the privileged bore responsibility for societal leadership. Though physically healthy and socially reserved as a boy, FDR exhibited self-assurance and optimism—traits that would later define his political persona.

Roosevelt's adult life blended elite confidence with resilience. After graduating from Harvard and attending Columbia Law School, he entered New York political life. Elected to the New York State Senate in 1910, Roosevelt emerged as a reform-minded Democrat and gained valuable administrative and political experience as Assistant Secretary of the Navy during World War I.

His promising rise was nearly halted in 1921 when polio left him permanently paralyzed from the waist down. Rather than withdraw, Roosevelt rebuilt his public life through discipline and quiet determination. Elected Governor of New York in 1928, he confronted the early Great Depression with pragmatic experimentation in relief and reform, sharpening the leadership style that propelled him to the presidency in 1932. His ascent reflected not only political skill and experience, but a personal transformation that deepened empathy, patience, and resolve—qualities central to his later leadership.

Domestic Life

Roosevelt married Eleanor Roosevelt in 1905, and together they had five children. Although early family life followed conventional upper-class norms, the relationship changed markedly after Roosevelt's 1918 affair with Lucy Mercer. Rather than dissolve, the marriage adapted: Eleanor pursued an increasingly independent public and moral role, while Franklin relied on mutual respect, loyalty, and shared political purpose rather than emotional intimacy. This unconventional arrangement provided stability while allowing both partners to function effectively in public life.

After Roosevelt's paralysis from polio in 1921, his domestic environment became carefully structured around his physical needs and emotional resilience. Warm Springs, Georgia, emerged as a second home and therapeutic center, offering privacy, routine, and psychological renewal.

Roosevelt's inner support circle was essential to both his private life and political effectiveness, particularly after polio confined him to a wheelchair. At its center was Eleanor, whose independence and activism complemented Franklin's leadership and expanded his access to social reform networks. His longtime political aide Louis Howe served as a surrogate conscience and strategist, fiercely protective of Roosevelt's career and instrumental in guiding his return to politics after illness. Howe's blunt counsel and loyalty helped anchor FDR during periods of doubt and transition.

Roosevelt also depended heavily on trusted personal aides and companions who managed daily logistics and emotional continuity. Missy LeHand, his devoted personal secretary, acted as gatekeeper, confidante, and emotional stabilizer, coordinating both household and political affairs. Later, figures such as Harry Hopkins became indispensable, blurring the line between domestic presence and policy influence by living in the White House and serving as an intimate adviser. This small, loyal circle—bound by discretion, trust, and constant proximity—allowed Roosevelt to mask physical vulnerability, manage information tightly, and maintain the confident, reassuring public persona that defined his leadership during crisis.

POLITICAL AFFILIATION AND GOVERNING STYLE

A Democrat elected amid economic collapse; Roosevelt governed as an experimental executive. Rejecting rigid ideology, he embraced pragmatic trial-and-error, famously asserting that the nation should "take a method and try it." His leadership style was flexible, improvisational, and highly centralized.

Roosevelt expanded presidential authority dramatically. He preferred action to theory, coalition-building to confrontation, and political maneuvering to constitutional debate. He managed a close but often contentious advisory circle, encouraging competition among aides to generate ideas and preserve executive dominance.

Roosevelt redefined the relationship of the presidency to the American public. Unlike the booming oratory of earlier presidents, FDR cultivated a calm, conversational style—measured pacing, simple vocabulary, and carefully structured explanations. He spoke with the public rather than at them, projecting confidence, warmth, and mastery without theatricality. His patrician accent was softened deliberately, and his delivery emphasized reassurance, clarity, and reason.

This approach was best characterized by his Fireside Chats, a series of informal radio addresses beginning in 1933. Framed as intimate conversations, the chats explained complex issues—banking crises, unemployment, war—using everyday language and analogies that listeners could easily grasp. Roosevelt often spoke as if seated in the listener's living room, fostering trust and personal connection while bypassing hostile press intermediaries. The Fireside Chats redefined presidential communication, transforming the office into a direct, empathetic voice in American homes and establishing mass communication as a core instrument of modern presidential leadership.

ACCOMPLISHMENTS AND VISION

Roosevelt's most enduring legacy is the New Deal, a sweeping redefinition of federal responsibility in response to the Great Depression.

The New Deal. The New Deal consisted of a flurry of laws and agencies enacted primarily between 1933 and 1938 under Roosevelt. Immediate stabilization came through the Emergency Banking Act (1933) and Glass–Steagall Act (1933), which restored confidence by separating commercial and investment banking and creating the FDIC. Agricultural collapse was addressed through the Agricultural Adjustment Act (AAA), while industrial recovery efforts included the National Industrial Recovery Act (NIRA), which created the Public Works Administration (PWA). Direct employment and relief were provided through programs such as the Civilian Conservation Corps (CCC) and later the Works Progress Administration (WPA), which together employed millions of Americans in infrastructure, conservation, and public works.

Long-term structural reform followed. The Social Security Act of 1935 established old-age pensions, unemployment insurance, and aid to dependent families. Labor relations were transformed by the National Labor Relations Act (Wagner Act), which guaranteed collective bargaining rights and created the NLRB. Financial markets were regulated through the Securities Act (1933) and Securities Exchange Act (1934), creating the SEC. Additional measures such as the Tennessee Valley Authority (TVA) reshaped regional development, while the Fair

Labor Standards Act (1938) set minimum wages, maximum hours, and child labor restrictions. Collectively, these laws did not end the Great Depression outright, but they permanently redefined federal responsibility for economic stability, labor protection, and social welfare.

Throughout the late 1930s, Roosevelt recognized the danger posed by Nazi Germany and Imperial Japan but faced strong isolationist sentiment at home. He pursued incremental measures—such as rearmament, the Lend-Lease Act[54], and naval patrols in the Atlantic—to support Britain and other Allies while avoiding formal war. The turning point came on December 7, 1941, when Japan attacked Pearl Harbor. Roosevelt responded with clarity and resolve, framing the attack as a direct assault on American sovereignty. His address to Congress the following day—declaring December 7 "a date which will live in infamy"—secured overwhelming public and congressional support for war, formally bringing the United States into World War II (Figure 12).

As a wartime leader, Roosevelt exercised strategic vision and political mastery rather than battlefield command. He coordinated closely with military leaders and forged the Allied "Grand Alliance" with Winston Churchill and Joseph Stalin. He prioritized industrial mobilization, transforming the American economy into an unmatched arsenal of democracy. FDR orchestrated an unprecedented partnership between the federal government and private enterprise, transforming a depression-scarred economy into the world's most powerful war machine. Roosevelt created centralized agencies—most notably the War Production Board (WPB)—to coordinate raw materials, set production priorities, and convert civilian factories to military output. Automobile plants shifted to tanks and aircraft, shipyards adopted assembly-line techniques, and standardized designs allowed for rapid mass production. The federal government financed factory expansion, guaranteed contracts, and absorbed risk, enabling industry to scale at speeds no market system could achieve independently.

---

54 Enacted in March 1941 under President Franklin D. Roosevelt, the Lend-Lease Act authorized the United States to supply military equipment, food, and other strategic materials to Allied nations—principally Great Britain, the Soviet Union, and China—whose defense was deemed vital to American security. By allowing aid without immediate payment, the act ended formal U.S. neutrality and positioned the United States as the "arsenal of democracy," providing crucial support that sustained Allied resistance prior to America's direct entry into World War II.

Equally critical was Roosevelt's management of labor, resources, and public morale. Through agencies such as the Office of Price Administration (OPA) and the War Manpower Commission, the administration managed inflation, rationed scarce goods, and allocated labor to essential industries while negotiating with unions to limit strikes. Roosevelt framed production itself as a form of patriotism, encouraging the entry of women and minorities into industrial work. By 1944, the United States was producing tens of thousands of aircraft annually, launching ships faster than enemies could sink them, and supplying not only its own forces but Allied armies worldwide. This industrial mobilization—directed from the White House but executed by private industry—proved decisive in securing Allied victory.

Under Roosevelt, the United States emerged as a global superpower, architect of postwar institutions including the United Nations, the World Bank, and the International Monetary Fund.

CRITICISMS AND CONTROVERSIES

Roosevelt's presidency has drawn criticism from across the political spectrum, particularly regarding the expansion of executive power. Critics argued that the New Deal dramatically enlarged the federal government, weakened states' rights, and set precedents for permanent intervention in the economy. Business leaders and conservatives condemned regulatory agencies, deficit spending, and labor protections as excessive and constitutionally suspect. The 1937 attempt to expand ("pack") the Supreme Court was widely viewed—even by some supporters—as an abuse of presidential authority.

Other criticisms focus on civil liberties, race, and policy limitations. Roosevelt's authorization of Japanese American internment during World War II, is now broadly regarded as a grave violation of constitutional rights. From the left, critics note that the New Deal often excluded or disadvantaged African Americans and agricultural laborers, allowing Roosevelt to preserve his political coalition. Economically, some argue the New Deal prolonged the Great Depression or failed to achieve full recovery before wartime mobilization. Taken together, these critiques frame Roosevelt as a transformative but deeply contested president—one whose leadership reshaped American government while raising enduring questions about expansion of the government.

LEGACY

Franklin D. Roosevelt is one of the most transformative presidents in American history. He preserved democratic governance during economic collapse and global war. He greatly expanded federal authority without abandoning constitutional order or electoral legitimacy.

Roosevelt ushered in the modern American presidency. Federal responsibility for economic stability, social welfare, and global leadership became permanent expectations rather than emergency measures.

Roosevelt demonstrated that democracy could survive—and even strengthen—under crisis-driven expansion of power. But he also left future generations the burden of defining limits. The presidency after Roosevelt would never again be modest, temporary, or purely administrative.

The Four Terms. Prior to Roosevelt, the two-term tradition, established by George Washington, functioned as a powerful informal constraint on presidential ambition. Roosevelt's decision to seek third and fourth terms occurred under extraordinary circumstances, but it also raised grave concerns about executive control.

The institutional response to Roosevelt's extended presidency was constitutional, not political. In 1951, the ratification of the Twenty-Second Amendment formally limited presidents to two elected terms. This amendment did not repudiate Roosevelt's leadership; rather, it acknowledged that democratic resilience depends not only on capable individuals but on structural safeguards.

THE POST AND COLD WAR
1945-1968

The post-war era represents a high-water mark of confidence in American governance. Following World War II, the United States emerged as a global superpower with unmatched economic capacity, military reach, and diplomatic influence. Unlike earlier postwar transitions, the return to peace did not diminish presidential authority. Instead, global leadership became a permanent condition of the office.

The United States accepted that communist governments—especially the Soviet Union—would continue to exist but sought to "contain" their influence by using economic aid, military alliances, political pressure, and, when necessary, force (containment doctrine). The goal was to block communism from spreading into vulnerable regions, on the assumption that if expansion were stopped, the system would eventually weaken or collapse on its own.

The creation of the Department of Defense, National Security Council, Central Intelligence Agency, and permanent military alliances institutionalized executive leadership in foreign affairs. War was no longer viewed as an exceptional event; therefore, preparedness became continuous.

Domestically, a broad political consensus emerged around the New Deal framework. Both major parties accepted federal responsibility for economic stability, infrastructure investment, social insurance, and regulatory oversight. The presidency functioned less as an engine of ideological transformation than as a manager of prosperity and stability. Economic growth, rising wages, and middle-class expansion reinforced confidence in the government.

Truman, Eisenhower, and Kennedy each exercised expansive authority, yet generally avoided dramatic institutional upheaval. Power was concentrated, but it was also embedded within professional bureaucracies and legislative partnerships. The presidency was strong, but it remained broadly trusted.

Civil rights emerged as the central domestic challenge to post-war consensus. Legal segregation and voting discrimination increasingly conflicted with democratic ideals promoted globally. Presidential intervention—sometimes cautious, sometimes decisive—signaled a growing federal role in enforcing constitutional equality.

By the mid-1960s, strains in the consensus were visible. The Vietnam War, justified initially through containment logic, escalated beyond public expectations and eroded trust in executive judgment. Social unrest, generational conflict, and media scrutiny weakened deference to institutional authority. The presidency remained powerful, but its legitimacy was contested.

By 1968, the Cold War consensus had fractured. What followed was not a return to prewar governance, but a period of skepticism, polarization, and institutional recalibration.

In historical perspective, this era represents the most stable and confident phase of the modern presidency. Executive power was expansive but broadly legitimate, constrained more by norms than by law. Its collapse set the stage for a new era defined not by consensus, but by doubt.

HARRY S. TRUMAN (1945–1953)

EARLY LIFE AND BACKGROUND

Born on May 8, 1884, in Lamar, Missouri, Harry S. Truman spent much of his youth in Independence, Missouri, a border-state town with deep Civil War memory. His father, John Anderson Truman, worked as a farmer and livestock trader. The family moved frequently in Truman's early years, reflecting economic instability common to rural Midwestern families in the late 19th century.

Truman was a serious, bookish child with poor eyesight. These traits limited sports but pushed him toward reading and music. He became an avid reader of history and biography—especially accounts of the American presidency and the Civil War. He also studied piano diligently. His mother, Martha Ellen Young Truman, was particularly influential, encouraging discipline, education, and moral responsibility. Although financially constrained, the household emphasized self-improvement, honesty, and civic duty—values that Truman later cited as foundational to his character and public service.

His service as an artillery officer in World War I proved formative. Truman demonstrated decisiveness under pressure, loyalty to subordinates, and organizational competence. After the war, he entered Missouri politics through the Democratic Party machine but gradually distinguished himself through administrative integrity rather than patronage. As a U.S. senator, Truman gained national recognition chairing the Truman Committee, which aggressively investigated waste and corruption in wartime procurement, saving billions of dollars and establishing his reputation as a capable steward of public resources.

When Truman assumed the presidency following Franklin Roosevelt's death in April 1945, he inherited unparalleled responsibility with little preparation for global leadership. He entered office amid global uncertainty, nuclear revolution, and rapidly deteriorating relations with the Soviet Union.

Domestic Life

Truman married Bess Truman (Elizabeth Virginia Wallace) in 1919 after a long courtship that began in their youth in Independence, Missouri. The marriage was affectionate and enduring, though decidedly private. Bess disliked public life and Washington society, preferring the familiarity of Independence. She avoided the political spotlight more than most First Ladies.

The Truman's had one child, Margaret Truman, born in 1924. Truman was a devoted father, closely involved in Margaret's education and later her music career, often attending her performances and defending her publicly when critics were harsh. Family letters reveal a warm, attentive husband and father who relied heavily on Bess for emotional support and counsel.

Despite the pressures of the presidency—especially during World War II's aftermath and the early Cold War—Truman maintained simple personal habits. He rose early, walked regularly, read history in the evenings, and wrote letters by hand. The family's emotional center remained their home in Independence. After leaving office in 1953,

Truman returned there permanently, living modestly and declining lucrative corporate opportunities. His domestic life reflected the same values that marked his public character: loyalty, restraint, plainspoken integrity, and a strong sense of personal responsibility.

POLITICAL AFFILIATION AND GOVERNING STYLE

A Democrat firmly rooted in New Deal liberalism, Truman governed with a blunt, personal, and centralized leadership style. He rejected the patrician distance cultivated by Roosevelt, preferring direct accountability and plainspoken communication. Truman believed presidential authority derived not from popularity or symbolism, but from the willingness to make decisions and accept responsibility for their consequences.

In foreign affairs, Truman relied on expert advisers but insisted on retaining final judgment, particularly in matters involving war, nuclear weapons, and alliance commitments. "Give 'em hell, Harry" came to define Truman's public persona—direct, unsentimental, and unapologetically confrontational—and remains one of the most enduring catchphrases associated with any American president.

ACCOMPLISHMENTS AND VISION

Truman's presidency established the foundational architecture of the Cold War world. Truman authorized the use of atomic bombs against Japan in August 1945 primarily to bring World War II to a rapid end and avoid enormous casualties. U.S. military planners projected that an invasion (Operation Downfall) could result in hundreds of thousands of American casualties and potentially millions of Japanese military and civilian deaths. Truman also faced the reality that Japan's leadership had not accepted unconditional surrender despite devastating aerial bombing. Using the atomic bomb was seen as a decisive shock that could compel surrender quickly, shorten the war, and save lives overall. Secondary considerations included demonstrating U.S. power to the Soviet Union as the postwar order took shape, but Truman consistently framed his decision as a tragic necessity driven by wartime responsibility, stating later that his overriding goal was to end the war as swiftly as possible and prevent further mass bloodshed.

Truman presided over the creation of several national security institutions. The National Security Act of 1947 created the Department of Defense, National Security Council, and Central Intelligence Agency, institutionalizing executive leadership in foreign and military affairs. These structures transformed the presidency into the central coordinating authority for global security.

The Truman Doctrine[55] articulated a commitment to resist authoritarian expansion through economic and military support, framing containment as a global responsibility rather than a regional concern. The Marshall Plan[56] stands as one of the most successful foreign policy initiatives in American history, stabilizing Western Europe, preventing economic collapse, and reinforcing democratic governance. Creation of NATO formalized alliance-based security, embedding American leadership in a multilateral framework.

Domestically, Truman desegregated the armed forces by executive order, marking the first major federal civil rights action since Reconstruction. His Fair Deal proposals—national health insurance, expanded housing, education funding, and labor protections—largely stalled in Congress, but they established policy foundations later realized during the LBJ's Great Society.

Criticisms and Controversies

Truman's decision to use atomic weapons remains one of the most ethically debated presidential actions. Critics emphasize civilian casualties and moral precedent; defenders cite invasion casualties avoided and wartime context. No subsequent president has faced an equivalent decision.

---

55 Announced by President Harry S. Truman in March 1947, the Truman Doctrine committed the United States to providing political, military, and economic assistance to nations threatened by communism. Framed as a defense of "free peoples" against external pressure or internal subversion, the doctrine marked a decisive shift from wartime alliance to Cold War containment and established the ideological foundation for subsequent U.S. foreign policy initiatives, including American engagement in global affairs.

56 Proposed in 1947 by U.S. Secretary of State George C. Marshall and implemented from 1948 to 1951, the Marshall Plan provided over $13 billion in U.S. economic assistance to Western European nations to rebuild war-torn economies, restore industrial and agricultural production, stabilize currencies, and promote trade. The program aimed to prevent economic collapse and political extremism in post-war Europe, and counter the spread of Soviet influence during the early Cold War. It is widely credited with accelerating European recovery and fostering long-term transatlantic cooperation.

The Korean War raised enduring constitutional concerns. Truman committed U.S. forces under United Nations authority without a formal congressional declaration of war. The conflict became protracted and politically divisive, contributing to declining public support.

Domestically, loyalty and security programs intended to counter espionage contributed to civil liberties violations and fueled McCarthy-era excesses[57]. Truman's confrontational relationship with a Republican led Congress limited legislative success. His approval ratings were low for much of his presidency, likely reflecting postwar fatigue amid partisan squabbling.

LEGACY

Truman's historical impact is defined foremost by his decisive role in shaping the post–World War II international order. Assuming the presidency unexpectedly in 1945, Truman made momentous choices under extraordinary pressure, including authorizing the use of atomic weapons to end the war with Japan and overseeing the transition from wartime alliance to Cold War rivalry. Through the Truman Doctrine, Marshall Plan, and creation of NATO, he articulated and institutionalized a policy of containment that framed U.S. foreign policy for decades. These initiatives helped stabilize Western Europe, deter Soviet expansion, and establish the United States as the central architect of the postwar liberal international system.

Domestically, Truman's impact was more contested but ultimately consequential. His Fair Deal proposals expanded the New Deal's moral vision, even when Congress blocked many of his initiatives, and he took bold executive action by desegregating the U.S. armed forces in 1948—one of the most significant civil rights steps taken before the 1960s. Truman also redefined the modern presidency as a center of direct, personal leadership, embracing plainspoken accountability rather than rhetorical distance. Though often unpopu-

---

57 McCarthyism refers to the period of intense anti-communist suspicion in the United States during the late 1940s and early 1950s, most closely associated with Joseph McCarthy. Amid Cold War anxieties, McCarthy and allied investigators alleged widespread communist infiltration of the federal government, the military, universities, and the entertainment industry. Congressional hearings—most notably those conducted by the Senate Permanent Subcommittee on Investigations—ruined careers and reputations, fostered a climate of fear, and narrowed acceptable political dissent. The movement began to collapse after McCarthy's reckless charges against the U.S. Army were exposed during the televised Army–McCarthy hearings in 1954.

lar while in office, his reputation has steadily risen as historians have emphasized his moral clarity, willingness to accept responsibility, and durable imprint on both American governance and global affairs.

DWIGHT D. EISENHOWER (1953–1961)

EARLY LIFE AND BACKGROUND

Dwight David Eisenhower was born on October 14, 1890, in Denison, Texas, but his formative years were spent in Abilene, Kansas, where his family settled when he was an infant. He grew up in a modest, disciplined household as the third of seven sons born to David Jacob Eisenhower and Ida Elizabeth Stover Eisenhower. The family was shaped by strong religious principles—his mother was a devout pacifist and a firm believer in hard work, self-restraint, and moral responsibility.

Money was scarce, and each boy was expected to contribute through chores and part-time work. Dwight worked at local jobs, including at a creamery, to help support the family. These early responsibilities fostered habits of discipline and cooperation that later became hallmarks of his leadership style.

He was an athletic and competitive boy, especially fond of football and baseball, though a serious knee injury in his teens curtailed his athletic ambitions. That setback redirected his focus toward academics and reading, particularly history and military subjects. He attended Abilene High School, where he developed a reputation as a dependable rather than flamboyant student.

Equally important was the contrast between his mother's pacifism and his own growing interest in military service, a tension that forced Eisenhower to reconcile moral conviction with pragmatic views of duty and national service. By the time he graduated high school in 1909, Eisenhower had internalized a worldview grounded in discipline, teamwork, humility, and quiet confidence.

After graduating from West Point in 1915, he spent World War I in stateside training and logistics roles. In the interwar years, his career advanced through exceptional staff work and mentorship, most notably under Major General Fox Conner in Panama, where he absorbed lessons in coalition warfare and civil–military relations. Later service as an aide to General Douglas MacArthur in Washington and the Philippines exposed Eisenhower to high-level planning and political dexterity.

World War II propelled Eisenhower into global leadership. In 1942 he was appointed Supreme Allied Commander in Europe, tasked with coordinating a multinational coalition whose success depended as much on diplomacy as on military strategy. His defining achievement was Operation Overlord (D-Day) in June 1944, the largest amphibious invasion in history. Eisenhower's leadership emphasized consensus-building and accountability. Indeed, he famously prepared an official statement accepting full blame if the invasion failed. Allied forces liberated Western Europe and secured Germany's surrender in 1945, establishing Eisenhower as the era's foremost coalition commander and setting the foundation for his ascent to the presidency.

Domestic Life

Eisenhower's domestic life was anchored by his long marriage to Mamie Doud Eisenhower (1916). Their relationship unfolded largely within the constraints of military life (frequent moves, long separations, and the emotional strain of command). The couple suffered a profound tragedy with the death of their first son, Doud Dwight ("Icky"), in 1921.

Despite his public image as a reserved and disciplined leader, Eisenhower valued privacy, routine, and domestic stability. Mamie played a central role in creating a warm, socially kind household, both during his military career and later in the White House. Eisenhower enjoyed painting, golf, and country life. Together, the Eisenhower's projected an image of steadiness and middle-class respectability that complemented his leadership style and reassured a nation emerging from world war.

POLITICAL AFFILIATION AND GOVERNING STYLE

Elected as a Republican, Eisenhower consciously rejected ideological governance in favor of pragmatic institutional stewardship. He accepted the core architecture of the New Deal while seeking to restrain its growth and ensure fiscal sustainability. Eisenhower believed that the legitimacy of executive power rested not in ideological assertion but in continuity and professional administration.

Eisenhower practiced what historians later termed the "hidden-hand presidency." Publicly, he projected calm detachment and avoided overt confrontation. Privately, he exercised firm control through disciplined staff oversight, detailed planning, and rigorous decision algorithms. He relied heavily on experienced cabinet officers and national security professionals but maintained a clear chain of command.

Unlike some of his predecessors, Eisenhower viewed presidential restraint as an exercise of power rather than a limitation.

ACCOMPLISHMENTS AND VISION

As president, Eisenhower brought a calm, steady hand to a nation exhausted by war and anxious about nuclear expansion. He ended active U.S. fighting in Korea soon after taking office, helping stabilize East Asia without expanding the conflict. He strengthened America's alliances, especially NATO, believing that shared defense reduced the risk of another world war. At home, Eisenhower resisted extreme political pressure during the Red Scare[58], quietly pushing back against reckless accusations while defending basic constitutional norms.

Eisenhower also left a lasting domestic legacy. He championed the Interstate Highway System, the largest public works project in American history, which transformed travel, commerce, and national defense. He balanced economic growth with fiscal responsibility, generally avoiding large deficits while expanding Social Security and supporting federal investment in science and education. By warning Americans about the dangers of the "military-industrial complex" in his farewell address, Eisenhower demonstrated rare foresight—reminding the nation that strength required not just weapons, but wisdom and democratic oversight[59].

He also took measured but consequential steps on civil rights, signing the Civil Rights Acts of 1957 and 1960, the first such laws since Reconstruction, aimed at protecting voting rights. Eisenhower's most dramatic civil rights action came in 1957, when he sent federal troops to Little Rock, Arkansas, to enforce school desegregation after state officials defied the Supreme Court. While personally cautious about rapid social change, he made clear that the rule of law would be upheld, even at political cost.

CRITICISMS AND CONTROVERSIES

Eisenhower faced criticism from both political opponents and later historians who viewed his leadership style as overly cautious and, at times, disengaged from domestic reform. Critics on the left argued that his moderate Republicanism and preference for incremental change slowed progress on civil rights and social welfare. Although Eisenhower ultimately enforced school desegregation in Little Rock, Arkansas, by deploying federal troops, some contemporaries faulted him for

---

58 The Red Scare refers to the period of intense anti-communist fear in the late 1940s and early 1950s, marked by investigations, blacklists, and public accusations. While Eisenhower shared concerns about Soviet espionage, he opposed demagoguery. Eisenhower worked behind the scenes to limit McCarthy's influence, defend due process, and support the Army during the televised Army-McCarthy hearings of 1954, which ultimately discredited McCarthy and brought the Red Scare to an end.

59 In his Farewell Address on January 17, 1961, President Dwight D. Eisenhower cautioned that the unprecedented peacetime alliance between the nation's military establishment and a large arms industry—what he termed the "military-industrial complex"—could acquire undue influence over public policy, democratic processes, and national priorities. Eisenhower urged vigilance to ensure that defense needs did not impair economic or scientific life. He emphasized the importance of balancing national security with civil liberties and responsible governance.

not taking a more forceful public stance in support of the Supreme Court's Brown v. Board of Education decision[60]. Others contended that his emphasis on balanced budgets and limited federal expansion constrained more ambitious responses to poverty, education funding, and urban development during a period of rapid postwar growth.

Eisenhower's Cold War policies also generated controversy. His reliance on nuclear deterrence and the doctrine of "massive retaliation" raised concerns about the risks of escalating global tensions and the potential for catastrophic conflict. Covert CIA-backed interventions in Iran (1953) and Guatemala (1954), undertaken to counter perceived communist influence, later drew criticism for undermining democratic governments and contributing to long-term regional instability. Additionally, some historians have debated whether Eisenhower's "hidden hand" leadership style—governing through private influence rather than public advocacy—limited transparency and masked policy disagreements within his administration. While many now credit him with maintaining stability during a tense era, these criticisms underscore ongoing debates about the scope and consequences of his domestic and foreign policies.

LEGACY

Eisenhower's legacy rests on his steady, pragmatic leadership during a formative decade of the Cold War and postwar prosperity. A former Supreme Allied Commander in World War II, he brought a disciplined, managerial style to the presidency, prioritizing stability at home and containment abroad. Eisenhower preserved and modestly expanded New Deal–era programs while maintaining fiscal restraint, balancing budgets in several years and keeping inflation relatively low. His most enduring domestic achievement was the creation of the Interstate Highway System in 1956, a transformative infrastructure project that reshaped American commerce, suburbanization, and national defense. He also signed the Civil Rights Acts of 1957 and 1960 and enforced school desegregation in Little Rock, establishing a cautious but meaningful federal role in advancing civil rights.

---

60 Brown v. Board of Education of Topeka, 347 U.S. 483 (1954), declared
state-sponsored segregation in public schools unconstitutional and marked
a foundational turning point in modern civil rights jurisprudence.

In foreign policy, Eisenhower pursued containment of communism while avoiding direct superpower war, relying on nuclear deterrence, alliances such as NATO, and covert operations through the CIA. He ended active combat in Korea and warned in his 1961 farewell address of the growing influence of the "military-industrial complex," reflecting concern about permanent militarization. Critics argue that his administration's reliance on nuclear brinkmanship and covert interventions in places like Iran and Guatemala contributed to long-term geopolitical instability. Nevertheless, historians generally rank Eisenhower as an effective, stabilizing president whose moderate governance, infrastructure investments, and measured Cold War strategy left a durable imprint on mid-20th-century America.

JOHN F. KENNEDY (1961–1963)

EARLY LIFE AND BACKGROUND

John F. Kennedy was born in 1917 into a wealthy and politically ambitious Irish Catholic family in Brookline, Massachusetts. His father, Joseph P. Kennedy Sr., was a powerful businessman and diplomat who expected his children to achieve public success, while his mother, Rose Kennedy, emphasized discipline, faith, and education. JFK's childhood was marked by frequent illness but also by intense competition with his siblings, especially his older brother Joe Jr. He attended elite schools, including Choate and Harvard, where he developed a strong interest in history and world affairs. His senior thesis on British unpreparedness before World War II was later published as Why England Slept, giving him early public credibility as a thoughtful observer of global politics.

Kennedy's path to the White House accelerated after World War II, where his service as a Navy officer and hero of the PT-109 incident helped redefine him as resilient and courageous. After the war, he entered politics as a Democrat, winning a seat in the U.S. House of Representatives in 1946 and a Senate seat in 1952. Though initially viewed as young and inexperienced, Kennedy built a national profile through his writing (Profiles in Courage), skillful use of television, and a disciplined campaign backed by family resources. In 1960, he secured the Democratic nomination and narrowly defeated Richard Nixon in one of the closest presidential elections in U.S. history. His youth, charisma, and promise of energetic leadership appealed to a nation ready for generational change, carrying him to the presidency at just 43 years old.

DOMESTIC LIFE

JFK's domestic life was marked by a carefully curated public image that contrasted with a far more complicated private reality. He married Jacqueline Bouvier Kennedy in 1953, and together they had four children, two of whom (Caroline and John F. Kennedy Jr.) survived infancy. As First Lady, Jackie transformed the White House into a cultural and historical showcase, emphasizing the arts and European-style elegance. The young Kennedy family projected vitality and modernity, reinforcing the "Camelot" image that came to define the administration.

Privately, Kennedy's home life was constrained by chronic illness and personal strain. He suffered from severe back pain, Addison's disease, and other health problems that required daily medication and limited his physical stamina. The marriage, while outwardly devoted, was tested by Kennedy's frequent absences and well-documented extramarital relationships. Jackie, for her part, endured multiple miscarriages and the loss of a premature son, Patrick, in 1963. Despite these challenges, Kennedy remained emotionally attached to his children, carving out moments of family life at the White House and the Kennedy compound in Hyannis Port.

Political Affiliation and Governing Style

A Democrat, Kennedy governed as a reform-minded pragmatist who emphasized flexibility and symbolic leadership. He consciously cultivated an image of rational, modern governance, surrounding himself with academic advisers and technocrats often referred to as the "best and the brightest." Kennedy viewed the presidency as both a command post for crisis management and a platform for inspiring national purpose.

He encouraged open debate among advisers before rendering final decisions, particularly in foreign policy. Kennedy relied heavily on secrecy, back-channel diplomacy, and incremental escalation, reflecting Cold War mindsets about control and deterrence. His rhetorical skills played a pivotal role in defining legitimacy, projecting confidence even when policy outcomes were uncertain.

Accomplishments and Vision

Kennedy guided the United States through the Cuban Missile Crisis in 1962, when the discovery of Soviet nuclear missiles in Cuba brought the world to the brink of nuclear war. Kennedy resisted pressure for immediate military action and instead chose a naval blockade combined with intense diplomacy. The crisis ended with the removal of Soviet missiles and is widely credited with preventing catastrophic conflict, showcasing Kennedy's calm judgment and willingness to balance strength with restraint.

Kennedy launched the Peace Corps, which sent young Americans abroad to assist with education, health, and development projects, strengthening U.S. influence through service rather than force. In space policy, he set the ambitious goal of landing a man on the Moon before the end of the decade, mobilizing science, industry, and national pride. Though he did not live to see the Moon landing, his commitment directly led to the Apollo program's success in 1969.

Domestically, Kennedy's record was more limited but still significant in direction and tone. He proposed major civil rights legislation, framing civil rights as a moral and constitutional issue, even when political disagreements slowed progress. He also advocated for tax cuts to stimulate economic growth and expand investment in education and science. While many of these initiatives were enacted after his assassination, Kennedy's presidency helped shift national priorities toward these goals leaving an impact that outlasted his short time in office.

CRITICISMS AND CONTROVERSIES

Kennedy's presidency has drawn criticism for both policy shortcomings and personal conduct. Early in his administration, the failed Bay of Pigs[61] invasion in 1961—an attempt to overthrow Fidel Castro's government in Cuba—was widely viewed as a major foreign policy miscalculation that embarrassed the United States and strengthened Cuba's ties to the Soviet Union. Kennedy also faced criticism for initially moving cautiously on civil rights, balancing moral support for racial equality with political concerns about maintaining support among Southern Democrats. While he ultimately proposed sweeping civil rights legislation in 1963 and used federal authority to enforce desegregation, some contemporaries and historians argue that stronger leadership earlier in his term might have accelerated progress.

Kennedy's conduct during the Cold War and aspects of his personal life have also generated controversy. The escalation of U.S. involvement in Vietnam through increased military advisers and support for the South Vietnamese government raised questions about the long-term consequences of American intervention. Additionally, revelations after his death about extramarital affairs and the concealment of significant health problems contributed to reassessments of his leadership and transparency. While Kennedy remains a widely admired and charismatic figure, historians continue to debate the effectiveness, risks, and unresolved challenges associated with his presidency.

LEGACY

Kennedy's historical impact lies less in the length of his presidency and more in the tone, direction, and expectations he set for American leadership. He came into office at a moment of Cold War anxiety and

---

61 The Bay of Pigs Invasion was a failed U.S.-backed attempt in April 1961 to overthrow Cuban leader Fidel Castro. Planned under the Eisenhower administration and executed early in Kennedy's presidency, the operation involved a CIA-trained force of Cuban exiles (Brigade 2506) landing at the Bay of Pigs on Cuba's southern coast. The invasion quickly collapsed due to poor intelligence, inadequate air support, and the Castro regime's rapid mobilization of Cuban forces. Its failure humiliated the Kennedy administration and strengthened Castro's hold on power.

generational change, and he redefined the presidency as energetic, forward-looking, and globally engaged. His handling of the Cuban Missile Crisis helped prevent nuclear war and established a model of crisis management that balanced military strength with diplomacy. Kennedy also elevated America's ambitions through initiatives like the Peace Corps and the Moon program, reinforcing the idea that national power could be expressed through service, innovation, and inspiration—not just force.

Equally important was the powerful symbolism of Kennedy's presidency. His youth, rhetoric, and emphasis on public service ("ask not what your country can do for you") reshaped how Americans viewed civic responsibility and political leadership. Although many of his domestic goals—especially on civil rights—were only fully realized after his assassination, his moral framing and early proposals helped accelerate national momentum. Kennedy's sudden death froze his presidency in the public imagination, creating an enduring legacy that blends real achievement with unrealized promise. As a result, JFK remains a defining figure of modern American history, remembered as much for the direction he pointed the country as for what he was able to accomplish in office.

The Kennedy Assassination. The assassination of Kennedy on November 22, 1963, in Dallas shocked the nation and marked one of the most traumatic moments in American history. Kennedy was killed while riding in a motorcade, and Vice President Lyndon B. Johnson was sworn in just hours later. In the aftermath, Johnson moved quickly to carry forward key parts of Kennedy's agenda, using the nation's grief to help pass major legislation—most notably the Civil Rights Act of 1964 and later the Voting Rights Act. In this way, Kennedy's death paradoxically accelerated the realization of parts of his vision, especially in civil rights.

At the same time, the assassination gave rise to decades of controversy and conspiracy theories. Although official investigations, including the Warren Commission, concluded that Lee Harvey Oswald acted alone, many Americans questioned the findings, citing inconsistencies, secrecy, and the broader Cold War context. Theories involving the CIA, the Mafia, the Soviets, or other actors have persisted, fueled by mistrust of government and the emotional impact of Kennedy's sudden death. As a result, the assassination remains not only a historical event but also a lasting source of national skepticism and debate, further complicating the mythic and unresolved nature of JFK's legacy.

Lyndon B. Johnson (1963–1969)

Early Life and Background

Lyndon B. Johnson was born in 1908 in the rural Texas Hill Country, near what would later be called Johnson City. He grew up in a large but struggling family. His father, Sam Johnson, was a local politician who talked constantly about public life and government but had limited financial success. As a result, the family experienced periods of instability, which made Lyndon deeply aware of insecurity, status, and the importance of power and networks from an early age.

Johnson was tall, intense, and ambitious even as a boy. He was not naturally academic, but he was highly social and competitive, with a strong desire to stand out and lead. A formative experience came after high school when he briefly taught impoverished Mexican American children in South Texas. Seeing firsthand the effects of poverty and limited opportunity left a lasting impression and helped shape his lifelong belief that government could—and should—play a role in improving ordinary people's lives.

As a young adult, Johnson threw himself into politics with relentless energy. After graduating from Southwest Texas State Teachers College, he worked as a congressional aide in Washington, where he quickly learned how power brokers functioned. He returned to Texas to run for Congress and won a House seat in 1937. During World War II he briefly served in the Navy, but his political career remained his focus. In 1948, after a famously close and controversial election, he won a seat in the U.S. Senate. Once there, Johnson rose at an unprecedented pace, using his intimidating presence, encyclopedic knowledge of Senate rules, and personal persuasion—often called the "Johnson Treatment"—to build alliances and outmaneuver rivals.

By the mid-1950s, Johnson had become Senate Majority Leader. He proved highly effective at passing legislation and keeping a deeply divided Senate functioning, earning respect from colleagues across party lines. However, his ambition extended beyond Congress. When John F. Kennedy sought the presidency in 1960, Johnson initially competed against him but ultimately accepted the vice-presidential nomination. Though uneasy and sometimes resentful in the role, Johnson's regional appeal in the South, legislative expertise, and experience were seen as crucial to balancing the ticket. His selection as vice president marked the culmination of decades of strategic advancement and positioned him just one step away from the presidency.

DOMESTIC LIFE

Johnson's domestic life was marked by ambition and a strong but complicated family bond. He married Lady Bird Johnson in 1934, and she became the stabilizing force in both his personal and professional life. Lady Bird provided emotional support, including crucial financial security through her successful business investments, which allowed Johnson to pursue politics with total focus. Their marriage, while durable, was often tense—Johnson was demanding, frequently absent, and consumed by his career, while Lady Bird managed much of the family life behind the scenes.

The couple had two daughters, Lynda Bird Johnson (born 1944) and Luci Baines Johnson (born 1947), who were raised largely under Lady Bird's careful supervision. Johnson loved his daughters but was often distant due to the pressures of political life. During his presidency, both daughters became more visible to the public, helping soften and humanize Johnson's image. At home, the Johnson family reflected the same intensity that defined his career—driven, stressful at times, but held together by loyalty, resilience, and a shared sense of purpose.

POLITICAL AFFILIATION AND GOVERNING STYLE

A Democrat committed to New Deal liberalism; Johnson governed as an activist legislative president. Unlike Kennedy's cerebral deliberation or Eisenhower's managerial restraint, Johnson pursued transformation through overwhelming political force. He believed power existed to be used decisively and viewed compromise as a tactical instrument rather than a guiding principle.

Johnson centralized his decision-making and relied heavily on personal authority, particularly in domestic policy. His leadership style emphasized urgency, pushing multiple major initiatives simultaneously to exploit political momentum created by Kennedy's assassination and the Democratic landslide of 1964.

In foreign policy, however, Johnson exhibited deep insecurity. Less confident than in domestic affairs, he deferred to military and Cold War orthodoxies, fearing political vulnerability more than strategic miscalculation.

ACCOMPLISHMENTS AND VISION

Johnson's greatest accomplishments came on the domestic front, where he launched an ambitious agenda known as the Great Society. Building on the momentum of the civil rights movement, Johnson pushed through landmark legislation that reshaped American society. This included the Civil Rights Act of 1964, which outlawed segregation and discrimination; the Voting Rights Act of 1965, which protected minority voting rights; and the Fair Housing Act, which addressed discrimination in housing. He also expanded the social safety net with programs such as Medicare and Medicaid, providing health care to the elderly and the poor, and increased federal support for education, urban development, and anti-poverty initiatives. These measures significantly expanded the role of the federal government in promoting social and economic equality.

In foreign policy, Johnson's record is more mixed but historically consequential. He strongly supported the Cold War goal of containing communism and oversaw a major escalation of U.S. involvement in the Vietnam War, believing that withdrawal would weaken America's global credibility. While this decision eventually overshadowed much of his domestic success and deeply divided the nation, Johnson also made important diplomatic and defense decisions, including arms control efforts and strengthening alliances. Taken together, his presidency left a lasting imprint: Johnson dramatically advanced civil rights and social welfare at home, even as Vietnam became a cautionary example of the limits and costs of American power abroad.

Criticisms and Controversies

Johnson faced his strongest criticism over the Vietnam War (Figure 13). Johnson steadily increased U.S. troop levels and military spending without ever formally declaring war, leading many Americans to feel the country had been drawn into a long, costly conflict without clear goals. As casualties mounted and progress lacked definition, public trust eroded. Johnson was also criticized for being overly optimistic in his public statements about the war, which later fueled a deep sense of government dishonesty resulting in organized protests, especially among young Americans.

At home, some of Johnson's ambitious domestic programs drew backlash as well. Conservatives argued that the Great Society expanded the federal government too far and created expensive programs that were fiscally irresponsible. Others questioned whether anti-poverty efforts achieved lasting results or unintentionally encouraged dependency. Johnson's personal style also generated criticism: he was known to be intimidating, domineering, and at times crude in private, which strained relationships and contributed to political fatigue. By the end of his presidency, these controversies had so overshadowed his achievements that Johnson chose not to seek reelection in 1968, leaving behind a legacy that was both transformative and deeply contested.

Legacy

Johnson left one of the most consequential domestic legacies of any U.S. president. His civil rights achievements permanently changed the nation's legal and moral landscape, ending segregation under federal law and securing voting protections that reshaped American democracy. Programs created under his Great Society—most notably Medicare and Medicaid—became enduring pillars of the social safety net, touching the lives of tens of millions of Americans long after his presidency. Johnson demonstrated how forceful presidential leadership and mastery of Congress could be used to enact sweeping reform in a short period of time.

At the same time, Johnson's legacy is inseparable from the Vietnam War, which deeply divided the country and eroded public trust in government. For many Americans, Vietnam overshadowed his domestic successes and came to symbolize the dangers of unchecked executive power and foreign policy overreach. Historically, Johnson is now often viewed as a tragic figure: a president who achieved remarkable progress on civil rights and social welfare, but whose decisions abroad undermined his political standing and personal confidence. His impact remains lasting and complex—proof that transformational leadership can produce both enduring progress and profound national skepticism of government involvement.

PUBLIC MISTRUST AND CRISIS MANAGEMENT
1969-1992

Unlike earlier eras defined by fluctuations in presidential power, this period is characterized by skepticism and contested authority. Changes in Cold War targets did not produce a new governing equilibrium; instead, it exposed deep fractures in public trust and institutional credibility that would take more than two decades to stabilize.

Public deference to executive judgment—central to postwar governance—essentially evaporated especially among younger activist Americans. Presidents were no longer presumed to act competently or in good faith. Media scrutiny intensified, congressional oversight expanded, and judicial influence increased. Executive authority remained formally powerful, but its genuineness was fragile.

Richard Nixon's presidency further exacerbated public mistrust. Nixon sought to restore executive control over foreign and national security while managing domestic dissent through centralized authority. His achievements in opening relations with China and pursuing arms control demonstrated presidential competence for strategic leadership. Yet Watergate exposed systemic abuse of power, transforming skepticism into full blown resentment. Congress responded with statutory constraints, ethics reforms, budget controls, and transparency requirements designed to curb executive overreach.

Economic disruption reinforced political cynicism. Stagflation in the 1970s discredited Keynesian demand management and undermined confidence in expert-led economic policy. Energy price increases, deindustrialization, and global competition challenged assumptions of perpetual growth.

Presidents Carter and Ford governed amid this mistrust. They emphasized moral restitution, transparency, and administrative competence. Yet their limited success reinforced perceptions of executive weakness. The presidency seemed constrained not only by law, but by diminished public trust.

The conservative realignment that culminated in Ronald Reagan's election did not simply reject liberal policy; it reframed the meaning of presidential leadership. Reagan restored confidence in the office through narrative persuasion, ideological clarity, and optimism. Markets, deregulation, and tax decreases became central tools of governance.

Despite Reagan's rhetorical success, structural constraints persisted. Deficits expanded, inequality widened, and institutional reforms enacted after Watergate were paralytic. The presidency regained public confidence but not unchecked authority. Executive power increasingly depended on communication and coalition rather than bureaucratic dominance.

Finally, the collapse of the Soviet Union removed the external threat that had structured American politics since 1945. George H. W. Bush presided over this transition with caution and diplomatic restraint, signaling the end of an era defined by crisis management.

RICHARD M. NIXON (1969–1974)

EARLY LIFE AND BACKGROUND

Richard Milhous Nixon was born on January 9, 1913, in Yorba Linda, California, the second of five sons in a working-class family. His father, Frank Nixon, struggled financially as a farmer and small businessman, while his mother, Hannah Nixon, was a devout Quaker whose moral seriousness and frugality left a lasting imprint on her son. The family endured repeated financial setbacks, and illness and death were ever-present realities: two of Nixon's brothers died young, an experience that reinforced a somber, inward, and resilient outlook.

The Nixon's eventually settled in Whittier, where Richard helped run the family grocery store and gas station while attending school. He was an excellent student but socially reserved, often feeling overshadowed by wealthier classmates. These early experiences fostered both a fierce work ethic and a lifelong sensitivity to status and perceived slights. By the time Nixon left Whittier for college, he had already internalized the themes that would define much of his life: ambition forged by adversity, emotional self-containment, and a determination to succeed without privilege.

After graduating from Whittier College, Nixon attended Duke University School of Law, where he distinguished himself academically before returning to California to practice law. During World War II, he served as a naval officer in the Pacific, gaining administrative experience and polishing his public credentials. The war years reinforced his sense of duty and organization, while also positioning him favorably for postwar politics.

Nixon entered politics in 1946, winning election to the U.S. House of Representatives by unseating a long-serving Democratic incumbent. He quickly rose to prominence as a leading anti-communist, most notably during the Alger Hiss investigations, which brought him national attention and a reputation as a relentless prosecutor. In 1950, he won a hard-fought Senate race in California, confirming his ability to mobilize grassroots support and exploit Cold War anxieties.

His ascent accelerated in 1952 when Dwight D. Eisenhower selected him as his vice-presidential running mate. Accusations of financial impropriety nearly derailed the ticket, but Nixon's nationally televised "Checkers speech" proved decisive—an emotional appeal that showcased his political resilience and mastery of the media. As vice president, Nixon gained extensive foreign policy experience and emerged as a seasoned national figure, setting the stage for his eventual return to the political forefront and the presidency.

Domestic Life

Nixon married Pat Nixon in 1940, and their marriage was built more on loyalty than on public displays of affection. Pat was practical, hardworking, and deeply supportive of her husband's ambitions, often managing the household and raising their children while Nixon focused intensely on his career. Friends and observers frequently noted that Nixon was emotionally reserved at home, but he was deeply dependent on Pat's steadiness and encouragement.

The couple had two daughters, Tricia Nixon and Julie Nixon Eisenhower, whom Nixon loved but interacted with in a formal, sometimes awkward way. Family life tended to be structured and disciplined, reflecting Nixon's own upbringing. Even in the White House, the Nixon's avoided elite social circles, preferring quiet family routines and projecting an image of normalcy rather than political celebrity.

Overall, Nixon's home life mirrored his personality: serious, controlled, and duty-bound. While not warm or expressive in the traditional sense, it was stable and enduring, providing him with a private anchor amid the pressures and turbulence of public life.

POLITICAL AFFILIATION AND GOVERNING STYLE

A Republican, Nixon governed with a highly centralized and secretive executive style. He distrusted both the press and the established bureaucracy, believing that institutional elites undermined presidential authority. In response, Nixon concentrated power within the White House, relying heavily on a small circle of loyal aides.

Nixon believed strongly in executive primacy in foreign affairs and sought to restore presidential control over national security after Vietnam-era erosion. His leadership style favored strategic calculation, secrecy, and decisive action—often at the expense of transparency and institutional norms.

ACCOMPLISHMENTS AND VISION

One of Nixon's most important achievements was reshaping U.S. foreign policy. He believed the Cold War could not be won simply through confrontation, so he pursued diplomacy with rivals. His historic trip to China in 1972 ended decades of isolation and fundamentally altered global politics, balancing China against the Soviet Union. At the same time, Nixon negotiated arms control agreements (SALT I) with the Soviet Union that slowed the nuclear arms race[62]. These efforts reflected his vision of a more stable, predictable world order based on power balance.

---

62 Initiated in 1969 and concluded in 1972, SALT I marked the first major U.S.–Soviet effort to restrain the nuclear arms race during the Cold War. The negotiations produced two principal agreements: the Anti-Ballistic Missile (ABM) Treaty, which limited each side to two (later one) ABM sites, and the Interim Agreement on Certain Measures with Respect to the Limitation of Strategic Offensive Arms, which capped the number of deployed intercontinental and submarine-launched ballistic mis-

At home, Nixon advanced policies that reshaped government in quieter but lasting ways. He supported environmental protection, signing legislation that created the Environmental Protection Agency and strengthened clean air and water laws. He also promoted a "New Federalism," aiming to shift power and funding from Washington to states and local governments, believing solutions worked best closer to the people. He also supported wage and price controls to combat inflation—measures that reflected pragmatic governance rather than conservative orthodoxy. He also advanced civil rights enforcement through school desegregation and affirmative action policies. While Nixon was politically conservative in tone, many of his domestic achievements were pragmatic rather than ideological, reflecting his broader vision: a strong America that relied on discipline and negotiation to navigate a complex modern era.

Nixon also sought to end U.S. involvement in the Vietnam War, which he recognized was deeply dividing the country and unsustainable in the long term. His strategy, often described as "Vietnamization," aimed to gradually withdraw American troops while strengthening South Vietnam's ability to defend itself. Although the process was controversial and prolonged, U.S. combat troop levels were sharply reduced during his presidency, and American prisoners of war were eventually returned. Nixon's underlying goal was to exit the war without appearing to abandon U.S. credibility abroad, reflecting an emphasis on pragmatism over idealism.

His administration carried out school desegregation in the South on a scale unmatched by previous presidents, significantly increasing the number of Black children attending integrated schools. He also supported affirmative action–style policies through federal contracting rules, aiming to expand economic opportunity without framing civil rights solely in rhetorical terms.

CRITICISMS AND CONTROVERSIES

The most damaging controversy was the Watergate scandal, which revealed a pattern of political espionage, abuse of power, and efforts to obstruct justice. What began as a break-in at Democratic Party offices expanded into a broader investigation showing that Nixon and

---

sile launchers. While SALT I did not reduce existing arsenals, it established verification through technology and set a precedent for subsequent arms control efforts.

his aides had used federal agencies, secret recordings, and legal pressure to protect the presidency and punish perceived enemies. Nixon's refusal to fully cooperate eroded public trust and led to impeachment proceedings. Facing near-certain removal from office, he resigned in 1974, becoming the first U.S. president to do so. For many Americans, Watergate permanently altered confidence in government.

Nixon was also criticized for his handling of the Vietnam War and domestic unrest. Although he reduced U.S. troop levels, the war expanded into Cambodia and Laos, fueling widespread protests and deepening social division. The administration's confrontational stance toward demonstrators, combined with events like the Kent State shootings, intensified public anger and mistrust.

More broadly, Nixon's leadership style drew criticism for its suspicion, secrecy, and tendency to view politics as warfare. His use of an "enemies list," aggressive campaign tactics, and centralized decision-making reinforced the image of a president who believed the ends justified the means. While supporters admired his toughness and strategic thinking, critics concluded that his willingness to bend—or break—ethical norms ultimately undermined the very institutions he sought to strengthen.

Legacy

Nixon's resignation triggered the most significant recalibration of executive power since Reconstruction. Congress enacted sweeping oversight reforms, ethics laws, and transparency requirements designed to prevent future abuses. The presidency emerged legally constrained, politically weakened, and permanently scrutinized.

Richard Nixon's legacy, with the benefit of time, is best understood as a story of complexity rather than redemption. He was never formally exonerated for Watergate, and the scandal remains a clear violation of public trust. Yet as decades passed, historians and the public came to recognize that Nixon was also a consequential president whose foreign policy decision reshaped global politics and whose domestic actions left lasting marks. In the end, Nixon is remembered neither as a simple villain nor as a misunderstood hero, but as a deeply capable and deeply flawed leader—one whose strategic brilliance was ultimately undone by suspicion and a failure to respect the limits of power.

GERALD R. FORD (1974–1977)

EARLY LIFE AND BACKGROUND

Gerald Rudolph Ford was born in 1913 in Omaha, Nebraska, but his childhood was spent almost entirely in Grand Rapids, Michigan, where he was raised after his mother left an abusive marriage and later remarried. Ford grew up believing his stepfather, Gerald R. Ford Sr., was his biological father; he did not learn the truth until he was a teenager.

Ford's upbringing was solidly middle-class and Midwestern. His stepfather ran a successful paint business, and the household emphasized hard work and personal responsibility. Ford worked part-time jobs from a young age and was active in the Boy Scouts, eventually becoming an Eagle Scout—the only U.S. president to earn that rank. The scouting experience reinforced discipline and teamwork, values that would later define his political style.

Athletics played a central role in Ford's youth. In high school and later at the University of Michigan, he excelled at football, becoming a standout center on national championship teams. Sports gave him confidence and structure. Taken together, Ford's childhood produced a man who valued teamwork, fairness, and honesty—traits that would later shape his understated leadership during one of the most unsettled moments in American political history.

After graduating from the University of Michigan, he turned down professional football offers and chose education and public service instead. He worked his way through Yale Law School as a boxing coach and assistant football coach, graduating in 1941. During World War II, Ford served in the U.S. Navy aboard an aircraft carrier in the Pacific, an experience that reinforced his reputation for teamwork and composure under pressure.

After the war, Ford settled into civilian life in Grand Rapids, opening a law practice and marrying Betty Bloomer. Betty Ford's candor and courage would later make her one of the most influential First Ladies in modern history. Encouraged by local Republicans, Ford ran for Congress in 1948 and won. What followed was an unusually long and stable legislative career: 25 years in the House of Representatives, where Ford was broadly respected across party lines. He was not an ideological firebrand; instead, colleagues saw him as fair-minded, reliable, and personally decent.

Ford's ascent accelerated in the 1960s when House Republicans selected him as House Minority Leader, a role he held for nearly a decade. His leadership style—transparent, collegial, and low-ego—earned trust during an era of growing political cynicism. That trust proved decisive in 1973, when President Nixon nominated Ford to be Vice President after Spiro Agnew resigned amid scandal. Ford was confirmed overwhelmingly by Congress.

In August 1974, following Richard Nixon's resignation, Ford became president without having run on a national ticket—the only person to assume the presidency under such circumstances. Ford's adult life and political ascent reflected the same qualities formed in childhood: composure, loyalty, and a belief that public service was about restoring trust rather than wielding power.

DOMESTIC LIFE

Ford partnership with Betty was central to his personal and public life. He was reserved, disciplined, and emotionally restrained; Betty was candid, outspoken, and socially progressive. Together, they raised four children—Michael, John ("Jack"), Steven, and Susan—while living a largely normal family life by Washington standards. Ford valued family time together and physical fitness, often swimming or golfing to unwind. He was a deeply devoted husband and father rather than a distant political figure.

As First Lady, Betty Ford reshaped public expectations of political spouses. She spoke openly about breast cancer, mental health, alcohol dependence, and prescription drug addiction, topics rarely discussed publicly in the 1970s. Her honesty sometimes created uneasiness in the White House, but it also humanized the Ford family and mirrored Gerald Ford's own commitment to truthfulness and humility. He supported her openness fully, even when it carried political risk.

After leaving the White House, the Fords remained close and publicly affectionate, settling into a long retirement marked by advocacy and family life. Their marriage is often cited as one of the most genuine and emotionally honest presidential partnerships, reinforcing Ford's broader legacy as a man whose private life matched his public reputation for decency.

POLITICAL AFFILIATION AND GOVERNING STYLE

A Republican, Ford assumed the presidency amid unprecedented constitutional crisis. His primary objective was to restore confidence in the presidency by demonstrating honesty, transparency, and respect for institutional norms.

Ford governed as a conciliator rather than an activist. He rejected secrecy, scaled back centralized executive control, and reestablished regular relations with Congress. His leadership style emphasized openness, consultation, and restraint, even at the expense of political advantage. Ford viewed the presidency as an institution to be stabilized rather than a platform for policy ambition.

ACCOMPLISHMENTS AND VISION

Ford's most accomplishment is that he stabilized the presidency after Watergate. By governing openly, respecting Congress, and avoiding personal aggrandizement, he re-established basic expectations of honesty and constitutional behavior. Over time, many scholars have reassessed his controversial pardon of Nixon as a statesmanlike—if politically costly—decision that shortened national trauma and prevented the presidency itself from being permanently weakened.

In foreign policy, Ford maintained continuity in détente and alliance management, overseeing the final stages of U.S. withdrawal from Vietnam and navigating complex Cold War dynamics. He supported the Helsinki Accords, which strengthened human rights norms and reinforced European stability[63].

Domestically, Ford confronted severe economic challenges, including inflation and recession. His administration pursued fiscal restraint and anti-inflation measures while resisting expansive federal intervention. Ford vetoed numerous spending bills, reinforcing the post-Watergate reassertion of congressional authority.

CRITICISMS AND CONTROVERSIES

By far the most enduring criticism was Ford's full pardon of Richard Nixon in September 1974. Many Americans believed the pardon denied accountability and reinforced the idea that powerful figures operated above the law. Although Ford argued it was necessary to spare the country a prolonged constitutional ordeal, the decision severely damaged public trust in the short term, triggered his lowest approval ratings, and likely contributed to his defeat in the 1976 election.

His "Whip Inflation Now" campaign was widely ridiculed as symbolic rather than substantive. Frequent veto battles with Congress reinforced the impression of drift and limited executive control over economic policy, even though many problems were structural and inherited.

Critics often described Ford as well-intentioned but uninspiring. He lacked rhetorical polish and sometimes appeared uncomfortable in the public spotlight. His administration was marked by policy caution and

---

63 The Helsinki Final Act, signed by 35 nations including the United States, the Soviet Union, and most European states, sought to reduce Cold War tensions by recognizing post–World War II European borders while promoting cooperation in security, economic exchange, and human rights. Although nonbinding, the Accords proved significant by legitimizing existing territorial arrangements in Europe and, more consequentially, by embedding human rights commitments that dissidents in Eastern Europe later used to challenge communist regimes.

compromise, which supporters viewed as stability, but critics saw as a lack of vision or direction during a time when voters wanted decisive leadership.

While Ford maintained détente, critics on the right accused him of being too accommodating to the Soviet Union. On the left, some faulted him for continuing Cold War assumptions rather than redefining U.S. global leadership after Vietnam. Additionally, the fall of Saigon and later events in Southeast Asia reinforced perceptions of American decline, even though Ford inherited those outcomes.

Ford's presidency is criticized less for wrongdoing than for controversial judgment (the pardon), economic frustration, and perceived political weakness. Yet even many critics concede that his shortcomings were inseparable from the extraordinary circumstances he inherited.

LEGACY

Ford's legacy is best understood as an exercise in institutional triage. He restored dignity and legality to an office deeply damaged by abuse of power, even as he sacrificed personal political standing in the process.

Historically, Ford demonstrated that restraint and integrity could preserve constitutional order during crisis, though not necessarily inspire public confidence or policy momentum. His presidency reaffirmed the importance of procedural legitimacy in democratic governance, even when outcomes appear unsatisfying.

Ford's tenure closed the immediate post-Watergate phase of executive retrenchment, setting the stage for renewed debate over the presidency's proper scope and purpose—debate that would intensify under his successor.

Finally, Ford is remembered as a man of personal decency and integrity, a reputation largely unchallenged even by critics. In an era increasingly defined by polarization and performative politics, his calm demeanor and lack of ideological extremism stand out. He treated political opponents as legitimate colleagues rather than enemies.

Jimmy E. Carter (1977–1981)

Early Life and Background

James Earl Carter Jr. was born on October 1, 1924, in Plains, Georgia, and spent his childhood in the nearby rural community of Archery. He grew up on a small family farm during the Great Depression, surrounded by cotton fields and hard-working agrarians. Carter helped with chores and learned the value of discipline, thrift, and persistence. His upbringing was modest but stable, rooted in a close-knit rural world where neighbors depended on one another.

Carter's parents exerted different but strong influences. His father, Earl Carter, was a hardworking businessman and farmer who valued self-reliance and personal responsibility. His mother, Lillian

Carter, was a nurse with strong humanitarian instincts who encouraged curiosity and compassion. Living in the segregated South, young Jimmy had close friendships with Black farmworkers' children—an experience that later shaped his views on racial justice and civil rights.

Education was central in the Carter household. Jimmy was a serious student, an avid reader, and intellectually curious. He was often described as quiet and introspective rather than flashy or charismatic. His early exposure to religion—especially the Southern Baptist tradition—also left a lasting mark, instilling a sense of moral accountability and service. By the time he left rural Georgia to enroll in the U.S. Naval Academy, Carter carried with him a strong ethical compass forged by faith, family, and hard work.

Carter graduated from the Navel Academy in 1946 and became an officer in the elite submarine service. Under the tutelage of Admiral Hyman Rickover, Carter was exposed to complex technical systems and hierarchical leadership—experiences that shaped his later technocratic and detail-oriented political style.

Carter's military career was halted abruptly in 1953 when his father died. He resigned his naval commission and returned to Plains to manage the struggling family peanut business. He modernized the operation, pulled it out of debt, and became a respected local businessman. At the same time, he immersed himself in civic life—serving on school boards, church committees, and local planning groups. These roles introduced him to grassroots politics and sharpened his reputation as a serious, competent problem-solver rather than a traditional courthouse politician.

His formal political ascent began in the early 1960s with election to the Georgia State Senate. Initially cautious on racial issues, Carter gradually evolved as the civil rights movement reshaped Southern politics. He learned how to navigate a changing electorate—balancing reform with cultural sensitivity—while cultivating a reputation for honesty and administrative competence. His narrow loss in the 1966 Georgia gubernatorial race convinced him that clarity and moral positioning mattered as much as caution.

In 1970, Carter won the governorship of Georgia by presenting himself as a reformer and political outsider. As governor, he reorganized state government, emphasized efficiency, and openly rejected segregationist rhetoric, declaring in his inaugural address that "the time for racial discrimination is over." This marked a decisive break with the Old South and positioned him as a New South leader.

By the mid-1970s, in the aftermath of Watergate, Carter leveraged his biography—naval officer, businessman, Southern reformer, and moral outsider—into a successful national campaign. Running explicitly as a Washington outsider who promised honesty and competence, he capitalized on public distrust of established political elites. His rise from a small-town peanut farmer to the presidency was built on discipline and an ability to adapt to moments of national transition.

Domestic Life

Carter married Rosalynn Carter in 1946. He had known her since childhood in Plains, Georgia. Their marriage is one of the longest and most enduring presidential partnerships in American history. Rosalynn was deeply involved in Carter's personal, business, and political life, serving as a trusted adviser.

The Carters raised four children—three sons (Jack, Chip, and Jeff) and a daughter (Amy). Their early family life was shaped by modest means, especially after Jimmy left the Navy and returned to Georgia to run the family peanut business. Rosalynn worked alongside him, handling accounting and management while raising the children.

The Carters emphasized simplicity in the White House—walking to the inauguration, carrying their own bags, and maintaining close involvement with their children's lives. Amy, the youngest, became one of the few presidential children to live in the White House while attending public school, reinforcing the Carters' preference for normalcy and privacy.

After leaving office, their domestic life was publicly admired. Returning to Plains, they lived in the same modest home they had owned for decades. Together, Jimmy and Rosalynn devoted themselves to humanitarian work, church involvement, and family, modeling a post-presidency centered on service rather than status. Their marriage and family life came to symbolize humility and shared commitment.

Political Affiliation and Governing Style

A Democrat, Carter governed as a moralist-administrator. He believed the presidency should model ethical behavior, transparency, and personal accountability. Carter sought to reduce the influence of entrenched interests and restore honesty to government.

However, Carter's outsider status proved a liability. He distrusted Congress and traditional party leadership, preferring direct engagement with policy details over coalition-building. His management style was highly hands-on, often micromanaging policy decisions and overwhelming institutional capacity. Carter's reluctance to delegate and inability to translate moral authority into political leverage weakened his effectiveness.

Accomplishments and Vision

Carter's presidency was guided by a vision of ethical leadership, human rights–centered foreign policy, and responsible government in the post-Watergate era. Emphasizing honesty and transparency, Carter sought to restore public trust in the presidency after the turmoil of Vietnam and Watergate. In foreign affairs, he made human rights a central pillar of U.S. diplomacy, influencing relations with Latin America, the Soviet Union, and other regions. His administration achieved notable diplomatic successes, most prominently the Camp David Accords of 1978, which produced a historic peace treaty between Egypt and Israel[64]. Carter also negotiated the Panama Canal Treaties, transferring control of the canal to Panama while preserving U.S. strategic interests, and signed the SALT II agreement[65] with the Soviet Union to limit strategic nuclear arms, reflecting his commitment to arms control and global stability.

---

64 The Camp David Accords were a set of agreements brokered by U.S. President Jimmy Carter between Egyptian President Anwar Sadat and Israeli Prime Minister Menachem Begin during secret negotiations at Camp David, Maryland, in September 1978. The accords produced two frameworks: one for a comprehensive peace between Egypt and Israel, and another outlining principles for Palestinian autonomy in the West Bank and Gaza. They led directly to the 1979 Egypt–Israel Peace Treaty, under which Egypt formally recognized Israel and Israel agreed to withdraw from the Sinai Peninsula, making Egypt the first Arab state to sign a peace treaty with Israel. While the accords significantly reduced the likelihood of large-scale Arab–Israeli war and earned Sadat and Begin the 1978 Nobel Peace Prize, the Palestinian framework was never fully implemented, leaving core issues—statehood, borders, refugees, and Jerusalem—unresolved.

65 The Strategic Arms Limitation Talks (SALT II) agreement was signed in June 1979 by U.S. President Jimmy Carter and Soviet General Secretary Leonid Brezhnev as a continuation of détente-era efforts to cap the nuclear arms race. The treaty set quantitative limits on strategic nuclear delivery vehicles—intercontinental ballistic missiles (ICBMs), submarine-launched ballistic missiles (SLBMs), and heavy bombers—and placed specific constraints on multiple independently targetable reentry vehicles (MIRVs). Although the

Domestically, Carter pursued an agenda focused on energy reform, environmental stewardship, and governmental efficiency. Responding to the energy crises of the 1970s, he promoted conservation, reduced dependence on foreign oil, and established the Department of Energy to coordinate national policy. He supported deregulation in key industries such as airlines, trucking, and telecommunications to encourage competition and lower costs for consumers. Carter also expanded environmental protections, increasing the size of national parks and protected lands, particularly in Alaska. Although many initiatives faced political and economic challenges, his presidency reflected a forward-looking vision that emphasized sustainability, diplomatic engagement, and principled governance in a period of economic uncertainty and global tension.

CRITICISMS AND CONTROVERSIES

Carter was often criticized for weak economic leadership. During his term, Americans faced high inflation, rising interest rates, and energy shortages that led to long gas lines. While many of these problems began before he took office, critics argued that Carter seemed unable to control them or explain clearly how his policies would bring relief. To many voters, daily life felt harder and more uncertain by the time he left office.

Carter's foreign policy was also seen as ineffective, especially after the Iran hostage crisis. When Iranian revolutionaries seized the U.S. embassy in Tehran and held American diplomats' hostage for over a year, Carter appeared powerless to resolve the situation. A failed rescue mission further damaged public confidence. Even supporters admitted that the prolonged crisis made the United States look weak on the world stage.

Carter had run as an outsider and often distrusted Congress, including members of his own party. As a result, he struggled to build strong alliances, and many of his proposals stalled or were watered down. Critics said he focused too much on details and morality and not enough on the political bargaining needed to get things done.

Finally, some Americans felt Carter's tone was too gloomy or moralizing. His famous warning about a national "crisis of confidence" struck some as honest, but others felt it sounded like a lec-

---

U.S. Senate never ratified SALT II following the Soviet invasion of Afghanistan later that year, both the United States and the Soviet Union largely observed its limits until 1986.

ture rather than leadership. By 1980, a large portion of the public wanted optimism, reassurance, and a stronger sense of direction—sentiments that helped fuel the backlash against his presidency.

LEGACY

The Camp David Accords remain one of the most durable peace agreements in the modern Middle East and stand as Carter's greatest presidential achievement. On energy, Carter was ahead of his time, warning about dependence on foreign oil and pushing conservation long before it became mainstream.

Politically, Carter's presidency exposed the limits of moral leadership without strong political coalition-building. He did not realign American politics or dominate Congress, and many of his domestic goals were only partially achieved. As a result, historians often rank his presidency as well-intentioned but ineffective, especially when judged by short-term results.

Carter's true legacy, however, was forged after he left office. Through the Carter Center, global election monitoring, disease eradication efforts, and decades of hands-on humanitarian work—including Habitat for Humanity—he redefined what a former president could be. Winning the Nobel Peace Prize in 2002 symbolized this transformation. Over time, public opinion softened: Americans came to separate Carter the president from Carter the person, increasingly admiring his honesty, humility, and lifelong commitment to service.

RONALD REAGAN (1981–1989)

EARLY LIFE AND BACKGROUND

Ronald Wilson Reagan was born in 1911 in Tampico, Illinois. His father, Jack Reagan, was a salesman whose struggles with alcohol were well known. His mother, Nelle Wilson Reagan, was a devout, optimistic woman who became the most formative influence in his life. The family bounced between small Midwestern towns before settling more permanently in Dixon, Illinois. Reagan later said he learned his core values—self-reliance, optimism, and empathy on society's margins.

His father's instability meant money was often tight, and young "Dutch" Reagan learned early to work. He delivered groceries, cleaned stores, and eventually served as a lifeguard on the Rock River, where he famously claimed to have saved dozens of swimmers. He absorbed his mother's moral clarity and storytelling flair; Nelle regularly took him to church and involved him in community theater, planting the seeds for his eventual expertise with public speaking and entertainment.

By adolescence, Reagan had developed an affable manner, confidence in front of crowds, and an instinctive faith that people could rise above hardship. He was not an exceptional student, but he was socially adept and ambitious. These traits were carried with him throughout his life. In Reagan's own telling, Dixon was where he learned what America was supposed to be—a theme he would return to repeatedly throughout his political life.

Reagan's ascent to the presidency was rooted more in communication skill than traditional political apprenticeship. After graduating from Eureka College, Reagan became a radio sports announcer and then a successful Hollywood actor in the 1930s and 1940s. While never a top-tier movie star, he was dependable, personable, and articulate—traits that led to leadership roles within the film industry, most notably as president of the Screen Actors Guild. That position introduced him to labor disputes, anti-communist politics, and national policy debates, marking his first real exposure to power and governance.

In the 1950s and early 1960s, Reagan reinvented himself. He served as a corporate spokesperson for General Electric. Traveling the country to speak at factories and civic gatherings, he honed a clear, optimistic political message emphasizing limited government, free markets, and individual responsibility. His nationally televised 1964 speech, "A Time for Choosing," transformed him overnight from a political commentator into a conservative rising star.

Reagan capitalized on that momentum by winning the California governorship in 1966, serving two terms. His administration successfully managed through a turbulent era of protests, budget pressures, and social change. Though he lost the Republican nomination to Gerald Ford in 1976, Reagan remained the party's standard-bearer. By 1980, amid economic stagflation and foreign policy anxiety, he successfully presented himself as a calm, confident alternative. He was subsequently elected president in a decisive victory over President Jimmy Carter.

Domestic Life

Reagan's domestic life was characterized by two very different marriages and, ultimately, by a deeply close and protective partnership with Nancy Reagan. In 1940, Reagan married actress Jane Wyman, with whom he had two adopted children (Maureen and Michael) and later a daughter, Christine, who died shortly after birth. The marriage struggled under the pressures of Hollywood careers, ending in divorce in 1949.

Reagan's second marriage, to Nancy Davis in 1952, became the emotional anchor of his life. Nancy was intensely loyal, highly attentive, and fiercely protective of her husband. Together they had two children, Patti and Ron. Reagan was affectionate and optimistic but also emotionally restrained because of his intense work ethic. Nancy managed much of the household and family logistics, creating stability that Reagan lacked from his own childhood. Their marriage was widely regarded as warm and enduring, with Reagan frequently expressing devotion to Nancy in letters and public remarks.

As president, Reagan valued privacy and routine at home. He enjoyed simple pleasures—watching movies, telling stories, and spending time at Rancho del Cielo, the couple's California ranch. The ranch was his sanctuary for renewal and reflection. Family relationships were sometimes strained, particularly with children who held differing political views, but Reagan remained emotionally steady and publicly restrained. In later years, his visible tenderness toward Nancy cemented the image of a man whose public confidence was matched by a deeply rooted domestic devotion.

Political Affiliation and Governing Style

A Republican, Reagan governed as a narrative president. He believed the central task of leadership was not administrative mastery but restoration of national confidence and moral clarity. Reagan delegated operational control to subordinates while retaining tight command over message, values, and strategic direction.

Reagan redefined presidential authority through optimism and ideological coherence. He framed government as a problem to be restrained rather than a solution to be expanded, shifting the political center without dismantling core New Deal institutions. Reagan's style emphasized persuasion over policy detail, coalition over bureaucracy, and symbolism over procedural control.

ACCOMPLISHMENTS AND VISION

Reagan's presidency marked a decisive ideological shift toward modern conservatism and a renewed emphasis on limited government, free markets, and strong national defense. Domestically, Reagan pursued a program of tax reduction, deregulation, and spending restraint—often described as "Reaganomics"—aimed at stimulating economic growth and curbing inflation that had plagued the 1970s. The Economic Recovery Tax Act of 1981 significantly lowered marginal tax rates, while deregulation in industries such as transportation, energy, and telecommunications sought to encourage competition and investment. Though federal deficits expanded due to increased defense spending and slower-than-expected revenue growth, the U.S. economy rebounded strongly after the 1981–82 recession, entering a prolonged period of expansion characterized by declining inflation and rising employment.

Reagan also placed great emphasis on restoring American confidence and projecting strength abroad. He authorized a substantial military buildup, modernizing U.S. nuclear and conventional forces while advocating the Strategic Defense Initiative (SDI), a proposed missile defense system designed to reduce reliance on nuclear deterrence. His administration initially took a hardline stance toward the Soviet Union but later pursued diplomacy with Soviet leader Mikhail Gorbachev. A series of high-profile summits culminated in the Intermediate-Range Nuclear Forces (INF) Treaty of 1987, which eliminated an entire class of nuclear missiles and marked a significant step toward easing Cold War tensions. Reagan's combination of military pressure and diplomatic engagement contributed to the broader thaw in U.S.–Soviet relations that preceded the Cold War's end.

Reagan's broader vision centered on a belief in American exceptionalism, individual initiative, and the transformative power of free enterprise. He sought to reduce the perceived overreach of the federal government while promoting personal responsibility and economic opportunity. His communication skills—earning him the nickname "The Great Communicator"—helped him articulate a message of national renewal and optimism that resonated with many Americans. By the end of his presidency, inflation had fallen dramatically, economic growth had stabilized, and U.S. global confidence had strengthened. Although debates persist over deficits, income inequality, and the long-term effects of his policies, Reagan's presidency reshaped the ideological direction of American politics and left a lasting imprint on both domestic governance and Cold War diplomacy.

CRITICISMS AND CONTROVERSIES

Reagan faced significant criticism during and after his presidency, even as many admired his leadership style and optimism. The most serious scandal was the Iran-Contra affair[66], in which members of his administration secretly sold arms to Iran (despite an embargo) and diverted some of the proceeds to support anti-communist rebels in Nicaragua. Reagan denied direct involvement and said he did not approve the diversion of funds. Critics argued the episode showed poor oversight and raised serious constitutional concerns about ignoring Congress. The scandal damaged public trust, even though Reagan personally remained relatively popular.

Reagan's economic policies were also controversial. While many credit his tax cuts and deregulatory approach with spurring growth, critics point out that federal deficits and the national debt grew sharply during his presidency. Wealth inequality widened, and opponents argued that the benefits of economic growth flowed disproportionately to the wealthy. Rising homelessness in many cities during the 1980s became a visible symbol for critics who believed Reagan's reduced role for government left vulnerable populations behind.

Finally, Reagan drew criticism for aspects of his social and foreign policies. Civil rights advocates argued he was slow to support certain protections, particularly early in his presidency, and AIDS activists sharply criticized the administration's delayed and muted response to the HIV/AIDS crisis. In foreign affairs, while he is praised for helping end the Cold War, critics contend that his support for

---

66 A major U.S. political scandal of the mid-1980s involving secret arms sales to Iran and the diversion of proceeds to support the Contra rebels in Nicaragua, in direct violation of congressional prohibitions. President Ronald Reagan publicly accepted responsibility for the actions of his administration but maintained that he did not authorize or have full knowledge of the diversion of funds. The affair raised enduring questions about presidential accountability, executive secrecy, and the limits of Cold War policymaking.

authoritarian anti-communist regimes in Latin America and elsewhere conflicted with America's stated commitment to human rights.

LEGACY

Reagan reinvigorated conservatism and successfully argued that government was often the problem rather than the solution. His emphasis on lower taxes, deregulation, strong national defense, and individual responsibility reset the political baseline. He also restored the president's role as a communicator, using optimism, simplicity, and storytelling to connect with ordinary Americans in a way few modern presidents have matched.

Internationally, Reagan is most remembered for his role in bringing the Cold War to a peaceful close. By combining military pressure with a willingness to negotiate, he helped reduce nuclear tensions and encouraged reforms within the Soviet system. While historians still debate how much credit he deserves relative to broader global forces, Reagan is widely seen as a key figure in easing decades of superpower hostility without a major war.

Overall, supporters view him as a president who restored American pride, revived the economy, and helped win the Cold War. Critics argue his policies worsened inequality, expanded deficits, and weakened parts of the social safety net. What is not disputed is that Reagan permanently altered the direction and tone of American public life—making him one of the most consequential presidents of the late 20th century.

Reagan's presidency closed this era by resolving its central dilemma: how to govern amid skepticism without abandoning authority. He did not eliminate constraints—but he made them politically tolerable.

George H. W. Bush (1989–1993)

Early Life and Background

George Herbert Walker Bush was born on June 12, 1924, in Milton, Massachusetts, and raised primarily in Greenwich, Connecticut. His father, Prescott Bush, was a successful banker and later U.S. senator, while his mother, Dorothy Walker Bush, emphasized charity and personal responsibility. The Bush household was affluent but disciplined, with a strong ethic of duty and modesty despite wealth.

Bush attended elite private schools, most notably Phillips Academy in Andover, Massachusetts. There he distinguished himself not as an intellectual prodigy but as a well-rounded leader, serving as captain of the baseball and soccer teams and president of his senior class. Teachers and classmates consistently described him as polite, reliable, and team-oriented rather than flamboyant, traits that would later define his political style.

A tragic but defining event of his childhood was the death of his younger sister, Robin, from leukemia when Bush was 20. Although this occurred just as he was entering adulthood, the loss deeply affected him and reinforced the family's stoic approach to adversity. More broadly, Bush grew up during the Great Depression, insulated from its worst effects yet keenly aware (through family example) of public service as an obligation of citizenship rather than a path to acclaim.

On his 18th birthday in 1942, he enlisted in the U.S. Navy, becoming one of the youngest naval aviators in World War II. Flying torpedo bombers in the Pacific, Bush completed 58 combat missions. In 1944, his aircraft was shot down during an attack on a Japanese installation; he successfully bailed out over water and was rescued by a U.S. submarine, while his crewmates were killed. The experience left him with lifelong humility about survival and a sober appreciation of sacrifice. He was awarded the Distinguished Flying Cross and several Air Medals.

After the war, Bush attended Yale University under the GI Bill, graduating in 1948. At Yale he again emerged as a team-oriented leader rather than an ideologue—most notably serving as captain of the baseball team. That same year he married Barbara Pierce, beginning a long and notably stable family life that would underpin his public career.

Rejecting the path of inherited Eastern establishment politics, Bush moved his family to Texas, where he built a successful career in the oil industry. Starting from entry-level positions, he eventually co-founded an independent oil company and became financially secure. This period cemented his pragmatic, business-oriented worldview and gave him political credibility as a self-made figure rather than simply a senator's son.

Bush entered politics in the 1960s, winning a U.S. House seat in Texas. Though he lost a Senate race in 1970, the defeat did not derail his ascent. Instead, it launched a series of appointed roles that broadened his experience: U.S. ambassador to the United Nations, chairman of the Republican National Committee during the Watergate crisis, U.S. envoy to China, and director of the Central Intelligence Agency. Few Americans accumulated such a wide-ranging resume across diplomacy, party leadership, and intelligence.

In 1980, Bush sought the Republican presidential nomination but lost to Ronald Reagan. He accepted the vice presidency, serving two terms and becoming deeply versed in foreign affairs and executive governance. By the time he ran for president in 1988, Bush presented himself not as a visionary reformer but as a steady, experienced hand—someone whose adulthood had been defined by service and loyalty and rather than personal ambition.

DOMESTIC LIFE

In 1945, while still a young naval officer, he married Barbara Pierce. Their marriage lasted more than 73 years, making it the longest presidential marriage in U.S. history. Barbara was not simply a spouse but a constant partner and deeply influential in shaping the family's values and tone.

Together they raised six children: George W., Robin (who died young), Jeb, Neil, Marvin, and Dorothy ("Doro"). Family life was warm but emphasized responsibility and competitiveness tempered by sportsmanship and humor. Bush was affectionate but emotionally reserved, expressing care through presence and reliability rather than overt sentiment. The death of their daughter Robin from leukemia profoundly shaped both parents, deepening their empathy and reinforcing their belief in resilience and faith.

Despite demanding careers, the Bush family maintained strong routines and traditions. Summers and holidays at Walker's Point in Kennebunkport, Maine, became a cornerstone of family identity—a place associated with sailing, informal gatherings, and continuity across generations. Bush prized these moments as grounding counterweights to public life and often described family as his greatest source of pride.

As a husband and father, Bush encouraged independence rather than ideology. He avoided pressuring his children into politics. His parenting style emphasized character—decency, loyalty, humility—over ambition. This ethos became part of the broader "Bush family" reputation, clarifying the cohesion and durability of the family under intense public scrutiny.

POLITICAL AFFILIATION AND GOVERNING STYLE

A Republican, Bush governed pragmatically. Unlike Reagan's narrative-driven leadership, Bush emphasized coalition-building and careful deliberation. He was skeptical of ideological absolutism and believed presidential authority was best exercised through alliances and institutional legitimacy.

His leadership style was cautious, detail-oriented, and respectful of professional expertise. Domestically, he accepted much of the conservative realignment that occurred under Reagan while acknowledging limits to fiscal policy.

ACCOMPLISHMENTS AND VISION

Bush's presidency coincided with the peaceful conclusion of the Cold War. He managed the collapse of the Soviet Union and the reunification of Germany with restraint and diplomatic skill, avoiding triumphalism that might have destabilized fragile transitions. His stewardship preserved alliances and laid groundwork for a cooperative post–Cold War order.

Bush also led a broad international coalition during the Persian Gulf War, responding decisively to Iraq's invasion of Kuwait (Figure 14). The war demonstrated effective multilateral leadership, clear objectives, and restrained use of force. Bush deliberately limited the conflict's scope, resisting pressure to occupy Iraq or pursue regime change—decisions that preserved coalition unity and regional stability.

Domestically, Bush signed major bipartisan legislation, including the Americans with Disabilities Act[67], expanding civil rights protections, and the Clean Air Act Amendments of 1990, strengthening environmental regulation[68]. He also confronted budget deficits, ultimately agreeing to tax increases in pursuit of fiscal discipline.

CRITICISMS AND CONTROVERSIES

The most politically damaging criticism centered on Bush's decision to approve tax increases after famously declaring, "Read my lips: no

---

67 A landmark civil rights law that makes it illegal to discriminate against people with disabilities. It requires employers, governments, and businesses open to the public to provide reasonable access and accommodations so individuals with disabilities can work, travel, communicate, and participate fully in everyday life.

68 A bipartisan overhaul of U.S. air-quality policy that expanded federal authority to regulate air pollution while introducing market-based mechanisms, most notably emissions trading, to achieve environmental goals at lower economic cost. The law strengthened standards for smog, acid rain, toxic pollutants, and ozone-depleting substances and is widely cited as a model for combining regulation with economic incentives.

new taxes." Faced with large federal deficits and pressure from Congress, he agreed to a 1990 budget deal that raised taxes. While fiscally pragmatic, the reversal alienated conservative Republicans, undermined trust among voters, and became a symbol of perceived political unreliability.

Bush was widely criticized for appearing detached from domestic economic concerns, especially during the 1990–1991 recession. Although the downturn was relatively mild, rising unemployment and slow recovery hurt middle-class confidence. His administration was seen as reactive rather than proactive on job creation, reinforcing an image of strength abroad but drift at home.

Compared with his foreign-policy achievements, Bush was faulted for lacking a clear, compelling domestic agenda. Initiatives such as the Americans with Disabilities Act and amendments to the Clean Air Act were substantial, but they were not effectively framed as part of a broader narrative. Critics argued that Bush governed competently but without a unifying domestic vision that resonated with voters.

Legacy

George H. W. Bush's legacy is defined by foreign-policy stewardship at a moment of extraordinary global transition. As president during the peaceful end of the Cold War, Bush managed the collapse of the Soviet Union with caution and restraint. His emphasis on alliance management and respect for former adversaries is widely credited with helping ensure that the Cold War ended without large-scale violence—an achievement that has grown in stature with time.

Bush's leadership during the 1991 Gulf War further cemented his reputation as a disciplined realist. By assembling a broad international coalition, securing United Nations authorization, and clearly limiting war aims to the liberation of Kuwait, he demonstrated a model of multilateral, rules-based use of force. His decision not to march on Baghdad remains debated, but many historians view it as consistent with his strategic restraint and understanding of postwar regional risks.

Domestically, Bush's impact is quieter but durable. Major bipartisan legislation—including the Americans with Disabilities Act and the 1990 Clean Air Act amendments—produced long-lasting improvements in civil rights and environmental protection.

These achievements underscore a governing style focused on incremental, practical gains rather than sweeping ideological change.

Scholars increasingly portray Bush as a bridge figure: the last Cold War president and a transitional leader between the Reagan era and the more polarized politics that followed. His willingness to compromise on taxes, once derided, is now often cited as an example of placing fiscal responsibility above short-term political advantage.

The Contemporary Presidency

1993-2025

This era marks the presidency's transition into a world without organizing consensus. The collapse of the Soviet Union removed the external threat that had structured American politics, justified executive authority, and enforced bipartisan cooperation for nearly half a century. In its absence, presidential leadership became simultaneously more powerful and more contested.

Globalization reshaped the economic foundations of governance. Trade liberalization, financial integration, and technological change generated prosperity while dislocating labor, weakening industrial communities, and accelerating inequality. Presidents increasingly confronted economic forces beyond direct national control, limiting the effectiveness of traditional policy tools and fueling public frustration with political institutions.

Domestically, political polarization intensified. Ideological barriers within parties reduced overlap and compromise, while cultural divisions displaced economic consensus. Governing coalitions narrowed, legislative productivity declined, and executive action expanded as presidents increasingly relied on administrative authority to achieve policy goals. Executive orders, regulatory reinterpretation, and unilateral foreign action became routine features of presidential governance.

Media transformation amplified these dynamics. The rise of 24-hour news, digital platforms, and social media fragmented public attention and collapsed traditional gatekeeping institutions. Presidential communication shifted from persuasion toward mobilization, prioritizing base loyalty over consensus-building. Visibility increased while trust declined.

Foreign policy during this era was defined by ambiguity rather than rivalry. Humanitarian intervention, terrorism, regional instability, and asymmetric conflict replaced Cold War containment. The attacks of September 11, 2001, temporarily restored unity and expanded executive authority dramatically, particularly in surveillance, military engagement, and national security. Over time, however, prolonged conflict and secrecy renewed skepticism toward presidential power.

Institutionally, this era is marked by strain rather than rupture. Courts remain active, elections competitive, and federalism intact. Yet norms governing restraint and compromise weakened. Presidents of both parties tested the boundaries of executive authority, while Congress struggled to assert coherent oversight.

In historical perspective, this era represents an unsettled presidency. Power is exercised continuously, visibly, and contentiously—without the legitimizing frameworks that sustained earlier eras. The central challenge of the contemporary presidency is not authority, but trust: how to govern effectively in a system that remains strong institutionally but fractured socially.

Evaluating the Contemporary Presidency

The presidents of this era are assessed using a modified historical framework appropriate to an unfinished era. Unlike earlier periods, where outcomes, institutional durability, and long-term consequences can be weighed with greater confidence, contemporary presidencies must be evaluated with explicit methodological restraint.

Accordingly, the assessments that follow prioritize structural context over personal verdict. Emphasis is placed on the conditions presidents inherit—economic globalization, partisan polarization, media fragmentation, and institutional constraint—rather than attributing outcomes solely to individual competence or intent. Policy initiatives are examined for their directionality and institutional impact, not for their final success or failure.

Evaluations also distinguish between immediate political controversy and durable historical consequence. Actions that dominate contemporary discourse may recede in long-term significance, while incremental institutional changes may prove decisive over time. Where evidence remains ambiguous, ambiguity is acknowledged rather than resolved prematurely.

Finally, this section avoids assigning definitive historical rankings. Instead, it frames each presidency as part of an evolving system under stress, recognizing that future events, archival access, and generational perspective will substantially alter present interpretations. This approach is intended not to diminish accountability, but to preserve analytical integrity in the face of proximity, partisanship, and incomplete evidence.

WILLIAM J. CLINTON (1993–2001)

EARLY LIFE AND BACKGROUND

William Jefferson Clinton was born on August 19, 1946, in the small railroad town of Hope, Arkansas. His father, a traveling salesman, was killed in a car accident just three months before Bill was born, leaving his mother, Virginia Kelley, to raise him largely on her own. For much of his early childhood, Clinton lived with his maternal grandparents, Eldridge and Edith Kelley. They provided financial stability and emotional grounding, and Clinton later credited them—especially his grandmother—with instilling in him a belief in education, responsibility, and social justice.

When Clinton was about four years old, his mother married Roger Clinton Sr., and the family moved to Hot Springs, Arkansas. The marriage proved difficult. Roger Clinton struggled with alcoholism and was often volatile, exposing young Bill to domestic instability and emotional stress. Clinton has spoken candidly about this period, describing how he sometimes intervened to protect his mother during violent episodes. These experiences deeply shaped his empathy for people and his later political focus on social programs, healthcare, and economic opportunity.

Despite challenges at home, Clinton excelled in school. He was a gifted student, an accomplished saxophonist, and a natural leader. At Hot Springs High School, he became active in student government and civic life, showing early signs of the charisma and ambition that would later define his political career. A pivotal moment came in 1963 when he met President John F. Kennedy as a delegate to Boys Nation in Washington, D.C.—an encounter Clinton later described as life-changing and decisive in setting him on the path to public service.

After graduating from Georgetown University in 1968, where he studied international affairs, Clinton won a Rhodes Scholarship to Oxford University. His time at Oxford broadened his worldview and exposed him to global politics, though it was also a period of personal exploration. He later earned a law degree from Yale Law School, where he met Hillary Rodham, a fellow law student who would become his closest political partner and adviser.

Clinton returned to Arkansas in the mid-1970s determined to enter public life. After a short stint teaching law at the University of Arkansas, he ran for Congress in 1974, narrowly losing but gaining valuable exposure and experience. Two years later, at just 30 years old, he was elected Attorney General of Arkansas, signaling his rapid rise within the state's Democratic Party. In 1978, Clinton won the governorship, becoming the youngest governor in the nation. His first term was rocky—marked by unpopular decisions and political inexperience—and he lost reelection in 1980, a setback that forced him to reassess his leadership style.

Clinton's comeback was swift and instructive. He won back the governorship in 1982 and served five consecutive terms (1983–1992), during which he reinvented himself as a pragmatic, results-oriented leader. As governor, he emphasized education reform, economic development, and a more centrist approach to governance, positioning himself as part of the emerging "New Democrat" movement. This blend of progressive goals and political moderation helped him build a national profile and made him appealing to a Democratic Party seeking to regain the White House after years of Republican dominance.

By 1992, Clinton leveraged his gubernatorial record, personal charisma, and message of economic renewal to mount a successful presidential campaign. Running as a youthful, energetic reformer focused on "putting people first," he defeated incumbent President George H. W. Bush and independent candidate Ross Perot. Clinton's ascent—from a small-town Arkansas upbringing to the presidency—reflected a combination of intellectual ability, political resilience, and a keen sense of how to adapt after failure, traits that would continue to define his leadership style in office.

DOMESTIC LIFE

Clinton's domestic life was closely intertwined with his political career and was marked by both partnership and strain. In 1975, he married Hillary Rodham Clinton, a fellow Yale Law School graduate whose intelligence, ambition, and policy expertise made her an unusually active partner in his public life. Their marriage was not unconventional for its time; Hillary maintained her own professional identity as a lawyer, policy advocate, and later an elected official, while also playing a central advisory role in Clinton's campaigns and governance.

The couple settled primarily in Arkansas during Clinton's rise in state politics, balancing demanding careers with family life. In 1980, they welcomed their daughter, Chelsea Clinton, who became the emotional center of the family. Clinton has often spoken of his devotion to Chelsea and his efforts—sometimes imperfect—to shield her from the pressures and scrutiny of political life. During his years as governor, family life was relatively private, though shaped by long hours, public expectations, and frequent campaigning.

As First Family in the White House, the Clintons projected an image of intellectual partnership and modern parenthood. Chelsea lived with them during most of Clinton's presidency, and the family made a deliberate effort to provide her with a stable, routine upbringing despite intense media attention. At the same time, Clinton's domestic life was strained by the personal controversies that emerged during his presidency, which placed significant stress on the marriage and tested public perceptions of his character.

POLITICAL AFFILIATION AND GOVERNING STYLE

A Democrat, Clinton governed as a pragmatic centrist and political triangulator. Confronted with divided government for much of his presidency, he adapted by borrowing selectively from both liberal and conservative policy frameworks. Clinton emphasized flexibility, policy experimentation, and rhetorical moderation rather than ideological rigidity.

His governing style was intensely personal and improvisational. Clinton relied heavily on policy detail, rapid synthesis, and interpersonal persuasion, often overwhelming advisers with his command of substance. At the same time, this adaptability sometimes produced inconsistency and reactive decision-making, particularly during early legislative efforts.

ACCOMPLISHMENTS AND VISION

Clinton entered the presidency with a clear, simple vision: strengthen the economy, expand opportunity, and modernize government for a post–Cold War America. His core belief was that economic growth, fiscal responsibility, and social progress could go hand in hand. He often described this approach as a "middle way," aiming to move beyond old ideological battles and focus on practical results that improved everyday life.

Economically, Clinton presided over one of the strongest periods of sustained growth in modern U.S. history. During his two terms, the nation experienced low unemployment, rising incomes, and a booming technology-driven economy. Perhaps his most cited achievement was turning large federal budget deficits into budget surpluses by the late 1990s. Clinton argued that paying down debt and maintaining fiscal discipline would strengthen the country long-term, free resources for private investment, and protect future generations.

Domestically, Clinton focused heavily on education, work, and family stability. He supported expanded access to college through student loan reforms, promoted higher academic standards, and emphasized lifelong learning. Welfare reform was another major and controversial achievement: Clinton pushed to overhaul the welfare system to encourage work while still providing support for children[69]. His administration also expanded health coverage for millions of children through the Children's Health Insurance Program (CHIP)[70], reflecting his belief that government should help working families, not replace them.

On the world stage, Clinton's vision centered on engagement rather than isolation. He worked to expand free trade, most notably through the North American Free Trade Agreement (NAFTA)[71], arguing that globalization was inevitable and that American workers would benefit if the U.S. helped shape the rules. He also supported NATO expansion and used diplomacy and limited military force to manage post–Cold War conflicts, particularly in the Balkans, where U.S. leadership helped end ethnic violence.

CRITICISMS AND CONTROVERSIES

Clinton's presidency was marked by significant accomplishments, but it was also overshadowed by persistent controversies that shaped public opinion and ultimately defined much of his historical reputation. The most damaging criticisms centered on personal conduct, trust, and character,

---

69 Enacted under President Bill Clinton, the Personal Responsibility and Work Opportunity Reconciliation Act of 1996 restructured the U.S. welfare system by ending the federal entitlement to cash assistance under Aid to Families with Dependent Children (AFDC) and replacing it with Temporary Assistance for Needy Families (TANF). The law-imposed work requirements, lifetime limits on benefits (generally five years), and granted states broad discretion in designing welfare programs through block grants. Supporters argued PRWORA promoted employment, reduced long-term dependency, and increased state flexibility, while critics contended it weakened the social safety net and left vulnerable populations more exposed during economic downturns, particularly single mothers and children.

70 Established under the Balanced Budget Act of 1997, the Children's Health Insurance Program (CHIP) provided low-cost health coverage to children in families whose incomes are too high to qualify for Medicaid but insufficient to afford private insurance. Administered jointly by the federal government and the states, CHIP significantly reduced the uninsured rate among low-income children and became a durable bipartisan component of the U.S. health-care safety net.

71 Implemented on January 1, 1994, NAFTA created a trilateral free-trade zone among the United States, Canada, and Mexico, eliminating most tariffs on goods and establishing rules governing investment, intellectual property, and dispute resolution. Proponents argued that the agreement expanded trade, lowered consumer prices, and strengthened North American supply chains, while critics contended it accelerated deindustrialization in the United States, contributed to wage pressures, and exposed regulatory and environmental gaps—particularly along the U.S.–Mexico border. NAFTA reshaped continental economic integration for more than two decades before being renegotiated and replaced by the United States–Mexico–Canada Agreement (USMCA), which took effect in 2020.

rather than on policy failures. These issues repeatedly distracted from his agenda and eroded confidence among supporters and critics alike.

The most serious controversy involved Clinton's relationship with White House intern Monica Lewinsky and his subsequent statements under oath. Clinton initially denied the relationship publicly and in legal testimony, which later proved false. This led to charges of perjury and obstruction of justice, and in 1998 the House of Representatives impeached him. Although he was acquitted by the Senate and remained in office, the episode deeply polarized the country. Critics argued that Clinton damaged the dignity of the presidency and undermined public trust by placing personal ambitions above honesty.

Beyond impeachment, Clinton faced long-running ethical controversies throughout his career. Investigations into the Whitewater real estate matter, campaign finance practices, and the handling of FBI background files created an ongoing atmosphere of scandal, even when no criminal charges were made. Supporters often argued that these investigations were politically motivated and disproportionate, while critics countered that Clinton's casual approach to ethical boundaries invited scrutiny and confusion.

Clinton also drew policy-based criticism from both the left and the right. Progressives faulted him for welfare reform, financial deregulation, and trade agreements like NAFTA, arguing these policies contributed to long-term inequality and job losses in certain communities. Conservatives criticized him for expanding government programs, moral laxity, and what they saw as an inconsistent or reactive foreign policy, particularly in response to terrorism during the 1990s.

Clinton's controversies highlight a central tension of his presidency: strong political skills and policy successes paired with personal behavior that weakened moral authority.

LEGACY

Governing during the calm between the Cold War and the War on Terror, Clinton presided over a period of economic expansion, technological transformation, and relative global stability. His administration helped define how the United States would operate in a new era—one less shaped by superpower rivalry and more by globalization, information technology, and economic interdependence.

Clinton's most durable impact lies in the economy. The combination of sustained growth, low unemployment, and federal budget surpluses in the late 1990s remains a benchmark against which later presidents are measured. Politically, Clinton reshaped the Democratic Party by advancing a pragmatic, centrist approach that accepted markets and trade while still emphasizing education, healthcare access, and support for working families. This "New Democrat" model influenced party strategy for decades, even as it later faced criticism from both progressives and conservatives.

On domestic policy, Clinton's legacy is mixed but consequential. Programs such as the Children's Health Insurance Program expanded the social safety net, while welfare reform fundamentally changed the relationship between government assistance and work.

In foreign affairs, Clinton's emphasis on alliances, diplomacy, and selective intervention helped stabilize post–Cold War Europe, though unresolved challenges—particularly terrorism and global instability—would confront his successors more sharply.

Ultimately, Clinton's historical impact is inseparable from the impeachment and personal scandals that clouded his presidency. While these controversies did not erase his policy achievements, they complicated his moral authority and reshaped public expectations of presidential accountability. Clinton stands as a reminder that effective governance and personal conduct are judged together. His presidency left behind a stronger economy and a reoriented Democratic Party, but also a cautionary lesson about character and trust.

GEORGE W. BUSH (2001–2009)

EARLY LIFE AND BACKGROUND

Born in 1946 in New Haven, Connecticut, George Walker Bush spent his childhood primarily in Texas. He was the first child of George H. W. Bush and Barbara Pierce Bush and, therefore, was raised in a family where public service, personal responsibility, and ambition were emphasized early. Although born into privilege, Bush's upbringing combined social advantage with a strong expectation of independence and resilience.

The Bush family moved frequently during George's early years as his father pursued business and political opportunities, eventually settling in Midland, Texas. Midland was a small, oil-driven town where Bush absorbed a distinctly Texan identity—informal, competitive, and socially grounded. He attended public schools, played baseball enthusiastically, and developed a reputation as sociable and outgoing, though not academically exceptional. His parents stressed character, faith, and loyalty, values that would later feature prominently in his public persona.

A defining influence on Bush's childhood was the early death of his younger sister, Robin, from leukemia in 1953. The loss deeply affected the family and reinforced themes of faith and emotional resilience within the household. Bush later described his childhood as loving but disciplined, shaped by high expectations and a constant awareness of his father's prominence. By adolescence, he had grown up accustomed to political conversation, public scrutiny, and the implicit pressure of legacy— conditions that quietly set the stage for his future path into leadership.

After graduating from Yale and Harvard Business School, he spent his early adult years in Texas's oil and energy sector. These experiences, along with struggles with alcohol that he later acknowledged, contributed to a period of personal reassessment in his forties, including a renewed commitment to Christian faith and discipline.

Bush first entered politics in 1994, when he ran for governor of Texas against the popular incumbent, Ann Richards. Campaigning as a pragmatic conservative with a personable style, Bush emphasized education reform, welfare reform, and bipartisan cooperation. He won decisively and, as governor, cultivated a reputation as a consensus builder, working with a Democratic legislature to pass education accountability measures and tax cuts. His gubernatorial record—combined with a relaxed, plainspoken demeanor—helped him project an image of approachability and resolve.

In 2000, Bush sought the presidency, positioning himself as a "compassionate conservative" who favored limited government, faith-based initiatives, and a strong national defense. His campaign emphasized character, values, and executive experience rather than detailed policy proposals. The election against Vice President Al Gore became one of the closest and most contested in U.S. history, ultimately decided by a narrow margin in Florida after a Supreme Court ruling ended recounts. Bush won the Electoral College while losing the national popular vote, entering office amid controversy but asserting a mandate to govern decisively.

DOMESTIC LIFE

Bush married Laura Welch in 1977, a partnership that proved to be stabilizing and enduring. Laura Bush, a former librarian and schoolteacher, maintained a low-key but influential presence throughout Bush's political career. Their marriage was widely regarded as supportive and private, with Laura often serving as a quiet counterbalance to her husband's more outgoing personality. Together they emphasized education, literacy, and family life, themes that later carried into Laura Bush's work as First Lady.

The couple raised twin daughters, Jenna and Barbara, born in 1981. Bush frequently spoke about the importance of family responsibility and personal example, particularly considering his own acknowledgment of youthful missteps. His decision to stop drinking alcohol in middle age became part of a broader narrative of personal accountability and faith. He framed this transition as essential to his role as a husband, father, and leader. Family life at the Bush ranch in Crawford, Texas, was portrayed as informal and grounded, reinforcing his public image as a plainspoken Texan despite his elite background.

As president, Bush worked to project normalcy and routine in family life amid the pressures of office. The Bush family maintained a relatively traditional household structure, with Laura Bush avoiding overt political advocacy and the daughters largely shielded from public life. After leaving the presidency, Bush devoted more time to family, painting, and philanthropy, reinforcing the impression that his domestic life was marked by stability and long-term personal commitment.

POLITICAL AFFILIATION AND GOVERNING STYLE

A Republican, Bush governed initially as a compassionate conservative, emphasizing tax reduction, education reform, and faith-based initiatives. His leadership style favored delegation, loyalty, and clear moral framing over policy micromanagement. Bush relied heavily on a close circle of advisers, valuing decisiveness and unity rather than internal dissent.

After the terrorist attacks of September 11, 2001, Bush's governing style shifted dramatically. The presidency assumed a national security–centered posture, with expanded executive authority justified by existential threat. Bush framed leadership in moral and civilizational terms, emphasizing resolve and clarity of purpose.

Accomplishments and Vision

Bush's presidency was fundamentally reshaped by September 11, 2001. Bush led a rapid reorientation of U.S. national security policy, launching the war in Afghanistan to dismantle al-Qaeda and remove the Taliban regime that had sheltered it. He also reorganized the federal government's security apparatus, creating the Department of Homeland Security to better coordinate intelligence, border protection, and emergency response and enacted the USA PATRIOT Act, expanding surveillance and counterterrorism powers[72].

Domestically, Bush pursued significant education reform with the passage of the No Child Left Behind Act[73], which expanded federal involvement in public education by emphasizing standardized testing, accountability, and measurable outcomes. While controversial in execution, the law reflected a bipartisan effort to address disparities in educational performance and represented one of the largest federal education initiatives since the 1960s. Bush also signed the Medicare Prescription Drug, Improvement, and Modernization Act, which added a prescription drug benefit (Medicare Part D), substantially expanding federal health benefits for seniors.

Bush's presidency also featured major tax policy changes. He enacted broad tax cuts aimed at stimulating economic growth,

---

72 Enacted shortly after the September 11, 2001, terrorist attacks, the USA PATRIOT Act (Uniting and Strengthening America by Providing Appropriate Tools Required to Intercept and Obstruct Terrorism) significantly expanded federal law enforcement and intelligence authorities to conduct surveillance, share information across agencies, and disrupt terrorist financing. While supporters argued the act enhanced national security and interagency coordination, critics raised civil liberties concerns—particularly regarding warrant standards, bulk data collection, and provisions such as roving wiretaps and delayed-notice ("sneak and peek") searches—leading to subsequent amendments and partial reforms, most notably under the USA FREEDOM Act of 2015.

73 The No Child Left Behind Act of 2001 (NCLB), signed into law by President George W. Bush, significantly expanded the federal government's role in K–12 education by emphasizing standards-based reform, annual standardized testing, and accountability measures tied to federal funding. The law required states to administer yearly assessments in reading and mathematics for grades 3–8 and once in high school, with schools expected to demonstrate "adequate yearly progress" (AYP) toward universal proficiency. While supporters argued that NCLB increased transparency and highlighted achievement gaps among student subgroups, critics contended that it encouraged excessive teaching to the test, imposed unrealistic performance targets, and penalized under-resourced schools. Widespread bipartisan dissatisfaction ultimately led to its replacement by the "Every Student Succeeds Act" (ESSA) in 2015, which returned greater flexibility to states while retaining federal oversight of educational equity.

reducing income tax rates, and increasing child tax credits. Supporters credited these policies with contributing to economic expansion in the mid-2000s, while critics questioned their long-term fiscal impact. In his second term, Bush confronted the 2008 financial crisis, authorizing emergency measures to stabilize the banking system. Though deeply unpopular at the time, these actions are widely viewed as having helped prevent a more severe economic collapse.

Bush also advanced major public health initiatives, including the President's Emergency Plan for AIDS Relief (PEPFAR), which became one of the most consequential global health programs in U.S. history[74].

CRITICISMS AND CONTROVERSIES

The defining controversy of Bush's presidency was the Iraq War. The decision to invade Iraq in 2003, justified by intelligence claims regarding weapons of mass destruction, profoundly damaged U.S. credibility when those weapons were not found. Prolonged insurgency, civilian casualties, and strategic miscalculations eroded public support and intensified global skepticism toward American leadership.

Domestically, critics argued that executive power expanded excessively, with detention practices, enhanced interrogation techniques, and warrantless surveillance raising constitutional and moral concerns. The federal response to Hurricane Katrina exposed administrative failures and undermined perceptions of competence. The response was widely criticized for slow coordination, inadequate preparedness, and poor communication, particularly in protecting vulnerable populations in New Orleans.

---

74 PEPFAR (President's Emergency Plan for AIDS Relief) was launched in 2003 under President George W. Bush as a U.S. global health initiative aimed at combating HIV/AIDS, particularly in sub-Saharan Africa and other heavily affected regions. Initially funded at $15 billion over five years, PEPFAR prioritized antiretroviral treatment, HIV prevention, and care for orphans and vulnerable children, while strengthening local health systems. Widely regarded as one of the most successful foreign aid programs in U.S. history, PEPFAR has been credited with saving more than 25 million lives and significantly reducing HIV-related mortality, while also generating bipartisan support and establishing a durable model for large-scale, results-driven global health intervention.

Bush's second term was further weakened by the 2008 financial crisis[75], which revealed regulatory shortcomings and contributed to severe economic contraction, though its origins extended beyond his administration.

LEGACY

Bush presided over the most consequential expansion of executive authority since World War II. The terrorist attacks of September 11, 2001, transformed his presidency and reshaped U.S. foreign and domestic policy for decades. Bush's emphasis on preventive war, expanded executive authority, and a global campaign against terrorism established precedents that subsequent administrations have largely maintained, even when rhetorically distancing themselves from his policies.

Domestically, Bush left a mixed but consequential record. Major initiatives such as expanded federal involvement in education and the creation of a prescription drug benefit for seniors permanently increased the federal government's role in social policy, despite his reputation as a small-government conservative. At the same time, the combination of tax cuts, prolonged military engagement, and emergency financial interventions contributed to long-term debates over fiscal responsibility and the proper scope of federal power in economic crises.

Public opinion of Bush improved modestly after he left office, aided by his withdrawal from partisan politics and a focus on humanitarian work and veterans' advocacy.

---

75 The 2008 financial crisis was the most severe global economic downturn since the Great Depression, originating from the collapse of the U.S. housing market and the widespread failure of complex financial machines tied to subprime mortgages Years of lax lending standards, securitization of high-risk mortgages, and heavy leverage by major financial institutions created systemic vulnerability. When housing prices declined and mortgage defaults surged, confidence in mortgage-backed securities and related derivatives evaporated, leading to the failure or forced rescue of major firms such as Lehman Brothers, Bear Stearns, AIG, and several large banks. The crisis triggered a global credit freeze, sharp contractions in output and employment, and unprecedented government intervention, including the Troubled Asset Relief Program (TARP), emergency Federal Reserve lending, and coordinated international stimulus. Its aftermath reshaped financial regulation, most notably through the Dodd–Frank Wall Street Reform and Consumer Protection Act, and prompted ongoing debate over moral hazard, "too big to fail," and the proper balance between market discipline and government oversight.

BARACK OBAMA (2009–2017)

EARLY LIFE AND BACKGROUND

Barack Obama was born on August 4, 1961, in Honolulu, Hawaii, at a time when the United States was still grappling with civil rights. His childhood was notably unconventional for a future president. His father, Barack Obama Sr., was a Kenyan economist studying in the United States, and his mother, Ann Dunham, was a white American from Kansas with a deep interest in anthropology and social justice. His parents separated when Obama was very young, and his father returned to Africa, a formative absence that would later shape Obama's reflections on identity and responsibility.

Obama spent most of his early years in Hawaii, raised primarily by his mother and his maternal grandparents, Stanley and Madelyn Dunham. His grandparents provided stability and middle-class values: his grandfather worked in sales, and his grandmother rose to become a bank vice president. Hawaii's racially diverse and relatively tolerant environment exposed Obama early to people of many backgrounds, helping him see race less as a rigid dividing line and more as a complex social reality.

Between the ages of six and ten, Obama lived in Indonesia after his mother remarried an Indonesian student. There, he attended local schools, learned basic Indonesian, and witnessed firsthand the challenges of poverty, political instability, and cultural difference. These years broadened his worldview and gave him an early sense that life in America, though imperfect, offered extraordinary opportunity. Returning to Hawaii, Obama attended the elite Punahou School on scholarship, where he excelled academically.

After attending and graduating from Occidental College, he transferred to Columbia University, where he earned a degree in political science and worked briefly in New York. Finding the work unsatisfying, Obama moved to Chicago in the mid-1980s to serve as a community organizer on the city's South Side. There, he worked with churches and local groups to address unemployment and housing challenges, experiences that grounded his political outlook in practical problem-solving and coalition-building rather than ideology alone.

Obama went on to attend Harvard Law School, where he distinguished himself academically and became the first Black president of the Harvard Law Review. The role brought him national attention and signaled his ability to navigate elite institutions while advocating consensus and civility. Returning to Chicago, he practiced civil rights law, taught constitutional law at the University of Chicago, and became increasingly involved in local politics. His marriage to Michelle Robinson further anchored him in Chicago's civic and professional life, reinforcing his reputation as a thoughtful, family-centered reformer.

Obama's formal political ascent began with his election to the Illinois State Senate in 1996, where he focused on ethics reform, criminal justice issues, and expanding access to health care for working families. His pragmatic approach and willingness to work across party lines helped build credibility beyond progressive circles. In 2004, his keynote address at the Democratic National Convention—emphasizing unity over division—propelled him onto the national stage and led to his election to the U.S. Senate later that year.

Although his tenure in the Senate was relatively brief, Obama quickly emerged as a national figure, known for his calm demeanor, rhetorical skill, and message of renewal. In 2008, he launched a presidential campaign centered on themes of hope, change, and restoring trust in government. Running amid public dissatisfaction with prolonged wars and economic instability, Obama built a broad coalition of younger voters, minorities, and independents. His election as the 44th president marked a historic milestone and represented the culmination of an adult life shaped by intellectual rigor, community engagement, and a steady ascent from local activism to national leadership.

Domestic Life

After meeting Michelle Robinson while working at a Chicago law firm, the two married in 1992 and established their family life firmly in Chicago. Their partnership was marked by a shared commitment to public service, professional achievement, and deliberate parenting.

The Obama's raised two daughters, Malia and Sasha, with an emphasis on stability and grounded expectations, even as Obama's political career accelerated. Michelle Obama has often described their effort to provide a "normal" childhood—home-cooked meals, schoolwork, chores, and family time—despite the extraordinary demands of public life. This focus on family cohesion and parental presence reflected Obama's desire to offer his children what he felt he had lacked at times: a consistent, engaged father in the household.

During Obama's presidency, the family sought to maintain these domestic priorities within the constraints of the White House. The Obama's kept their daughters enrolled in school, prioritized family dinners when possible, and shielded their children from unnecessary public exposure. Their domestic life in the White House reinforced Obama's public image as a family-oriented leader. Domestic life informed his policy rhetoric, particularly his emphasis on education, work–life balance, and opportunity for families striving to provide stability for the next generation.

Political Affiliation and Governing Style

A Democrat, Obama governed as a deliberative institutionalist. He valued process, consultation, and legal constraint, often favoring measured decision-making over executive spontaneity. Obama emphasized constitutional norms, multilateralism, and technocratic expertise, seeking to stabilize governance after the expansive executive assertions of the post-9/11 era.

Obama's leadership style prioritized persuasion and symbolism, particularly in rhetoric emphasizing unity and shared responsibility. While intellectually rigorous, this approach sometimes appeared detached or cautious in the face of rapidly evolving partisanship. Persistent polarization limited legislative ambition and pushed the administration increasingly toward executive action.

Accomplishments and Vision

During his two terms as president, Obama pursued an agenda aimed at stabilizing the economy, expanding access to health care, and repositioning the United States at home and abroad. He took office amid the worst financial collapse since the Great Depression, and his early presidency focused on preventing systemic economic failure. The American Recovery and Reinvestment Act combined tax relief, infrastructure spending, and aid to states, helping halt the economic freefall, stabilize financial markets, and set the stage for a long—if uneven—recovery. He also enacted the Dodd-Frank act that served to regulate the banking industry[76].

Obama's signature domestic achievement was the Affordable Care Act (ACA)[77], which significantly expanded health insurance cover-

---

76 Enacted in response to the 2008 financial crisis, the Dodd–Frank Act sought to reduce systemic risk and strengthen oversight of the U.S. financial system by expanding federal regulation of banks and non-bank financial institutions. Key provisions included the creation of the Consumer Financial Protection Bureau (CFPB) to police consumer lending practices; enhanced capital, liquidity, and stress-testing requirements for large, systemically important financial institutions; new regulatory authority for derivatives markets; and the Volcker Rule, which restricted proprietary trading by commercial banks. Supporters argued the law improved financial stability and consumer protection, while critics contended it increased compliance costs and constrained credit availability, leading to partial rollbacks and regulatory tailoring in subsequent years.

77 Enacted in 2010 under President Barack Obama, the Patient Protection and Affordable Care Act represented the most significant overhaul of the U.S. health care system since Medicare and Medicaid. The law expanded insurance coverage primarily through the creation of health

age through marketplaces, subsidies, and the expansion of Medicaid. While controversial and politically divisive, the law reduced the number of uninsured Americans by tens of millions and established consumer protections such as coverage for preexisting conditions.

In foreign policy, Obama emphasized multilateralism and restraint after a decade of war. He oversaw the drawdown of U.S. forces in Iraq, authorized the operation that killed Osama bin Laden, and sought to recalibrate U.S. counterterrorism strategy toward targeted operations rather than large-scale occupations. His administration negotiated the Iran nuclear agreement in coordination with international partners, aiming to limit Iran's nuclear capabilities through verification and diplomacy rather than military confrontation. Obama also reopened diplomatic relations with Cuba, ending more than five decades of formal isolation.

On climate and energy policy, Obama treated climate change as a central long-term challenge. His administration advanced fuel-efficiency standards, invested heavily in renewable energy, and negotiated the Paris Climate Agreement[78], committing the United States to international emissions-reduction goals. The EPA's 2009 Endangerment Finding determined that greenhouse gases threaten public health and welfare, providing the legal basis for federal regulation of carbon emissions under the Clean Air Act.

CRITICISMS AND CONTROVERSIES

Despite his historic election and significant policy achievements, Obama's presidency was marked by sustained criticism from across the political spectrum, reflecting both ideological polarization and concerns regarding the limits of executive power. One of the most per-

---

insurance exchanges, subsidies for low- and middle-income individuals, and the expansion of Medicaid eligibility, while prohibiting insurers from denying coverage based on preexisting conditions. It also introduced an individual mandate (later reduced to a zero penalty), emphasized preventive care, and sought to slow cost growth through payment reforms and regulatory oversight. Although the ACA substantially reduced the uninsured rate, it remained politically contentious and unevenly implemented across states, reflecting enduring debates over federal authority, market regulation, and the balance between cost control and access.

78 International treaty adopted December 12, 2015, at the 21st Conference of the Parties (COP21) to the United Nations Framework Convention on Climate Change (UNFCCC), committing participating nations to limit global temperature rise to well below 2°C above pre-industrial levels and to pursue efforts to limit warming to 1.5°C through nationally determined contributions (NDCs), emissions reductions, and international cooperation on climate mitigation and adaptation..

sistent critiques came from conservatives who opposed the Affordable Care Act, arguing that it expanded federal authority too far, disrupted existing insurance markets, and relied on mandates and regulations that burdened businesses and individuals. Legal challenges and repeated congressional efforts to repeal the law underscored its controversial status, even as it became more embedded in the health care system.

Critics argue that the 2009 Endangerment Finding expanded federal regulatory authority beyond congressional intent, relied on uncertain long-term climate projections, and imposed significant economic and energy costs through sweeping emissions regulations under the Clean Air Act.

Obama also faced criticism for his reliance on executive actions, particularly in areas where Congress was gridlocked. His use of executive orders on immigration—most notably the Deferred Action for Childhood Arrivals (DACA) program—was praised by supporters as a humane response to legislative inaction but criticized by opponents as an overreach of presidential authority.

In foreign policy, critics on the right argued that Obama projected weakness, especially in relations with adversaries such as Russia and China, and faulted him for not enforcing his stated "red line" after Syria's use of chemical weapons. On the left, he was criticized for continuing drone strikes, expanding surveillance programs, and failing to close the detention facility at Guantánamo Bay—policies that appeared to contradict his earlier civil liberties rhetoric. The intervention in Libya, which contributed to long-term instability after the fall of Muammar Gaddafi, became another focal point for debate over Obama's foreign policy judgment.

Obama's presidency was also shaped by unusually intense partisan and personal opposition. The "birther" movement, which falsely questioned his citizenship, reflected deeper racial and cultural tensions and forced the White House to address issues that previous presidents never faced. While Obama largely avoided personalizing these attacks, critics argued that his measured, professorial style sometimes came across as detached or insufficiently responsive to public frustration, particularly during moments of economic anxiety.

LEGACY

As the nation's first African American president, Obama's election marked a milestone in U.S. history and reshaped perceptions of who could attain the highest office, expanding the nation's civic imagination. That symbolic achievement, however, existed alongside persistent racial tensions, underscoring both the progress made and the divisions that remained unresolved.

Substantively, Obama's most enduring policy legacy is the Affordable Care Act, which permanently altered the U.S. health care landscape. Even after years of political opposition and partial rollbacks, the core framework of the law has endured, suggesting institutional durability rather than fleeting reform. His climate and energy initiatives, including U.S. participation in the Paris Climate Agreement, helped elevate climate change to a central policy issue.

In foreign affairs, Obama is often remembered for his emphasis on multilateralism, restraint, and diplomacy after a period of prolonged war. The operation that killed Osama bin Laden stands as a decisive moment, while efforts such as the Iran nuclear agreement and the opening to Cuba reflect a preference for negotiated solutions over military escalation. Critics argue these approaches were naïve or insufficiently forceful; supporters contend they reduced long-term risk and restored U.S. credibility abroad.

Politically, Obama's presidency coincided with—and in some ways intensified—an era of deep partisan polarization. His calm, technocratic style and emphasis on evidence-based governance appealed strongly to supporters but failed to bridge the widening cultural and ideological divides he often sought to heal.

DONALD J. TRUMP (2017–2021)

EARLY LIFE AND BACKGROUND

Donald John Trump was born on June 14, 1946, in Queens, New York City, the fourth of five children. He grew up primarily in the Jamaica Estates neighborhood, an affluent area that reflected his family's rising social and economic status. Trump's father, Fred Trump, was a successful real-estate developer specializing in middle-income housing in New York's outer boroughs, while his mother, Mary Anne Trump, was a Scottish immigrant who emphasized manners, appearance, and social status.

Trump's childhood was marked by strong discipline and a clear hierarchy within the family. Fred Trump exerted a powerful influence, stressing toughness, self-reliance, and winning. Donald was described as energetic, willful, and confrontational, traits that often put him at odds with authority figures. Concerned about his behavior, his parents sent him at age 13 to the New York Military Academy, a private boarding school that emphasized order, obedience, and leadership training. There, Trump thrived within a rigid system, excelling in athletics and rising to student leadership roles, while absorbing a worldview shaped by rank, loyalty, and command.

The combination of privilege, strict discipline, and early exposure to real-estate business left a lasting imprint on Trump's personality. His childhood fostered confidence bordering on bravado, a belief in dominance and control, and an instinct to frame interactions in terms of winners and losers. These formative experiences help explain the assertive, confrontational style and emphasis on strength and success that later defined Trump's public persona and political career.

After graduating from the Wharton School of Business in 1968, Trump entered his father's real-estate business. Unlike Fred Trump, who focused on steady, low-risk housing projects, Donald was drawn to high-visibility ventures. In the 1970s he began shifting the family business toward Manhattan, pursuing hotels, office towers, and branding opportunities that emphasized scale, luxury, and personal recognition. The construction of Trump Tower on Fifth Avenue in the early 1980s became a defining symbol of this approach and established Trump as a national figure in business and popular culture.

Trump's adult life was marked by dramatic highs and lows. He expanded aggressively into casinos, hotels, airlines, and entertainment, often financing projects with heavy debt. Several ventures failed, leading to multiple corporate bankruptcies in the late 1980s and 1990s. Trump nonetheless survived financially by restructuring debt, leveraging his name as a brand, and cultivating constant media attention. This ability to reframe setbacks as temporary or strategic reinforced his self-image as a resilient entrepreneur rather than a conventional corporate executive.

In the 2000s, Trump's visibility surged again through television. As host of The Apprentice, he became widely known to millions of Americans as a decisive authority figure who rewarded loyalty and punished failure. By the time Trump entered politics, he was defined less as a businessman than as a cultural symbol of toughness, success, and outsider defiance.

Trump's ascent to the presidency began formally in 2015, when he announced his candidacy as a Republican. Running as a political outsider with no prior elected office experience, his campaign was based on opposition to political elites, skepticism toward globalization, and a promise to restore national strength. His blunt rhetoric, confrontational style, and heavy use of mass media and social media platforms energized supporters while polarizing critics. In the 2016 election, Trump defeated a field of experienced politicians in the Republican primaries and went on to win the presidency, completing an unconventional rise from inherited wealth and celebrity to the highest office in American government.

DOMESTIC LIFE

Trump has had a highly visible personal and family life, shaped by multiple marriages, a large family, and a long-standing intersection between private relationships and public business activities. His first marriage, to Ivana Trump, produced three children—Donald Jr., Ivanka, and Eric—who were raised amid the expansion of the Trump real-estate and branding enterprises. Trump's later marriages, to Marla Maples and then Melania Trump, added two more children, including Barron Trump, born in 2006.

Family has played a prominent role in Trump's adult life, particularly in business. His older children were gradually integrated into the Trump Organization and became public representatives of the family brand, appearing at corporate events, interviews, and later political functions. Trump has frequently emphasized loyalty and trust within the family, preferring to rely on relatives rather than external executives for key responsibilities. This family-centered structure reinforced the close overlap between his domestic and professional spheres.

As a public figure, Trump's personal life has often attracted media attention, sometimes overshadowing conventional distinctions between private and public roles. During his presidency, members of his family maintained a visible presence, reflecting a continuation of patterns established long before he entered politics. Overall, Trump's domestic life has been characterized by continuity with his broader worldview: an emphasis on family loyalty, personal relationships as sources of authority, and the integration of home, business, and public identity.

POLITICAL AFFILIATION AND GOVERNING STYLE

Elected as a Republican but often operating at arm's length from traditional party leadership, Trump governed through a highly personalized executive style. He prioritized loyalty, public messaging, and rapid agenda gesturing, frequently using high-volume media engagement—including social media—to bypass intermediaries and sustain continuous political mobilization. Decision-making was often centralized around the president and a narrow circle of advisers. Supporters viewed this approach as an overdue break from bureaucratic inertia and orthodoxy; critics viewed it as destabilizing to administrative norms and reliant on rhetorical confrontation rather than institutional persuasion. Regardless of interpretation, Trump's presidency clearly accelerated a modern trend toward executive-centered governance under legislative gridlock.

ACCOMPLISHMENTS AND VISION

In domestic policy, Trump prioritized tax reduction, deregulation, and economic growth. The 2017 tax overhaul lowered corporate tax rates and altered individual tax brackets, reflecting his belief that business expansion and investment would drive broader prosperity. His administration also rolled back numerous federal regulations, particularly in energy, environmental policy, and financial oversight, with the stated goal of reducing costs and accelerating growth. In trade policy, Trump shifted the Republican approach away from reflexive free-trade consensus toward tariff leverage and bilateral bargaining, particularly toward China. He supported replacement of NAFTA with the U.S.–Mexico–Canada Agreement (USMCA), which entered into force on July 1, 2020[79]. In criminal justice, he signed the First Step Act (2018), a bipartisan reform package focused on sentencing and prison policy[80].

---

79 United States–Mexico–Canada Agreement (USMCA), signed November 30, 2018, and entered into force July 1, 2020, replaced the North American Free Trade Agreement (NAFTA) and updated regional trade rules by strengthening labor and environmental standards, modernizing digital trade and intellectual property provisions, and revising automotive rules of origin to encourage North American production.

80 The First Step Act, signed into law by President Donald Trump in December 2018, was a bipartisan criminal justice reform aimed at reducing federal prison sentences and improving rehabilitation outcomes. The law expanded judicial discretion in sentencing, retroactively applied provisions of the Fair Sentencing Act of 2010 to reduce disparities between crack and powder cocaine offenses and increased the availability of "good time"

Before the COVID-19 pandemic, these policies coincided with low unemployment and steady economic expansion, outcomes frequently cited by the administration as validation of its economic strategy.

On immigration and border security, Trump advanced a vision of stricter enforcement and national control. He increased border enforcement measures, restricted certain forms of immigration, and made construction of a border wall a central symbolic and policy priority. These efforts reflected his broader emphasis on law, order, and sovereignty.

In foreign policy, Trump questioned multilateral institutions and longstanding agreements, favoring bilateral negotiations and transactional diplomacy. At the same time, Trump sought high-profile engagement with adversaries, arguing that personal diplomacy could reduce long-standing tensions. The Trump administration also facilitated agreements between Israel and several Arab states (commonly referred to as the Abraham Accords), reinforcing a transactional, deal-oriented approach to diplomacy[81].

During the COVID-19 pandemic, the federal response included major economic relief legislation (notably the CARES Act, signed March 27, 2020) and a large-scale vaccine development initiative commonly known as Operation Warp Speed[82].

---

credits for incarcerated individuals. It also emphasized recidivism reduction through evidence-based programs, vocational training, and incentives for participation, while modestly limiting the use of mandatory minimum sentences for certain nonviolent offenses. Although critics argued it did not go far enough in addressing mass incarceration, the First Step Act marked the most significant federal criminal justice reform in a generation and reflected a rare moment of bipartisan consensus on sentencing and prison reform.

81 The Abraham Accords refer to a series of U.S.-brokered agreements announced in 2020 that normalized diplomatic relations between Israel and several Arab states, beginning with the United Arab Emirates and Bahrain, followed later by Sudan and Morocco. Departing from decades of Arab League consensus that conditioned recognition of Israel on the establishment of a Palestinian state, the accords emphasized bilateral normalization, economic cooperation, security coordination, and technological exchange. Supporters argued that the agreements strengthened regional stability, enhanced cooperation against shared threats—particularly Iran—and created new economic and diplomatic opportunities. Critics contended that the accords sidelined the Israeli–Palestinian conflict, weakened Palestinian leverage, and rewarded unilateral actions without resolving core issues of occupation, borders, or statehood.

82 Operation Warp Speed was a U.S. government public–private partnership launched in May 2020 under the Trump administration to accelerate the development, manufacturing, and distribution of COVID-19 vaccines, therapeutics, and diagnostics. By combining substantial federal funding, advance purchase agreements, and regulatory flexibility—while maintaining FDA safety and efficacy standards—the program significantly reduced financial risk for manufacturers and enabled multiple vaccines to reach emergency authorization within roughly

Viewed in historical context—particularly given ongoing political developments—Trump's accomplishments and vision should be interpreted through shifting lenses. As with other recent presidencies, fuller historical assessment will depend on temporal distance and evolving scholarship.

CRITICISMS AND CONTROVERSIES

Trump's presidency was unusually controversy-saturated, with disputes spanning ethical norms, administrative process, and democratic guardrails. The House impeached Trump twice. In December 2019, the House adopted articles alleging abuse of power and obstruction of Congress; the Senate acquitted him in February 2020. In January 2021, following the events of January 6, 2021, the House impeached Trump for incitement of insurrection; the Senate acquitted him in February 2021.

The administration's immigration enforcement posture, use of executive authority, and confrontational relationship with the press and parts of the civil service intensified debate over institutional legitimacy and presidential restraint. The COVID-19 period became a particularly polarizing stress test: critics emphasize inconsistent federal messaging, politicization of public-health measures, and uneven intergovernmental coordination; supporters emphasize rapid private–public mobilization for vaccines and the scale of economic relief.

Finally, Trump's refusal to concede the 2020 election and his role in the post-election period became central to arguments that his presidency represented an unprecedented challenge to norms surrounding peaceful transfer of power—a point that remains both historically consequential and politically contested in emphasis and framing.

LEGACY

The legacy of Donald J. Trump remains unsettled, shaped by recency, polarization, and the continuing evolution of American politics. More than most modern presidents, Trump altered the style of the presidency as much as its policy direction. He normalized a confrontational, highly personalized approach to leadership, relied heav-

---

a year, far faster than traditional timelines. Although widely credited with speeding vaccine availability, Operation Warp Speed also drew criticism for its military branding, uneven transparency, and the persistence of logistical and vaccine-hesitancy challenges during the rollout.

ily on direct communication with the public, and treated political conflict as a central feature rather than a byproduct of governance.

Institutionally, Trump's influence is likely to be most durable in areas where presidential actions have long time horizons. His judicial appointments—particularly to the Supreme Court and federal appellate courts—reshaped the federal judiciary in ways that may affect constitutional interpretation, regulatory authority, and social policy for decades. In economic and regulatory policy, his emphasis on deregulation and tax reduction reinforced a market-oriented conservative agenda, while his skepticism of globalization and free trade accelerated a broader reassessment of U.S. economic strategy.

Politically, Trump transformed the Republican Party and, by extension, the broader party system. He mobilized voters who felt disconnected from traditional political institutions and redefined conservative politics around themes of nationalism, cultural identity, and distrust of elites. At the same time, his presidency intensified partisan divisions and hardened political identities, contributing to a more adversarial and less consensus-driven political environment.

Joseph R. Biden (2021–2025)

Early Life and Background

Joseph Robinette Biden Jr. was born on November 20, 1942, in Scranton, Pennsylvania, an industrial city centered around coal mining and railroads. He was the first of four children born to Joseph Sr. and Catherine "Jean" Biden. His early childhood coincided with the economic aftershocks of the Great Depression and World War II. Biden often noted that his father experienced periods of financial instability, moving between jobs and struggling to regain a secure footing.

When Biden was ten, the family relocated to Claymont, Delaware, in search of better economic prospects. The move marked a transition from Scranton's tight-knit ethnic neighborhoods to a suburban environment. Biden attended Catholic schools and struggled academically at times, particularly due to a pronounced stutter. Overcoming this speech impediment—through deliberate practice and persistence—became a formative personal challenge and a defining feature of his character.

Biden's upbringing was strongly influenced by family, faith, and a sense of moral obligation. His mother emphasized empathy and standing up for others, while his father stressed self-respect and recovery after failure. These early lessons, shaped by modest means and personal adversity rather than privilege, provided the emotional and ethical framework that Biden would later cite as foundational to his worldview.

After earning a bachelor's degree from the University of Delaware and a law degree from Syracuse University, he returned to Delaware to practice law and quickly entered local politics. In 1972, at just 29 years old, Biden won election to the U.S. Senate, becoming one of the youngest senators in American history. Weeks later, before he could be sworn in, his wife Neilia and infant daughter Naomi were killed in an automobile accident, leaving Biden to raise his two young sons alone. He considered resigning but ultimately chose to serve, commuting daily by train from Delaware to Washington.

Over the next three decades, Biden established himself as a durable and pragmatic figure in the Senate. He served on, and later chaired, the Judiciary Committee and the Foreign Relations Committee, playing prominent roles in debates over crime legislation, judicial confirmations, arms control, and U.S. foreign policy after the Cold War. His style was marked by a mix of personal engagement, deal-making, and institutional loyalty, earning him respect across party lines.

Biden first sought the presidency in 1988, but his campaign ended early amid controversy over speaking skills and questions about stamina. A second bid in 2008 gained limited traction, though it positioned him as a seasoned statesman. That same year, Barack Obama selected Biden as his running mate, valuing his legislative experience and foreign-policy background. As vice president from 2009 to 2017, Biden became a central adviser to the president, overseeing aspects of economic recovery, foreign diplomacy, and congressional negotiations, while cultivating a reputation as a loyal and empathetic partner.

After leaving office, Biden initially signaled retirement, particularly following the death of his son Beau in 2015. However, amid growing political polarization and concern about democratic norms, he entered the 2020 presidential race framing himself as an experienced, steady alternative during a period of national turmoil. His campaign emphasized restoration of institutional stability and broad appeal to moderate and working-class voters. Winning the Democratic nomination and the general election, Biden was inaugurated in January 2021, completing a long and unconventional ascent to the presidency.

Domestic Life

Joe Biden's domestic life has been marked by close family bonds, enduring partnerships, and significant personal loss. He married Neilia Hunter in 1966, and together they had three children: Beau, Hunter, and Naomi. In 1972, shortly after Biden's election to the U.S. Senate, Neilia and their daughter Naomi were killed in a car accident, a tragedy that profoundly affected his private life. Biden became a single father to Beau and Hunter, prioritizing their upbringing while maintaining his Senate duties—a balance he often cited as central to his identity and values.

In 1977, Biden married Jill Tracy Jacobs, an educator who would remain professionally active throughout their marriage. They had one daughter together, Ashley. Jill Biden continued her career in education, including teaching at community colleges while serving as Second Lady and later First Lady. Biden frequently credited his wife with providing stability and emotional grounding during demanding political years.

Family remained a defining element of Biden's life, particularly his close relationship with his children and grandchildren. The death of his eldest son, Beau, from brain cancer in 2015 was another profound personal loss. His younger son, Hunter, has faced well-documented struggles with addiction and legal issues, matters Biden has addressed publicly with an emphasis on compassion, responsibility, and family support rather than denial or distance.

Political Affiliation and Governing Style

A Democrat, Biden governs as an institutionalist and coalition manager. His leadership style reflects a deliberate contrast with his immediate predecessor, emphasizing restoration of norms, predictability, and respect for administrative process. Biden values consultation, delegation, and continuity, relying heavily on experienced advisers and established bureaucratic channels.

Biden's presidency has prioritized stabilization over transformation. He has sought to reassert conventional expectations of presidential behavior—measured rhetoric, deference to expertise, and procedural regularity—while navigating extreme polarization and narrow legislative margins. His approach emphasizes incrementalism and alliance maintenance rather than charismatic persuasion or executive confrontation.

ACCOMPLISHMENTS AND VISION

Biden assumed office amid overlapping crises: the COVID-19 pandemic, economic disruption, institutional distrust, and global instability. Early actions focused on pandemic management, economic relief, and vaccine distribution, building upon initiatives already underway while expanding federal coordination.

Domestically, Biden secured passage of significant legislation, including large-scale infrastructure investment and targeted industrial policy aimed at supply-chain resilience, domestic manufacturing, and climate mitigation. These initiatives marked a partial departure from late-20th-century market orthodoxy, signaling renewed federal involvement in long-term economic planning.

In foreign policy, Biden prioritized alliance renewal and multilateral coordination. His administration re-engaged traditional partners and emphasized collective responses to global challenges. The U.S. response to Russia's invasion of Ukraine was centered on coalition-based sanctions, military assistance, and diplomatic coordination.

CRITICISMS AND CONTROVERSIES

One of the most significant controversies arose from the U.S. withdrawal from Afghanistan in 2021. Although the decision to end the war reflected long-standing bipartisan fatigue and followed agreements negotiated under the prior administration, the rapid collapse of the Afghan government and chaotic evacuation from Kabul drew sharp bipartisan criticism. The episode raised concerns about planning, intelligence assessments, and the limits of U.S. nation-building, becoming an early defining challenge of Biden's term.

Economic conditions formed a second major area of criticism. While the administration emphasized job growth and recovery from the COVID-19 pandemic, elevated inflation in 2021 became a persistent political liability. Critics argued that expansive federal spending, including pandemic relief and later domestic investments, contributed to inflationary pressures, while supporters countered that inflation was a global phenomenon and that U.S. recovery compared favorably with peer nations. High interest rates and housing affordability further shaped public dissatisfaction, even as employment remained strong.

Immigration and border management also generated sustained controversy. Record levels of migrants arriving at the southern border strained federal, state, and local systems, prompting criticism from Republicans and some Democrats alike. Biden faced pressure from multiple directions: accusations of weak enforcement from critics, and concerns from advocates about humanitarian conditions and legal bottlenecks. Efforts to balance enforcement with asylum protections proved politically contentious and difficult to resolve legislatively.

Finally, Biden's age and public presentation became a recurring point of criticism throughout his presidency. Gaffes, halting speech, and limited public appearances fueled debate about cognitive stamina and succession planning, often amplified by partisan media. While medical evaluations reported him fit for duty, questions about leadership longevity became an unavoidable backdrop to policy debates and electoral considerations.

Legacy (Provisional)

Any assessment of Biden's presidency must remain explicitly provisional. His legacy is likely to be assessed through the lens of stabilization, institutional repair, and long-term investment rather than sweeping ideological transformation. Taking office amid a global pandemic, economic disruption, and heightened political polarization, Biden prioritized restoring what he described as the "normal functioning" of government—reemphasizing alliances, and administrative continuity. For supporters, this emphasis on norms and process represented a corrective to a period of political volatility; for critics, it reflected a cautious style that struggled to generate public confidence or momentum.

Domestically, Biden's legacy will center on large-scale federal investments in infrastructure, manufacturing, and clean energy, including legislation aimed at rebuilding roads and bridges, expanding domestic semiconductor production, and accelerating the energy transition. These measures were designed with long time horizons, making their full effects more visible to future administrations than to voters during his term. Historians are likely to debate whether these initiatives marked a durable reorientation of federal economic policy or a temporary response to extraordinary post-pandemic conditions.

In foreign policy, Biden's presidency reinforced U.S. alliances, particularly in Europe and the Indo-Pacific, while confronting renewed great-power competition. His strong support for Ukraine following Russia's invasion underscored a recommitment to collective security and democratic norms, though critics raised concerns about escalation risks and long-term costs. Conversely, the withdrawal from Afghanistan stands as a defining and controversial endpoint to America's longest war—praised by some as overdue and criticized by others for its execution and humanitarian consequences.

DONALD J. TRUMP (2025–PRESENT)

Donald J. Trump's return to the presidency represents one of the most remarkable political comebacks in American history. After electoral defeat, impeachment, criminal indictments, and relentless institutional opposition, Trump reassembled a winning national coalition by consolidating populist support, reasserting dominance within the Republican Party, and reframing his political survival as necessary. His return underscores the durability of personal political identity in an era of polarized loyalty. Moreover, it highlights the extent to which modern presidential power is intertwined with media ecosystems, cultural grievance, and partisan realignment.

Trump's second return to the presidency has, by design, begun with a markedly more assertive and implementation-focused posture than his first term. A central theme of the first year has been speed: rapid reversal of prior administration actions, expedited staffing and personnel control, and early efforts to consolidate executive direction over the administrative state. Generally relying on executive orders, proclamations, and agency rulemaking rather than waiting for Congress to act. This "move-first" approach is consistent with the campaign premise that institutional inertia—not lack of electoral mandate—was the principal barrier to delivering results in the first term.

On the legislative front, the signature first-year enactment appears to be a major tax law—signed July 4, 2025—framed by the administration as a comprehensive economic package with immediate effects in the 2025 tax year. On the executive governance front, the administration moved quickly to reconfigure federal personnel in a manner consistent with "administrative state" reform pledges, including reinstating a Schedule F–style framework intended to expand political control over policy-influencing roles. In trade and industrial policy, the administration has pursued tariff actions (and tariff-related authorities) consistent with "America First" protectionist commitments. In the regulatory domain, outside trackers characterize the first year as a broad deregulatory push across multiple agencies—again aligned with campaign commitments to reduce regulatory constraints—though the durability of these moves will often depend on judicial review and future administrative reversals.

Immigration has emerged as one of the clearest areas where President Trump's second term has sought to align early action with campaign pledges. Throughout the campaign, Trump emphasized border control, deterrence, and executive enforcement as priorities frustrated by institutional resistance during his first term. In the opening year of the second term, the administration has moved rapidly to reassert a restrictive enforcement posture through executive authority, agency direction, and regulatory interpretation rather than comprehensive legislation. These actions reflect continuity with first-term objectives—border security, expedited removals, and limits on asylum access—while placing greater emphasis on administrative control and speed of implementation. Supporters view these measures as fulfillment of explicit electoral promises and a reassertion of executive responsibility over immigration enforcement; critics argue they raise humanitarian, legal, and federal-state coordination concerns. As with other early second-term initiatives, the long-term effectiveness and durability of these immigration actions remain contingent on judicial review, administrative capacity, and sustained political support, requiring continued caution in historical assessment.

Any assessment at the one-year mark must remain provisional for at least two reasons. First, the second term's agenda is still being implemented—through ongoing rulemaking, litigation, appropriation cycles, and inter-branch conflict—so "accomplishment" often means initiation plus partial execution rather than settled outcomes. Second, the political meaning of these actions is unusually contested: supporters tend to interpret early consolidation and rapid policy reversal as long-overdue, while critics tend to interpret the same pattern as institutional stress and overreach. A historically careful approach therefore distinguishes (a) what has plainly been done (statutes signed, orders issued, rules proposed), from (b) what is still indeterminate (ultimate economic effects, institutional durability, and long-run constitutional consequences).

THE ARC OF THE OFFICE

Across more than two centuries, the American presidency has proven to be neither static nor fragile. It has expanded, contracted, adapted, and recalibrated in response to war, economic upheaval, technological change, and social transformation. Yet despite repeated claims that the office has been fundamentally altered or irreparably damaged, the presidency has remained recognizably constitutional in structure and function.

The earliest presidents defined the office through restraint. Washington's voluntary limitations, Adams' struggle with dissent, and Jefferson's tension between ideals and power established norms that mattered as much as formal authority. These early precedents demonstrated that the presidency would be shaped not only by constitutional text, but by human judgment.

The nineteenth century tested the presidency under existential strain. Jackson personalized executive authority; Lincoln expanded it dramatically in defense of the Union; Reconstruction exposed the limits of presidential power when political legitimacy fractured. Industrialization and the Gilded Age further transformed the office, as economic scale outpaced institutional capacity and corruption exposed weaknesses in governance. Yet reform followed excess, and institutional adaptation followed crisis.

The twentieth century marked the presidency's transformation into a modern executive institution. World wars, economic collapse, and global leadership demands expanded presidential authority permanently. Franklin Roosevelt's four terms—later constrained by constitutional amendment—demonstrated both the necessity and danger of concentrated power. The Cold War institutionalized executive leadership within a framework of alliances, deterrence, and bureaucratic governance, while preserving congressional and judicial counterweights.

Post-Watergate retrenchment reminded the nation that presidential power is contingent, not absolute. Subsequent presidents navigated diminished trust, economic complexity, and cultural division. The late twentieth and early twenty-first centuries introduced new pressures: globalization, media saturation, permanent campaigning, and polarized electorates. Presidents increasingly relied on executive action not because of unchecked ambition alone, but because legislative consensus became harder to achieve.

Throughout this evolution, a consistent pattern emerges. Periods of expansion provoke correction. Overreach invites resistance. Norms erode, then reform. The presidency bends under pressure, but it does not break. Courts intervene. Elections redirect authority. Congress reasserts itself unevenly but persistently. Public opinion fluctuates, but legitimacy ultimately rests on institutional continuity rather than individual dominance.

Importantly, this history cautions against both complacency and alarmism. The presidency is powerful, but not omnipotent. It is constrained not only by law, but by tradition, political opposition, administrative reality, and human limitation. No president governs alone; none governs indefinitely. Even the most disruptive figures operate within a system that absorbs, moderates, and eventually recalibrates their influence.

This book has approached the presidency not as a moral referendum on individual leaders, but as a long-running institutional experiment shaped by human actors operating under pressure. Some presidents expanded liberty; others restricted it. Some strengthened institutions: others strained them. Most did both, often unintentionally. History's verdicts evolve with time, distance, and evidence.

What remains constant is the presidency's role as a mirror of the nation itself—reflecting its fears, ambitions, divisions, and aspirations. The office changes because the country changes. Understanding that evolution requires neither cynicism nor hero worship, but perspective.

It is with that perspective that this book now turns, deliberately and transparently, from analysis to reflection.

WHY DEMOCRACY WILL PREVAIL

AUTHOR'S REFLECTION

American democracy is not a fragile experiment perpetually on the verge of collapse. It is a remarkably resilient system—one that has endured more than 250 years of division, crisis, corruption, and aggressive leadership without breaking. Time and again, the United States has confronted moments that felt existential to those living through them, only to emerge altered, corrected, and ultimately intact.

History provides essential perspective. The nation has faced periods of polarization far deeper than those of the present day, and corruption that was once far more open, systemic, and unapologetic. In the nineteenth and early twentieth centuries, political machines openly bought votes, bribery was routine, and scandals such as Crédit Mobilier and Teapot Dome implicated the highest levels of government. Yet even then, democratic institutions responded—sometimes slowly, sometimes imperfectly—through reform, exposure, and public pressure.

Presidential power has also been tested repeatedly. Leaders such as Andrew Jackson, Theodore Roosevelt, and Franklin D. Roosevelt pushed executive authority aggressively, at times defying norms, pressuring institutions, or acting unilaterally in moments of crisis. They were controversial in their own eras and often sharply criticized as dangerous or destabilizing. Yet the system absorbed their actions, constrained excesses, and—where necessary—responded with correction. Even grave failures, such as Jackson's Indian removal policies or Franklin Roosevelt's internment order during World War II, eventually provoked moral reckoning, legal reassessment, and institutional reform.

Seen in this historical context, contemporary debates—over executive orders, institutional pressure, or political norms—remain serious but not unprecedented. Modern governance is, in many respects, less corrupt and more transparent than in earlier eras. Civil service protections, post-Watergate ethics rules, judicial review, investigative journalism, and electoral accountability have made crude abuses of power more difficult to sustain. While public trust has fluctuated, the constitutional architecture has continued to function.

This record justifies cautious optimism. The United States has survived civil war, economic collapse, global conflict, political scandal, and prolonged internal division without descending into autocracy. The Constitution's design—separation of powers, federalism, an independent judiciary, regular elections, and a free press—was not intended to prevent conflict, but to manage it. Democracy in America has never been static or serene; it has been adaptive.

The presidency, as this book has shown, is powerful but not absolute. It bends under pressure, but it does not exist in isolation. Authority is constrained by institutions, contested by rivals, shaped by public opinion, and ultimately limited by time. No individual leader, however dominant or disruptive, has proven capable of overriding the system indefinitely.

The enduring strength of American democracy lies not in the perfection of its leaders, but in the durability of its institutions and the willingness of its citizens to hold them accountable. The system corrects itself not in moments, but over generations—through law, elections, norms, and civic engagement.

The experiment in liberty continues. It is imperfect, often frustrating, and frequently contentious. Yet its long arc suggests not fragility, but resilience. American democracy has endured precisely because it allows conflict, absorbs pressure, and adapts without surrendering its core principles. There is every reason to believe it will continue to do so.

Appendix A (Tables)

Enlightenment Ideals	American Example
Natural Rights	Declaration of Independence
Popular Sovereignty	"We The People"
Social Contract	Written Constitution
Rule of Law	Constitutional Supremacy
Separation of Powers	Three Branches
Checks and Balances	Institutional Restraints
Individual Liberty	Bill of Rights
Religious Toleration	First Amendment
Human Design/Logic	Constitutional Design
Civic Virtue	Republican Government

Enlightenment ideals formed the intellectual foundation of American democracy, emphasizing reason, natural rights, and government by consent rather than hereditary authority. Political philosophers such as John Locke argued that individuals possessed inherent rights to life, liberty, and property, and that legitimate governments derived authority from a social contract with the governed. These ideas profoundly shaped the American governing philosophy, most clearly reflected in the Declaration of Independence's assertion that governments derive "their just powers from the consent of the governed." Montesquieu's theory of separation of powers further influenced the structure of the U.S. Constitution, encouraging the creation of three coequal branches of government and a system of checks and balances designed to prevent tyranny and safeguard liberty.

The Enlightenment also fostered enduring democratic norms including rule of law, religious tolerance, civic participation, and faith in rational public discourse. The framers sought to balance majority rule with protections for minority rights through a written constitution and an independent judiciary, reflecting Enlightenment confidence in structured liberty and institutional restraint. Although early American democracy did not fully extend these ideals to all inhabitants—excluding women, enslaved individuals, and many others—the Enlightenment framework provided the philosophical basis for later expansions of suffrage and civil rights.

American democracy thus remains an evolving political system grounded in Enlightenment principles of liberty, reason, and self-government.

The Founding Fathers
Architects of the Republic

George Washington. Commander-in-chief of the Continental Army during the American Revolution; presided over the Constitutional Convention; established key precedents as the first president, including civilian control of the military and the two-term tradition.

John Adams. Leading advocate for independence; diplomatic leader who helped secure French and Dutch support; key negotiator of the Treaty of Paris; strong proponent of republican government and constitutional checks and balances.

Thomas Jefferson. Principal author of the Declaration of Independence; articulated natural rights philosophy rooted in Enlightenment thought; later advanced republican expansion and religious liberty (Virginia Statute for Religious Freedom).

James Madison. Often called the "Father of the Constitution"; central architect of the Constitutional Convention; co-author of The Federalist Papers; key sponsor of the Bill of Rights, shaping the structure of American constitutional government.

Alexander Hamilton. Major contributor to The Federalist Papers; leading advocate for ratification of the Constitution; first Secretary of the Treasury who designed the early national financial system (national bank, federal credit, assumption of state debts).

Benjamin Franklin. Senior statesman and diplomat; secured critical French alliance during the Revolution; influential voice at the Constitutional Convention advocating compromise and unity; symbol of Enlightenment rationalism and civic virtue.

John Jay. Co-author of The Federalist Papers; diplomat who negotiated the Treaty of Paris ; first Chief Justice of the United States, helping establish judicial authority and precedent.

GEORGE MASON. Author of the Virginia Declaration of Rights, a model for the U.S. Bill of Rights; influential at the Constitutional Convention but refused to sign the Constitution due to lack of explicit protections for individual liberties.

PATRICK HENRY. Powerful orator and revolutionary leader ("Give me liberty or give me death"); strong Anti-Federalist voice who pushed for a Bill of Rights to protect individual freedoms.

SAMUEL ADAMS. Key organizer of resistance to British rule; leader in the Sons of Liberty and Boston Tea Party; influential in mobilizing colonial support for independence and republican governance.

GOUVERNEUR MORRIS. Delegate to the Constitutional Convention; principal stylist and final drafter of the Constitution's text, including the Preamble; strong advocate for a robust national government.

ROGER SHERMAN. Proposed the Connecticut (Great) Compromise, establishing bicameralism with proportional representation in the House and equal representation in the Senate; signed the Declaration, Articles of Confederation, Constitution, and Treaty of Paris.

JAMES WILSON. Leading legal theorist of popular sovereignty; major contributor at the Constitutional Convention; early Supreme Court justice; advocated that government authority derived directly from the people.

Appendix B
Historical Maps and Battles

Figure 1. Major Battles of the Revolutionary War.

The Revolutionary War was not decided by a single engagement but by a sequence of battles that shifted momentum, sustained the Continental Army, and ultimately drew in decisive foreign support. Several key engagements, spread across distinct geographic theaters, shaped the path to American independence.

Lexington and Concord (April 1775) marked the outbreak of open warfare when British troops attempted to seize colonial military supplies near Boston. Colonial militia resistance forced a British withdrawal and demonstrated that armed opposition was both possible and effective, transforming political protest into sustained rebellion.

Bunker Hill (June 1775), though technically a British victory, the battle convinced both sides that the conflict would not be easily resolved and strengthened colonial confidence that regular British troops could be repelled in conventional combat.

The New York Campaign (1776) brought major British victories, including the Battle of Long Island, and forced General George Washington to retreat across New Jersey. Despite battlefield losses, Washington preserved the Continental Army.

In a dramatic reversal, **Trenton and Princeton** (December 1776–January 1777) revitalized the American cause. Washington's surprise attack on Hessian forces at Trenton, followed by victory at Princeton, restored morale, encouraged reenlistments, and demonstrated effective use of mobility and surprise.

The war's turning point came at **Saratoga** (September–October 1777), where American forces captured an entire British army under General John Burgoyne. This victory persuaded France to formally ally with the United States, providing naval power, troops, and financial assistance that fundamentally altered the balance of the war.

Meanwhile, the British captured Philadelphia during the **Philadelphia Campaign** (1777–1778), but failed to destroy Washington's army. The Continental Army's survival and subsequent training during the winter at Valley Forge strengthened its long-term effectiveness.

After shifting focus to the South, the British initially gained ground, but American victories such as **Cowpens** (January 1781) severely weakened British field forces through tactical ingenuity and attrition. These setbacks forced British commander Lord Cornwallis to move his army toward the Virginia coast.

The war effectively ended at **Yorktown** (September–October 1781), where American and French forces, supported by French naval control, trapped Cornwallis and compelled his surrender.

Figure 2. The Siege of Yorktown.

The Siege of Yorktown (September–October 1781) unfolded as a meticulously coordinated Franco-American operation designed to trap British General Charles Cornwallis on the Virginia Peninsula. After feinting toward New York, General George Washington and French General Rochambeau marched their combined forces south to join the Marquis de Lafayette, who had been shadowing Cornwallis's army. By late September, approximately 17,000 American and French troops surrounded Yorktown forced the British into a defensive perimeter anchored on earthworks and redoubts around the town and at Gloucester Point across the York River. Crucially, the French fleet under Admiral de Grasse defeated the British navy at the Battle of the Chesapeake (September 5, 1781), sealing off Cornwallis's escape or reinforcement by sea and transforming the engagement into a full-scale siege rather than a mobile campaign.

Once encirclement was complete, allied forces constructed successive siege parallels—trenches and artillery positions gradually advancing toward British defenses—allowing heavy bombardment of Yorktown. On October 14, American and French light infantry launched coordinated nighttime assaults on British Redoubts No. 9 and No. 10, key forward defensive positions; their capture enabled the allies to complete a second parallel within musket range of the main British line. Continuous artillery fire and tightening siege works rendered Cornwallis's position untenable, and a failed attempt to evacuate across the York River was thwarted by a storm. With supplies exhausted and defenses collapsing, Cornwallis formally surrendered on October 19, 1781. The outcome effectively ended major combat operations in the American Revolutionary War, compelled Britain to enter peace negotiations, and secured American independence with decisive French military and naval support.

Figure 3. Geopolitical Boundaries After The Treaty of Paris (1783).

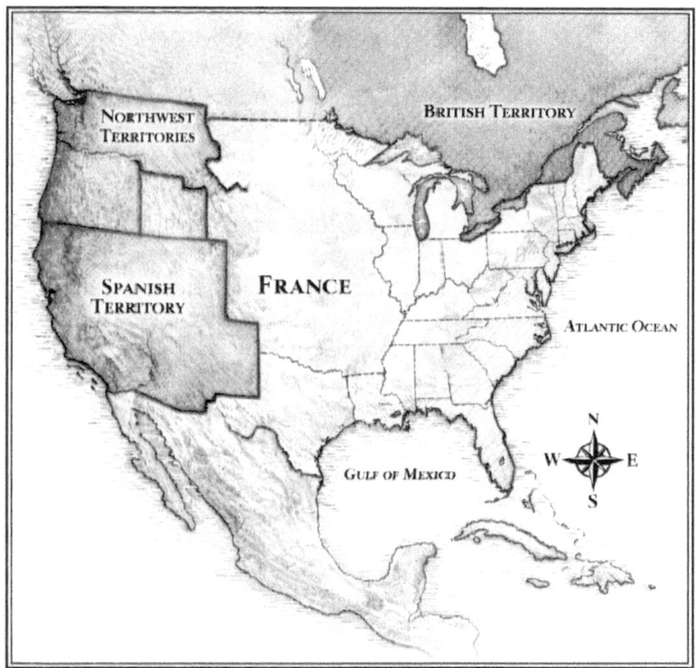

The Treaty of Paris, signed on September 3, 1783, formally ended
the American Revolutionary War and marked the international recognition of the United States from Great Britain. Although fighting had largely ceased after the American victory at Yorktown in 1781,
the treaty provided the legal and diplomatic framework that concluded the conflict and reshaped the political map of North America.

Negotiations took place in Paris between American commissioners—most notably Benjamin Franklin, John Adams, and John
Jay—and British representatives. France, Spain, and the Dutch
Republic were also involved in parallel treaties with Britain, but
the American negotiators ultimately reached an agreement directly
with Britain. The treaty was ratified by the Continental Congress in January 1784, bringing the war officially to a close.

The most significant provision of the Treaty of Paris was Britain's
unequivocal recognition of the United States as a "free, sovereign,

and independent" nation. This recognition was not merely symbolic; it allowed the United States to enter treaties, conduct foreign trade, and engage in diplomacy on equal footing with other nations. The treaty also established generous territorial boundaries for the new nation. The United States was granted land extending west to the Mississippi River, north to the Great Lakes, and south to Spanish Florida. These boundaries more than doubled the territory controlled by the former colonies and laid the groundwork for westward expansion.

In addition to sovereignty and boundaries, the treaty addressed several unresolved wartime issues. Britain agreed to withdraw its troops from U.S. territory "with all convenient speed." Both sides pledged to allow creditors to collect prewar debts, an important concession aimed at stabilizing transatlantic commerce. The treaty also included provisions concerning Loyalists—colonists who had remained loyal to the British Crown. While Congress agreed to recommend that states restore confiscated Loyalist property, enforcement was left to individual states, resulting in uneven compliance and lingering resentment.

Fishing rights were another key element. American fishermen were granted continued access to the rich fisheries off Newfoundland and in the Gulf of St. Lawrence, preserving an industry vital to the New England economy.

The Treaty of Paris had profound long-term consequences. By securing expansive territory and international recognition, it positioned the United States for rapid growth and emergence as a continental power. At the same time, ambiguities in enforcement—particularly regarding Loyalist compensation and British troop withdrawal from frontier forts—contributed to ongoing tensions between the two nations, tensions that would resurface in the decades leading up to the War of 1812.

Figure 4. The Political Party System From 1789-Present.

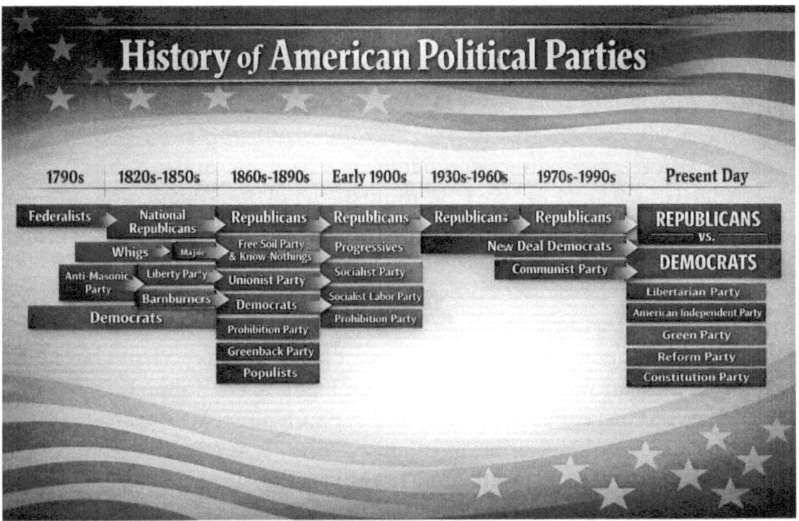

The early party system emerged from foundational constitutional disagreements. The Federalists advocated a strong national government, commercial development, a national bank, and closer ties to Britain, reflecting the priorities of urban merchants and financial elites. Opposing them, the Democratic-Republicans emphasized agrarian republicanism, states' rights, and a stricter interpretation of the Constitution. Out of this Jeffersonian tradition evolved the modern Democratic Party, which, over time, shifted from a coalition of southern agrarians and western expansionists to the party of Jacksonian populism, and later to the New Deal coalition emphasizing federal economic intervention, labor protections, and civil rights. Splinter reform movements—such as the Liberty Party (abolitionism), Free Soil Party (opposition to slavery's expansion), and the Anti-Masonic Party (anti-elite institutional distrust)—reflected moral reform currents that influenced the emerging Republican Party in the 1850s. The Republicans coalesced primarily around opposition to the expansion of slavery, national economic modernization, and preservation of the Union.

During the mid-19th century realignment, the Whigs promoted congressional supremacy, infrastructure investment ("internal improvements"), and cautious economic nationalism, but collapsed over sectional tensions. Reformist and protest movements proliferated: the Know-Nothing (American) Party centered on nativism; the Greenback Party focused on currency expansion and debt relief; the Populists advocated agrarian economic reform, railroad regulation, and monetary inflation; and the Prohibition Party advanced moral legislation against alcohol. Labor-oriented and socialist movements—including the Socialist Labor Party and later the Socialist Party of America—pressed for worker protections, public ownership, and structural economic reform. In the early 20th century, the Progressive movement (appearing within both major parties and briefly as a separate Progressive Party) emphasized regulatory reform, antitrust enforcement, direct democracy mechanisms, and administrative expertise. Meanwhile, the Communist Party USA emerged from Marxist traditions advocating revolutionary or systemic transformation of capitalism, though it remained marginal in electoral politics.

From the 1930s forward, ideological sorting intensified. The New Deal Democrats consolidated a coalition of labor unions, urban voters, minorities, and southern whites around federal economic intervention, social insurance programs, and expanded regulatory authority. Post-1960s civil rights legislation catalyzed long-term partisan realignment, particularly in the South, contributing to the modern ideological contrast between the contemporary Democratic Party (generally favoring an active federal role in economic management, social welfare expansion, civil rights protections, and multilateral foreign policy) and the modern Republican Party (emphasizing limited government, market-oriented economic policy, lower taxation, deregulation, and a stronger emphasis on federalism and traditional social structures). Smaller contemporary parties—such as the Libertarian Party (individual liberty and minimal state intervention), Green Party (environmentalism and social justice), Reform Party (centrist institutional reform), Constitution Party (originalist constitutionalism), and various independent movements—reflect enduring currents of fiscal restraint, environmental advocacy, populism, or constitutional literalism that continue to influence the broader political discourse even when not electorally dominant.

Figure 5. The Louisiana Purchase.

The Louisiana Purchase (1803) was a landmark agreement in which
the United States, under President Thomas Jefferson, acquired approximately 828,000 square miles of territory from France for $15 million,
effectively doubling the nation's size and securing control of the Mississippi River and the vital port of New Orleans. The deal removed France as
a major colonial power in North America and greatly reduced the influence of Britain and Spain in the region. In addition, it ensured American farmers permanent access to global markets through river trade.
Although Jefferson worried about the constitutionality of acquiring foreign land without explicit authorization, he proceeded under the trea-
ty-making power, and the Senate quickly ratified the agreement. The
purchase accelerated westward expansion, strengthened national security, and set the United States on a path to becoming a global power, while
also intensifying long-term conflicts over slavery, Native American displacement, and the balance of power between free and slave states.

Figure 6. The Major Battles of The War of 1812.

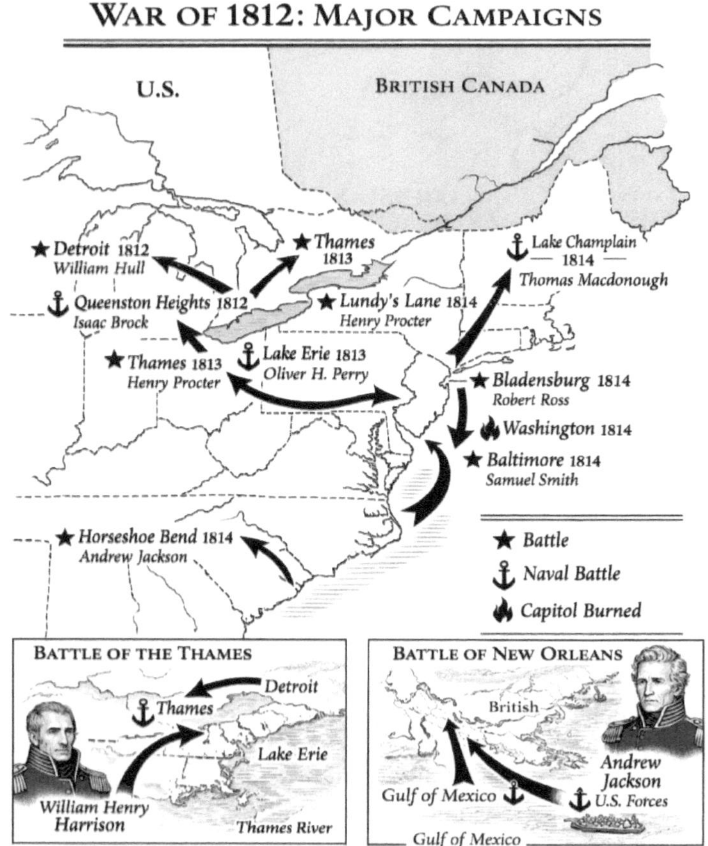

The War of 1812 opened with American attempts to seize British Canada, but early operations met with mixed results. U.S. forces under William Hull surrendered Detroit in 1812, and American militia attacks along the Niagara frontier failed to secure lasting gains. Control of the Great Lakes soon became decisive. In 1813, Commodore Oliver Hazard Perry's victory on Lake Erie secured American command of the western lakes and enabled General William Henry Harrison to defeat British and Native forces at the Battle of the Thames, where Tecumseh was killed and British influence in the Old Northwest collapsed. Fighting continued along the Niagara frontier, culminating in the hard-fought and indecisive Battle of Lundy's Lane in 1814. Meanwhile, on Lake Champlain, Thomas Macdonough's naval victory at Plattsburgh halted a major British invasion from Canada and preserved American control of the northern frontier.

In 1814 the British shifted strategy to direct attacks on the American coast. A British expedition defeated U.S. forces at Bladensburg and burned Washington, D.C., before being repelled at Baltimore, where the defense of Fort McHenry became a symbol of national resilience. In the South, Andrew Jackson crushed the Red Stick Creek forces at Horseshoe Bend, securing the southwestern frontier and freeing troops for coastal defense. The climactic Battle of New Orleans in January 1815 saw Jackson's entrenched army decisively defeat a veteran British force under General Edward Pakenham, inflicting heavy casualties and cementing Jackson's national reputation. Although the Treaty of Ghent restored prewar boundaries, the conflict strengthened American sovereignty, weakened Native resistance in the Northwest, and fostered a surge of national identity that shaped the nation's political trajectory in the decades that followed.

Treaty of Ghent. Signed on December 24, 1814, in Ghent (present-day Belgium), the Treaty of Ghent formally ended the War of 1812 between the United States and Great Britain. The agreement largely restored relations to the status quo ante bellum, requiring both sides to return conquered territory and make no changes to prewar borders. It did not address the maritime issues—such as impressment and neutral trade rights—that had helped spark the conflict, but it succeeded in halting hostilities and paved the way for improved Anglo-American relations in the decades that followed. The U.S. Senate ratified the treaty on February 16, 1815, after which news reached America and the war officially concluded.

Figure 7. **Territorial Expansion During the Polk Administration.**

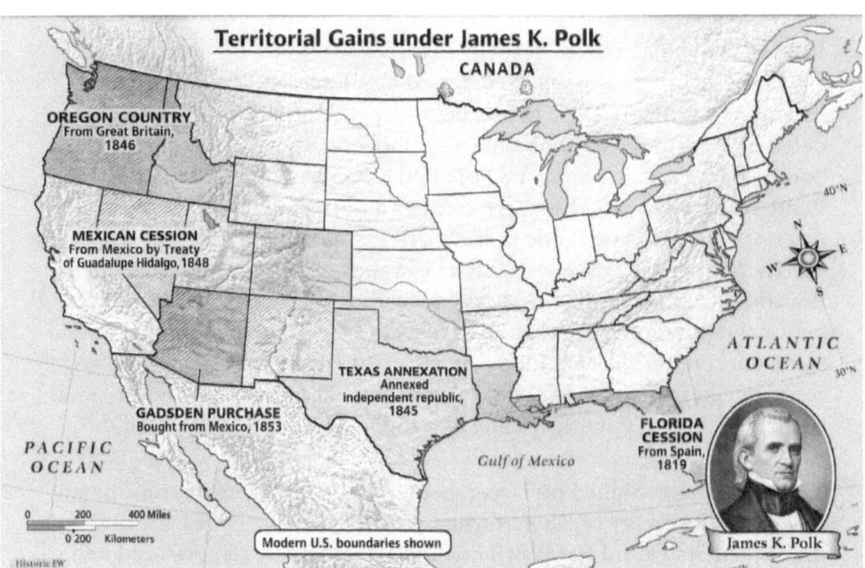

This map illustrates the dramatic westward expansion of the United States
during the Polk administration; a period closely associated with the ideology of **Manifest Destiny**. In 1845, the United States annexed Texas, significantly expanding its southern border. The Oregon Treaty of 1846
peacefully resolved competing claims with Great Britain, extending
U.S. territory to the Pacific Northwest along the 49th parallel. The largest acquisition followed the Mexican–American War, when the Treaty
of Guadalupe Hidalgo (1848) transferred vast lands from Mexico to
the United States, including present-day California, Nevada, Utah, Arizona, and parts of New Mexico, Colorado, and Wyoming. Together,
these acquisitions nearly doubled the nation's land area and dramatically reshaped the political and economic future of the United States.

Manifest Destiny was the 19th-century belief that the United States was
divinely ordained to expand westward across the North American continent. The term was popularized in 1845 by journalist John L. O'Sul-
livan, who argued that American expansion was both inevitable and
morally justified. In practice, Manifest Destiny encouraged territorial
growth through settlement, treaties, and war—most notably the annexation of Texas, the Oregon settlement, and the Mexican–American

War—while also contributing to the displacement of Native American nations and intensifying sectional conflict over the expansion of slavery.

Figure 8. **The Mexican-American War.**

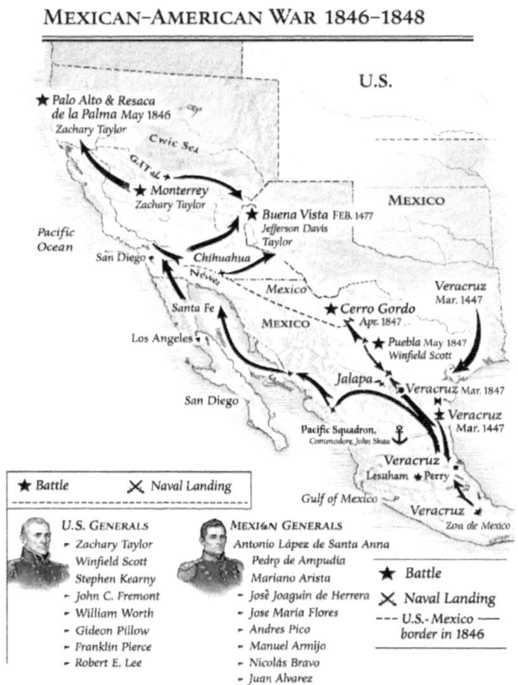

The Mexican–American War began in 1846 with clashes along the disputed Texas–Mexico border, where General Zachary Taylor defeated Mexican forces under Mariano Arista at Palo Alto and Resaca de la Palma. Taylor then advanced into northern Mexico, capturing Monterrey and later securing a major defensive victory at Buena Vista against the larger army of General Antonio López de Santa Anna. Simultaneously, U.S. forces under Stephen Kearny and John C. Frémont moved westward to seize New Mexico and California, while naval squadrons established American control along the Pacific coast. These early campaigns established U.S. dominance in the northern provinces and opened multiple fronts that stretched Mexican defensive capacity.

In 1847 the United States launched a decisive campaign against the Mexican heartland. General Winfield Scott conducted the first large-scale American amphibious landing at Veracruz and marched inland toward Mexico City, defeating Mexican forces at Cerro Gordo, Contreras, Churubusco, and Molino del Rey before storming Chapultepec and capturing the capital. Santa Anna's repeated efforts to halt the advance failed as American forces demonstrated superior logistics, artillery, and coordinated maneuvers. The fall of Mexico City forced negotiations that produced the Treaty of Guadalupe Hidalgo in 1848, through which Mexico ceded vast territories—including present-day California, Nevada, Utah, Arizona, and New Mexico—to the United States, dramatically reshaping the continental balance of power and accelerating sectional tensions within the expanding republic.

Importance and Historical Relevance. The Mexican–American War was a watershed event in nineteenth-century North American history. Its outcome dramatically reshaped the territorial map of the United States through the **Treaty of Guadalupe Hidalgo** (1848), by which Mexico ceded vast lands that would become California, Nevada, Utah, most of Arizona and New Mexico, and parts of Colorado and Wyoming. This territorial expansion fulfilled key ambitions of Manifest Destiny but came at significant political and moral cost.

Domestically, the war intensified sectional tensions over the expansion of slavery into newly acquired territories, accelerating the chain of events that led to the American Civil War. Internationally, it marked the emergence of the United States as a continental power while leaving Mexico politically destabilized and economically weakened for decades. The campaigns depicted on this map also had lasting military significance, serving as a training ground for many officers—on both sides of the later Civil War—who gained critical combat experience during the conflict.

Figure 9. **The American Civil War.**

The American Civil War unfolded across two primary theaters, with the Union pursuing a coordinated strategy to divide and defeat the Confederacy while Confederate forces sought to defend territory and erode Northern will. Early fighting centered in the Eastern Theater between Washington, D.C., and Richmond, where Confederate General Robert E. Lee and the Army of Northern Virginia confronted successive Union commanders. Initial Confederate successes at First Bull Run and Fredericksburg bolstered Southern morale, but the bloody Battle of Antietam in 1862 halted Lee's first invasion of the North and provided President Abraham Lincoln the opportunity to issue the Emancipation Proclamation. The turning point in the East came at Gettysburg in July 1863, where Union forces under General George G. Meade repelled Lee's second northern invasion and ended Confederate offensive capacity in that theater.

In the Western Theater, Union strategy focused on controlling major river systems and transportation corridors. General Ulysses S. Grant's victories at Forts Henry and Donelson and the hard-fought Battle of Shiloh opened the Tennessee River valley, while the capture of New Orleans in 1862 gave the Union control of the Confederacy's largest port. The decisive campaign for Vicksburg in 1863 secured Union control of the Mississippi River, effectively splitting the Confederacy in two and isolating its western territories. These victories demonstrated the Union's growing logistical and industrial advantages and elevated Grant to overall command of Union forces.

By 1864 the Union launched coordinated offensives designed to exhaust Confederate armies and infrastructure. Grant's Overland Campaign forced Lee into a prolonged defensive struggle culminating in the siege of Petersburg, which eventually cut off Richmond's supply lines. Simultaneously, General William Tecumseh Sherman captured Atlanta and conducted his March to the Sea, destroying key rail lines and economic resources across Georgia and the Carolinas. Confederate resistance gradually collapsed under sustained military pressure and dwindling supplies. In April 1865 Lee surrendered to Grant at Appomattox Court House, effectively ending major combat operations and preserving the Union while fundamentally transforming the nation through the abolition of slavery and the expansion of federal authority.

Figure 10. **World War 1 Triggers and Major Battles.**

The First World War emerged from a volatile mix of militarism, alliance commitments, imperial rivalry, and intense nationalism, particularly in the Balkans. The assassination of Archduke Franz Ferdinand in June 1914 triggered a chain reaction among Europe's great powers, activating rigid alliance systems and leading to general war. Germany's implementation of the Schlieffen Plan drew Britain into the conflict after the invasion of Belgium, and by late 1914 Europe was divided between the Allied Powers and the Central Powers. The United States, under President Woodrow Wilson, initially pursued neutrality, reflecting both public opinion and a belief that America could serve as a mediator. However, German unrestricted submarine warfare, the sinking of American ships, and the Zimmermann Telegram proposing a German–Mexican alliance gradually shifted public and political sentiment toward intervention.

The map illustrates the principal theaters of combat and the strategic movements that defined the war's course. On the Western Front, Germany's early advance was halted near Paris, leading to entrenched trench warfare from the North Sea to Switzerland. Battles such as Verdun and Ypres symbolized the brutal attritional struggle between France, Britain, and Germany. On the Eastern Front, German victories at Tannenberg and subsequent offensives weakened Russia, contributing to revolutionary upheaval and Russia's withdrawal in 1917. Peripheral campaigns unfolded in Gallipoli and the Middle East, reflecting Allied efforts to break the stalemate and undermine the Ottoman Empire. By 1917, however, the war had reached a strategic deadlock that neither side could decisively break.

The entry of the United States in April 1917 altered the balance of power. President Wilson framed intervention not merely as retaliation for German aggression but as a defense of democratic governance and international order, later articulating his Fourteen Points as a blueprint for a just peace. American Expeditionary Forces under General John J. Pershing reinforced exhausted Allied armies and played a critical role in the Second Battle of the Marne—highlighted in the inset—as well as subsequent offensives during the Hundred Days Campaign. The influx of American manpower, industrial production, and financial support tipped the strategic balance against Germany. By November 1918, mounting battlefield losses, economic collapse, and domestic unrest compelled the Central Powers to seek armistice, reshaping the political map of Europe and laying the groundwork for both postwar reconstruction and future instability.

Figure 11. **Post-World War I Geopolitical Boundaries.**

This map illustrates the political restructuring of Europe following the
First World War and the peace settlements that culminated in the Treaty
of Versailles and related agreements between 1919 and 1920. The defeat
of the Central Powers led to the collapse of four major empires—German,
Austro-Hungarian, Russian, and Ottoman—resulting in a redrawing
of national boundaries across Central and Eastern Europe. New or reconstituted
nations such as Poland, Czechoslovakia, Finland, and Yugoslavia
emerged from former imperial territories, reflecting both the principle
of national self-determination and the strategic interests of the victorious
Allied powers. Germany lost territory to France, Belgium, and the newly

restored Poland, while Austria-Hungary fragmented into several independent states, dramatically altering the balance of power on the continent.

The map also highlights the broader geopolitical consequences of the war's end. Eastern Europe became a patchwork of newly established states with fragile borders and diverse ethnic populations, creating persistent tensions and unresolved territorial disputes. The Soviet Union, formed after the Russian Revolution and civil war, stood largely isolated but remained a significant presence along Europe's eastern frontier. Meanwhile, the weakening of Germany and the emergence of smaller successor states created both opportunities for democratic governance and conditions of instability that would later be exploited by nationalist movements. The postwar settlement reshaped Europe's political landscape but left unresolved grievances and structural weaknesses that contributed to renewed conflict in the decades that followed.

Figure 12. Europe's Shifting Geopolitical Balance after WW II(1939 vs 1949).

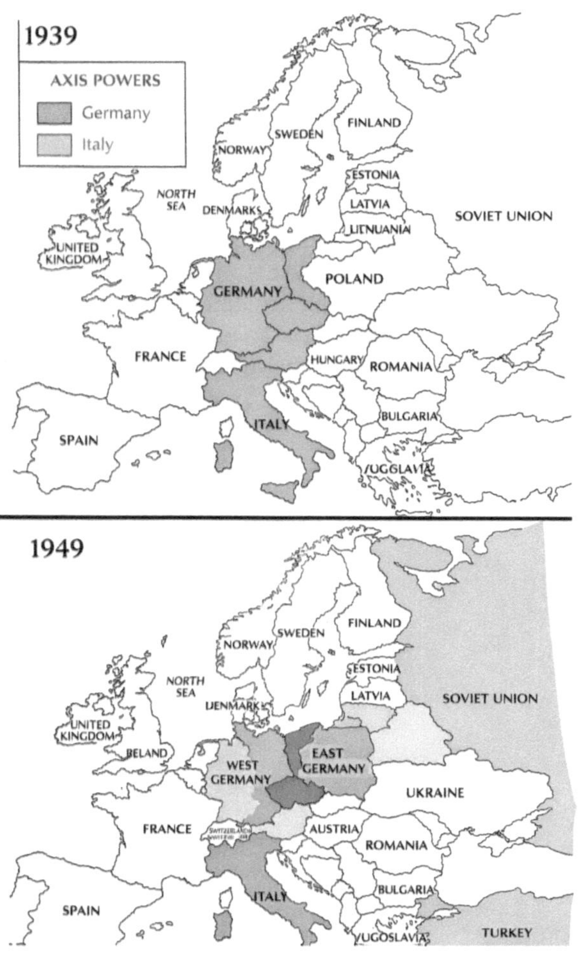

The upper map (1939) captures Europe at the moment of maximum instability before general war. Germany, under Adolf Hitler, had already dismantled the Versailles framework through remilitarization, the Anschluss with Austria, and the dismemberment of Czechoslovakia. Italy, led by Benito Mussolini, aligned itself with Berlin in the so-called "Pact of Steel," seeking Mediterranean expansion and imperial prestige. Poland sat at the geographic and strategic center of the crisis, wedged between Germany and the Soviet Union, with the contested

Polish Corridor and the Free City of Danzig serving as immediate flash-points. France and the United Kingdom, though still powerful, were strategically defensive and politically cautious after years of appeasement.

The 1939 configuration reveals a Europe still composed of numerous sovereign states in Central and Eastern Europe—Hungary, Romania, Yugoslavia, Bulgaria, and the Baltic republics—many of which were diplomatically fragile and militarily exposed. The Soviet Union, under Joseph Stalin, pursued a security strategy rooted in buffer zones, culminating in the Molotov–Ribbentrop Pact of August 1939, which secretly partitioned Eastern Europe into spheres of influence. This pact cleared the path for Germany's invasion of Poland and the formal beginning of World War II, transforming a tense geopolitical standoff into total war.

The lower map (1949) illustrates the dramatic territorial and ideological transformation produced by that conflict. Germany is divided into West Germany (Federal Republic of Germany) and East Germany (German Democratic Republic), symbolizing the emerging Cold War. The Soviet Union has consolidated control over Eastern Europe, incorporating the Baltic states directly and exercising political dominance over Poland, Romania, Bulgaria, and others through communist governments. The wartime alliances have hardened into opposing blocs, and the Iron Curtain—though not physically marked—effectively bisects the continent.

By 1949, the principal actors are no longer simply nation-states competing for territory but ideological systems competing for global influence. The United States and the Soviet Union now define European security architecture, with Western Europe moving toward integration and collective defense (NATO founded in 1949) while Eastern Europe is aligned under Soviet influence. Italy and France reemerge within the Western orbit, while Germany becomes the central geopolitical fault line of the Cold War. Together, these two maps vividly illustrate the transition from revisionist authoritarian expansion in 1939 to bipolar ideological division by 1949—a fundamental reordering of European power that would shape international politics for the next four decades.

Figure 13. The Vietnam Conflict.

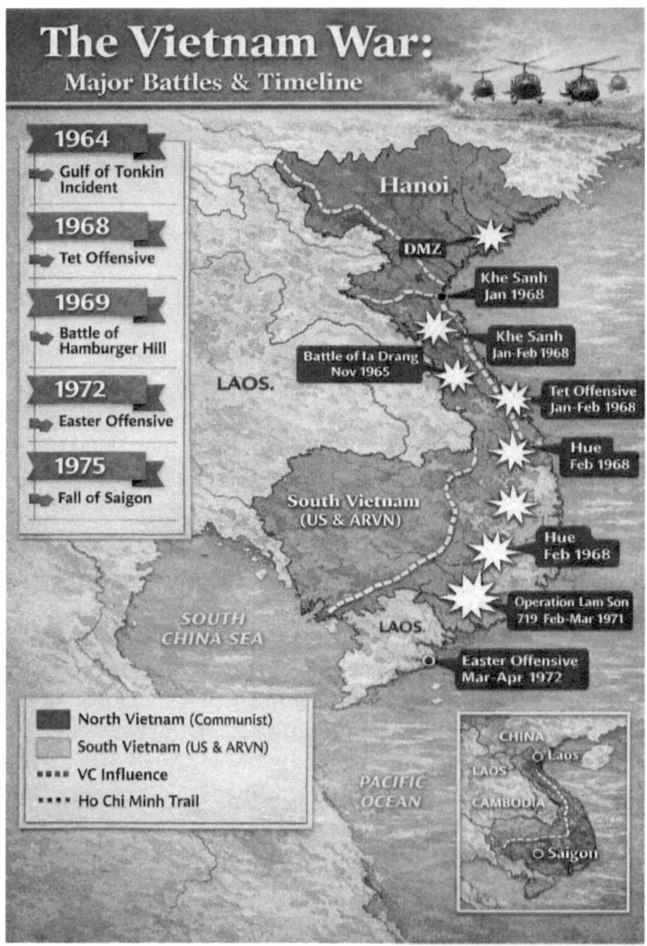

This map traces the Vietnam War over time, highlighting major battles, major offensives, and critical logistical networks that shaped the conflict. It depicts the division of Vietnam at the Demilitarized Zone (DMZ), the central role of the Ho Chi Minh Trail through Laos and Cambodia, and key engagements such as Ia Drang (1965), Khe Sanh and Huế during the Tet Offensive (1968), Hamburger Hill (1969), the Easter Offensive (1972), and the final North Vietnamese advance culminating in the Fall of Saigon in 1975.

Despite deploying overwhelming military force, the United States pursued a strategy heavily reliant on attrition, body counts, and technological superiority, while underestimating the political, nationalist, and ideological motivations driving North Vietnamese and Viet Cong forces. U.S. leaders often misread the conflict as a conventional front in the Cold War rather than a decolonization struggle rooted in Vietnamese history and nationalism. Widespread bombing campaigns, search-and-destroy operations, and forced population relocations weakened rural support for the South Vietnamese government and eroded domestic and international confidence in U.S. leadership. The inability to sever enemy supply lines, build durable South Vietnamese institutions, or sustain public support at home ultimately revealed the limits of American military power in achieving political objectives, leading to U.S. withdrawal and the reunification of Vietnam under communist control in 1975.

Figure 14. **The Persian Gulf War.**

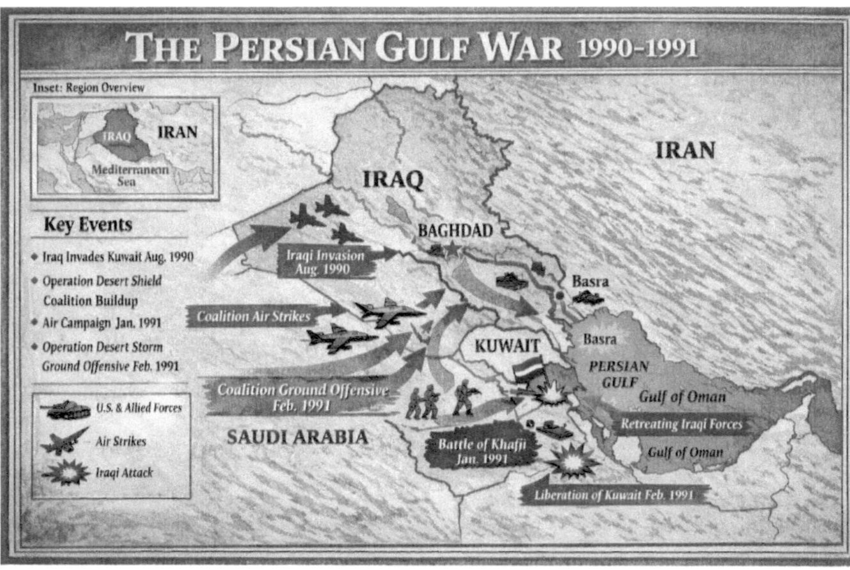

This map illustrates Iraq's August 1990 invasion of Kuwait, the subsequent
U.S.-led coalition response, and the major phases of the conflict, including Operation Desert Shield, the intensive air campaign beginning in January 1991, and the swift ground offensive (Operation Desert Storm) that
culminated in the liberation of Kuwait. Key troop movements, air strikes,
and major engagements—such as the Battle of Khafji—are shown to highlight the coalition's strategy of overwhelming force and maneuver warfare.

After months of coalition buildup in Saudi Arabia under Operation Desert Shield, the war began with a sustained air campaign that system-
atically degraded Iraq's command-and-control systems, air defenses,
armored formations, and logistical networks. The Battle of Khafji in January 1991, the only significant ground engagement prior to the main offensive, demonstrated both Iraqi limitations and coalition coordination, as
Iraqi forces briefly seized the town before being repelled by Saudi, U.S.,
and allied units. In late February 1991, coalition ground forces launched
a rapid, multi-pronged assault—often described as the "left hook"—that
bypassed heavily fortified Iraqi positions, encircled Republican Guard

units, and shattered organized resistance in just 100 hours. The overwhelming speed, air supremacy, and technological advantage of the coalition led to a clear military victory, the liberation of Kuwait, and a ceasefire that reaffirmed Iraqi sovereignty, but left Saddam Hussein's regime weakened, isolated, and subject to long-term international sanctions.

GLOSSARY

Administrative State—The network of federal agencies, departments, and regulatory bodies responsible for implementing and enforcing laws enacted by Congress. Often discussed in debates about executive authority, democratic accountability, and bureaucratic independence.

Alliance-Based Foreign Policy—An approach to international relations that emphasizes cooperation with formal allies and multilateral institutions rather than unilateral action.

Anti-Establishment Politics—Political movements or leadership styles that portray established political institutions, elites, or governing norms as obstacles to popular will or effective governance.

Authoritarianism—A governing system or tendency in which political power becomes highly concentrated and institutional constraints are weakened. In this book, the term is used descriptively in historical comparison rather than as a general label.

Bipartisan Consensus—A governing condition in which major political parties broadly agree on core policy goals or institutional frameworks despite ongoing electoral competition.

Caretaker Presidency—A presidency focused primarily on stabilization, continuity, or institutional maintenance rather than major policy transformation.

Checks and Balances—Constitutional mechanisms through which each branch of government limits the powers of the others.

Civil Service Protections—Legal safeguards designed to protect government employees from political retaliation and to maintain continuity across administrations.

Cold War Consensus—The broad post–World War II agreement among U.S. leaders on containment of communism, alliance leadership, strong defense, and an expanded executive role in foreign policy.

Constitutional Norms—Unwritten but widely accepted expectations governing behavior within constitutional institutions, including restraint in the use of power, respect for electoral outcomes, and adherence to lawful process.

Deliberative Institutionalism—A governing style emphasizing consultation, legal constraint, institutional process, and incremental decision-making rather than rapid or unilateral executive action.

Deregulation—The reduction or removal of government rules or oversight, typically intended to increase market competition or reduce regulatory burdens.

Divided Government—A political condition in which the presidency and at least one chamber of Congress are controlled by different political parties.

Electoral Mandate—The perceived authority granted to an elected official by voters, often cited to justify policy initiatives following an election.

Executive Action—Presidential directives—such as executive orders, proclamations, or memoranda—that guide federal operations without requiring new legislation.

Executive-Centered Governance—A governing pattern in which the presidency becomes the primary driver of policy due to legislative gridlock, national crisis, or administrative necessity.

Executive Overreach—The perception or allegation that a president has exceeded constitutional, statutory, or customary limits on executive authority.

Executive Restraint—The practice by which presidents voluntarily limit the use of formal powers to preserve institutional balance, public trust, and constitutional legitimacy, even when broader authority may be legally available.

Federalism—The constitutional division of authority between national and state governments.

Gridlock—A condition in which political institutions are unable to enact legislation due to partisan division, procedural barriers, or competing priorities.

Humanitarian Intervention—The use of military, economic, or diplomatic power to address humanitarian crises abroad, often debated in terms of legality and effectiveness.

Institutional Legitimacy—Public acceptance of governing institutions as lawful and deserving of compliance, even amid political disagreement.

Judicial Review—The authority of courts to interpret the Constitution and invalidate laws or executive actions that conflict with it.

Managed Capitalism—An economic system combining private enterprise with government regulation, monetary policy, and social welfare programs.

Moral Authority—Influence derived from perceived integrity, credibility, or ethical conduct rather than formal institutional power.

Narrative Presidency—A leadership style emphasizing public messaging, symbolism, and persuasion as central tools of governance.

Norm Erosion—The weakening of informal but influential behavioral expectations that traditionally constrain political actors.

Partisan Polarization—The process by which political parties become more ideologically distinct and less willing to compromise.

Personalized Executive Power—A form of presidential leadership in which authority becomes closely associated with the individual officeholder rather than the institutional presidency.

Populism—A political approach that claims to represent "the people" in opposition to perceived elites, institutions, or established power structures. In presidential leadership, populism often emphasizes direct appeals to popular mandate over institutional mediation.

Post–Watergate Retrenchment—The reduction and oversight of presidential authority following the Watergate scandal through legislative reforms, investigations, and renewed institutional constraints.

Pragmatic Internationalism—A foreign policy approach that prioritizes stability, alliances, and practical outcomes over ideological objectives.

Separation of Powers—The constitutional division of authority among legislative, executive, and judicial branches of government.

Stagflation—An economic condition characterized by high inflation, slow economic growth, and elevated unemployment occurring simultaneously.

Stewardship Theory of the Presidency—The view that the president may act broadly in the national interest unless explicitly prohibited by the Constitution or law, contrasting with more limited interpretations of executive authority.

Technocratic Governance—Policymaking driven primarily by technical expertise, data analysis, and administrative competence rather than political mobilization.

Unilateralism—Action taken by a government independently rather than in coordination with allies or multilateral institutions.

ANNOTATED BIBLIOGRAPHY

The following works informed the historical synthesis presented in this volume and are recommended for readers seeking deeper study of each presidential era. Wherever possible, widely respected scholarly and interpretive biographies have been selected to provide balance, context, and durability.

Readers should note that biographies of more recent presidents are written in closer proximity to the events they describe and therefore rely more heavily on contemporary reporting, memoir, and evolving historical interpretation. As archival materials are released and scholarly reassessments emerge over time, interpretations of modern presidencies may continue to develop. Accordingly, works on earlier presidents often benefit from greater historical distance and documentation, while those on contemporary leaders should be read with an understanding of their immediacy and provisional nature.

THE FOUNDING ERA (1789–1829)

Bailyn, Bernard. The Ideological Origins of the American
       Revolution. Cambridge, MA: Harvard University Press, 1967.
       Foundational study of revolutionary political thought and
       the intellectual origins of American constitutionalism.

Bolles, Blair. *Jefferson: Architect of American Liberty.*
       New York: W. W. Norton, 1967.
       Readable mid-century biography emphasizing Jefferson's political philosophy and institutional vision.

Brands, H. W. *The First American: The Life and Times of
       Benjamin Franklin.* New York: Doubleday, 2000.
       Comprehensive modern biography highlighting Franklin's diplomatic and intellectual influence on the founding generation.

Chernow, Ron. *Alexander Hamilton.* New York: Penguin Press, 2004.
       Definitive modern account of Hamilton's financial system and lasting institutional impact.

Chernow, Ron. *Washington: A Life*. New York: Penguin Press, 2010.
Authoritative biography emphasizing Washington's role in establishing presidential norms and executive restraint.

Cheney, Lynne. *James Madison: A Life Reconsidered.*
New York: Viking, 2014.
Accessible study of Madison's constitutional thought and presidency.

Ellis, Joseph J. *American Creation*. New York: Knopf, 2007.
Interpretive overview of the political achievements and tensions of the early republic.

Ellis, Joseph J. *Founding Brothers*. New York: Knopf, 2000.
Pulitzer-winning exploration of relationships and conflicts among the founding generation.

Feldman, Noah. *The Three Lives of James Madison.*
New York: Random House, 2017.
Modern reassessment of Madison as constitutional theorist, partisan leader, and wartime president.

Isaacson, Walter. *Benjamin Franklin: An American Life*. New York: Simon & Schuster, 2003.
Widely read biography emphasizing Franklin's diplomacy and civic influence.

McCullough, David. *John Adams*. New York: Simon & Schuster, 2001.
Pulitzer Prize–winning biography restoring Adams to central importance in the founding era.

Meacham, Jon. *Thomas Jefferson: The Art of Power.*
New York: Random House, 2012.
Balanced modern interpretation of Jefferson's political skill and presidential leadership.

Rakove, Jack N. *Original Meanings*. New York: Knopf, 1996.
Important constitutional study of founding debates and interpretive traditions.

Wood, Gordon S. *Empire of Liberty*. New York: Oxford University Press, 2009.
Comprehensive history of the early republic and Jeffersonian era.

Wood, Gordon S. *The Radicalism of the American Revolution*. New York: Knopf, 1992. Classic interpretation of the Revolution's social and political consequences.

POPULISM AND ANTEBELLUM AMERICA (1829–1861)

Bradley, Mark E. *Martin Van Buren: America's First Politician*. New York: Oxford University Press, 2012. Modern scholarly reassessment of Van Buren and the emergence of party-centered politics.

Brands, H. W. *Andrew Jackson: His Life and Times*. New York: Doubleday, 2005. Accessible modern biography of Jackson's populist presidency and expansion of executive power.

Borneman, Walter R. *Polk*. New York: Random House, 2008. Strong narrative of Polk's single-term presidency and territorial expansion.

Howe, Daniel Walker. *What Hath God Wrought*. New York: Oxford University Press, 2007. Pulitzer-winning synthesis of political, economic, and cultural change in antebellum America.

McGrath, Tim. *James Monroe: A Life*. New York: Dutton, 2020. Comprehensive modern biography of Monroe and the "Era of Good Feelings."

Rayback, Joseph. *Millard Fillmore*. Buffalo: Henry Stewart, 1959. Still the standard scholarly biography of Fillmore and Compromise-era politics.

Remini, Robert V. *Andrew Jackson and the Course of American Democracy*. New York: Harper & Row, 1984. Detailed scholarly study of Jacksonian political transformation.

Traub, James. *John Quincy Adams: Militant Spirit*. New York: Basic Books, 2016. Modern interpretation of Adams's diplomatic and antislavery legacy.

Wilentz, Sean. *The Rise of American Democracy*. New York: Norton, 2005.
Major synthesis of political democratization from Jefferson through Jackson.

THE CIVIL WAR AND RECONSTRUCTION (1861–1877)

Blight, David. *Race and Reunion*. Cambridge, MA: Harvard University Press, 2001.
Influential study of Civil War memory and national reconciliation.

Chernow, Ron. *Grant*. New York: Penguin Press, 2017.
Definitive modern biography reassessing Grant's presidency and civil rights enforcement.

Foner, Eric. *Reconstruction*. New York: Harper & Row, 1988.
Authoritative account of Reconstruction policy and constitutional transformation.

Goodwin, Doris Kearns. *Team of Rivals*. New York: Simon & Schuster, 2005.
Widely read study of Lincoln's political leadership and cabinet governance.

McPherson, James. *Battle Cry of Freedom*. New York: Oxford University Press, 1988.
Pulitzer-winning single-volume history of the Civil War era.

Meacham, Jon. *And There Was Light*. New York: Random House, 2022.
Recent synthesis of Lincoln's moral and political development.

White, Ronald C. *A. Lincoln*. New York: Random House, 2009.
Comprehensive modern biography emphasizing Lincoln's constitutional leadership.

THE GILDED AGE (1877–1901)

Brands, H. W. *American Colossus*. New York: Doubleday, 2010.
Survey of industrial growth and political transformation after the Civil War.

Calhoun, Charles. *The Gilded Age*. Lanham,
    MD: Rowman & Littlefield, 2007.
    Concise scholarly overview of late-19th-century politics and society.

Chernow, Ron. *Titan*. New York: Random House, 1998.
    Definitive biography of Rockefeller and the rise of corporate capitalism.

Goodyear, William A. *President Garfield*. Kent, OH:
    Kent State University Press, 2006.
    Scholarly reassessment of Garfield's brief but consequential presidency.

Greenberger, Robert. *Chester A. Arthur*. New York: Kaplan, 2017.
    Accessible modern biography highlighting civil service reform.

Hogenboom, Ari. *Rutherford B. Hayes*. Lawrence:
    University Press of Kansas, 1995.
    Balanced scholarly study of Hayes and Reconstruction's end.

Merry, Robert. *President McKinley*. New York: Simon & Schuster, 2017.
    Modern reassessment of McKinley's leadership and global strategy.

Senik, Joseph. *A Man of Iron*. New York: Skyhorse, 2022.
    Recent biography of Grover Cleveland empha-
    sizing institutional conservatism.

White, Richard. *The Republic for Which It Stands*.
    New York: Oxford University Press, 2017.
    Major synthesis of politics, economy, and society in the Gilded Age.

THE PROGRESSIVE ERA (1901–1921)

Berg, A. Scott. *Wilson*. New York: Putnam, 2013.
    Definitive modern biography of Wilson's aca-
    demic and presidential career.

Cooper, John Milton. *Woodrow Wilson*. New York: Knopf, 2009.
    Scholarly interpretation of Wilson's domes-
    tic and international leadership.

Goodwin, Doris Kearns. *The Bully Pulpit*. New
    York: Simon & Schuster, 2013.
    Study of Roosevelt, Taft, and the rise of modern media politics.

Morris, Edmund. *The Rise of Theodore Roosevelt*. New York: 1979.
Pulitzer-winning first volume of the definitive Roosevelt trilogy.

Morris, Edmund. *Theodore Rex*. New York: Random House, 2001.
Detailed account of Roosevelt's presidency and reform agenda.

Morris, Edmund. *Colonel Roosevelt*. New York: Random House, 2010.
Final volume covering Roosevelt's later political career.

Market Autonomy (1921–1929)

Brands, H. W. *The Money Men: Capitalism, Democracy, and the Hundred Years' War Over the American Dollar*. New York: W. W. Norton, 2006.
Explores the evolution of American financial policy and debates over monetary control shaping early 20th-century governance.

Kennedy, David M. *Freedom from Fear: The American People in Depression and War, 1929–1945*. New York: Oxford University Press, 1999.
Pulitzer-winning synthesis providing essential context for late-1920s economic collapse and the transition to the New Deal.

Leuchtenburg, William E. *The Perils of Prosperity, 1914–1932*. Chicago: University of Chicago Press, 1958.
Classic account of the 1920s political economy and limits of market-centered governance.

Whyte, Kenneth. *Hoover: An Extraordinary Life in Extraordinary Times*. New York: Knopf, 2017.
Major modern biography reassessing Hoover's administrative capacity and pre-presidential influence.

The New Deal and World War (1929–1945)

Brands, H. W. *Traitor to His Class: The Privileged Life and Radical Presidency of Franklin Delano Roosevelt*. New York: Doubleday, 2008.
Balanced modern interpretation of Roosevelt's political transformation and New Deal leadership.

Brinkley, Alan. *The End of Reform: New Deal Liberalism in Recession and War*. New York: Vintage, 1995.
Influential study of the limits and evolution of New Deal reform.

Goodwin, Doris Kearns. *No Ordinary Time: Franklin and Eleanor Roosevelt: The Home Front in World War II*. New York: Simon & Schuster, 1994.
Pulitzer Prize–winning account of wartime leadership and domestic mobilization.

Kennedy, David M. *Freedom from Fear*. New York: Oxford University Press, 1999.
Definitive single-volume history of the Great Depression and World War II home front.

Leuchtenburg, William E. *Franklin D. Roosevelt and the New Deal*. New York: Harper & Row, 1963.
Classic scholarly analysis of New Deal legislation and institutional transformation.

Smith, Jean Edward. *FDR*. New York: Random House, 2007.
Comprehensive modern biography emphasizing Roosevelt's political skill and wartime leadership.

The Cold War (1945–1968)

Ambrose, Stephen E. *Eisenhower: Soldier and President*. New York: Simon & Schuster, 1990.
Accessible study of Eisenhower's military background and consensus-based presidency.

Caro, Robert A. *The Passage of Power*. New York: Knopf, 2012.
Detailed narrative of the Kennedy–Johnson transition and the early Johnson presidency.

Dallek, Robert. *Flawed Giant: Lyndon Johnson and His Times, 1961–1973*. New York: Oxford University Press, 1998.
Major scholarly biography of Johnson's domestic achievements and Vietnam-era challenges.

Goodwin, Doris Kearns. *Lyndon Johnson and the American Dream*. New York: Harper & Row, 1976.
Early interpretive biography exploring Johnson's political ambition and legislative mastery.

Logevall, Fredrik. JFK: *Coming of Age in the American Century,
  1917–1956*. New York: Random House, 2020.
  First volume of a major modern Kennedy biography emphasizing formative influences.

Logevall, Fredrik. *Embers of War: The Fall of an Empire and the
  Making of America's Vietnam*. New York: Random House, 2012.
  Pulitzer Prize–winning history tracing ori-
  gins of U.S. involvement in Vietnam.

McCullough, David. *Truman*. New York: Simon & Schuster, 1992.
  Pulitzer-winning biography restoring Truman's central place in early Cold War leadership.

Smith, Jean Edward. *Eisenhower in War and Peace*.
  New York: Random House, 2012.
  Comprehensive modern reassessment of Eisenhow-
  er's strategic and presidential leadership.

PUBLIC MISTRUST AND CRISIS MANAGEMENT(1969–1992)

Beschloss, Michael. *The Crisis Years: Kennedy and Khrushchev,
  1960–1963*. New York: Edward Burlingame Books, 1999.
  Study of Cold War decision-making and executive crisis management.

Bird, Kai. The Outlier: *The Unfinished Presidency of
  Jimmy Carter*. New York: Crown, 2021.
  Recent reinterpretation of Carter's presi-
  dency and post-presidential legacy.

Brands, H. W. *Reagan: The Life*. New York: Doubleday, 2015.
  Comprehensive modern biography of Rea-
  gan's political rise and presidency.

Cannon, James. Time and Chance: *Gerald Ford's Appointment
  with History*. New York: Harper & Row, 1994.
  Insider account of Ford's presidency and the post-Watergate transition.

Farrell, John A. *Richard Nixon: The Life*. New York: Doubleday, 2017.
  Definitive modern biography examining Nix-
  on's political career and presidency.

Kutler, Stanley I. The Wars of Watergate. New York: Knopf, 1990.
Comprehensive history of Watergate and its constitutional consequences.

Meacham, Jon. *Destiny and Power: The American Odyssey of George Herbert Walker Bush*. New York: Random House, 2015.
Balanced modern biography of Bush's foreign policy leadership and presidency.

The Contemporary Presidency (1993–2025)

Dallek, Robert. *The American Presidency: An Intellectual History*. New York: Oxford University Press, 2021.
Survey of presidential leadership and institutional development across U.S. history.

Greenstein, Fred I. *The Presidential Difference*. Princeton: Princeton University Press, 2000.
Comparative study of presidential leadership styles and performance.

Packer, George. *The Unwinding*. New York: Farrar, Straus and Giroux, 2013.
Narrative account of economic and political change shaping modern governance.

Skowronek, Stephen. *Presidential Leadership in Political Time*. Lawrence: University Press of Kansas, 2008.
Influential theory of recurring presidential leadership cycles.

O'Reilly, Bill, and Martin Dugard. *The United States of Trump: How the President Really Sees America*. New York: Henry Holt, 2019.
Journalistic account of the Trump presidency emphasizing leadership style, political messaging, and decision-making from a contemporary media perspective.

Remnick, David. *The Bridge: The Life and Rise of Barack Obama*. New York: Knopf, 2010.
Best single-volume serious biography; contextual and non-hagiographic.

Draper, Robert. *Dead Certain: The Presidency of George
    W. Bush*. New York: Free Press, 2007.
    Balanced insider account of Bush's govern-
    ing style and decision-making culture.

Osnos, Evan. *Joe Biden: The Life, the Run, and What
    Matters Now*. New York: Scribner, 2020.
    Best balanced modern biography; pre-presidential but essential context.

Haberman, Maggie. *Confidence Man: The Making of Donald Trump
    and the Breaking of America*. New York: Penguin Press, 2022.
    Widely regarded as the most comprehensive journalis-
    tic account of Trump's political rise and presidency.

RELEVANT CONSTITUTIONAL AND PRESIDENCY WORKS

Gerhardt, Michael J. *The Forgotten Presidents: Their Untold
    Constitutional Legacy*. New York: Oxford University Press, 2013.
    Explores overlooked constitutional contribu-
    tions of lesser-known presidents.

Greenstein, Fred I. *Inventing the Job of President*.
    Princeton: Princeton University Press, 2009.
    Study of how early presidents shaped the modern executive role.

Neustadt, Richard E. *Presidential Power and the Modern
    Presidents*. New York: Free Press, 1990.
    Classic analysis of presidential influence and political leadership.

Skowronek, Stephen. *The Politics Presidents Make*.
    Cambridge, MA: Harvard University Press, 1993.
    Seminal work on presidential authority and political development.

The American Presidents Series. New York: Times
    Books/Henry Holt, ongoing.
    Concise scholarly biographies of each U.S. president writ-
    ten by leading historians; useful for readers seek-
    ing brief, focused studies of individual presidencies.

INDEX

Y